The
Clinical Assessment
of Memory

Dennis Reeves, CDR, MSC, USN, PhD, is a Commander, Medical Service Corps, U.S. Navy, and an experimental and clinical psychologist in the Department of Psychology, National Naval Medical Center, Bethesda, Maryland. He currently serves as Associate Head of Training and Research, and Head of the Assessment Division for the medical center's internship program.

Dr. Reeves obtained his doctoral degree in experimental psychology from the University of Kansas, has completed a 3-year postdoctoral retraining program in clinical psychology at The George Washington University, and has received postdoctoral training in clinical neuropsychology at Georgetown University, Walter Reed Army Medical Center, and the National Naval Medical Center.

Dr. Reeves has served as Deputy Chairman of a major joint-services research program coordinating psychometric development projects among 23 civilian and military laboratories. Concurrently, he served as Chairman of the Neuropsychology Task Area Group for the Office of Military Performance Assessment Technology. In this capacity he directs the development of automated neuropsychological assessment instruments.

Danny Wedding, PhD, is a clinical psychologist and a professor in the Department of Psychiatry at the University of Missouri–Columbia. He currently serves as Director of the Missouri Institute of Mental Health (MIMH), a mental health policy, research, and training center located in St. Louis

Dr. Wedding received a doctoral degree in clinical psychology from the University of Hawaii, has completed a clinical psychology internship at Hawaii State Hospital, and spent a postdoctoral year training in clinical neuropsychology and behavioral medicine at the University of Mississippi Medical Center.

Dr. Wedding has taught in the medical schools of East Tennessee State University and Marshall University. He has also completed two years working for the U.S. Congress in fellowship programs administered by the Institute of Medicine and American Association for the Advancement of Science (AAAS). Dr. Wedding is the coauthor, with Arthur MacNeill Horton, Jr., and Jeffrey Webster, of *The Neuropsychology Handbook* (1986), and with Richard Berg and Michael Franzen of *Screening for Brain Impairment* (1987)—both published by Springer Publishing.

The
Clinical Assessment
of Memory

—————— ## A Practical Guide

Dennis Reeves, PhD
Danny Wedding, PhD

SPRINGER PUBLISHING COMPANY
New York

Copyright© 1994 by Springer Publishing Company, Inc.

Springer Publishing Company, Inc.
536 Broadway
New York, NY 10012

94 95 96 97 98 / 5 4 3 2

Library of Congress Cataloging in Publication Data

Reeves, Dennis,
    The clinical assessment of memory : a practical guide / Dennis Reeves, Danny Wedding.
        p.   cm.
    Includes bibliographical references and index.
    ISBN 0-8261-7920-7
    1. Memory disorders—Diagnosis.   I. Wedding, Danny.   II. Title
    RC394.M46R44   1994
    616.8'4—dc20   93-36920
                                              CIP

Printed in the United States of America

To Andrea, Michael, Joshua, and Jeremiah . . .
The Very Best of Our Memories

Contents

CONTENTS

CONTENTS

CONTENTS

Foreword

Memory poses a problem for patients and clinicians. For patients, memory difficulty is by far the most common presenting complaint. For clinicians, the problem with memory is a result of the complexity of the neuroanatomy, the divergent cognitive theories (and terminology), the wide range of amnestic syndromes, and the difficulty in applying this information to the evaluation of patients. Today there are so many tests of memory functioning that the clinician is likely to find selecting the proper test(s) for a particular patient to be quite daunting.

This volume addresses the needs of the clinician in evaluation of memory functioning. It provides a welcome review and update of the various approaches taken by cognitive psychologists in the classification of memory processes. Reeves and Wedding have managed to translate cognitive psychology's complex and overlapping descriptions of memory processes into a framework that demonstrates the relationship between these processes and the underlying neuroanatomy. This relationship is especially well demonstrated through a description of amnestic syndromes.

Studies conducted with amnestic patients in clinical settings and with normal individuals in the laboratories of cognitive psychologists gave rise to a panoply of memory-testing procedures that have now found their way into the hands of clinicians. However, aside from this volume there is little to guide the clinician in selecting which test to give which patient. The authors describe dozens of the most common memory procedures in terms of the memory processes assessed by each test. They address the influence of age and education on test performance, the adequacy of existing normative groups, and the pattern of test performance associated with different amnestic groups.

FOREWORD

Although not a substitute for a careful reading of test manuals, this volume will give the reader a clear sense of the administration, scoring, and interpretation of these test procedures.

Reeves and Wedding demonstrate their dedication to teaching neuropsychology. Their scholarship and effort in integrating knowledge from neuroanatomy, neuropharmacology, behavioral neurology, neuropsychology, and cognitive psychology are evident in this highly practical guide.

GARY KAY, PHD
Georgetown University

Preface

This book was constructed to provide a useful reference during the formal assessment of memory. It reviews current theories of memory, provides a summary of the neuroanatomy of memory, and offers guidelines for administration and interpretation of selected memory tests.

Each chapter has been constructed as a "stand alone" unit, and it is not necessary to read the chapters in sequence to benefit from the book. The references provided will guide the reader who wishes to learn more about the fascinating topic of human memory.

We are both practicing clinicians and draw heavily on our own experiences as neuropsychologists in describing various memory disorders. Personalizing the book in this way makes for more interesting reading, and we genuinely appreciate those patients who have allowed us to share their stories.

We have not attempted to provide a compendium of information about memory disorders, nor do we survey all available assessment instruments. At every decision point in planning *The Clinical Assessment of Memory*, we were guided by a simple question: Will this information be helpful for the average clinician working in a typical mental health center? We hope the answer is a resounding yes.

Acknowledgments

First and foremost we would like to acknowledge David Silber, who challenged us to "create something useful" and then followed through with encouragement to publish. Further, we greatly appreciate the assistance of a number of colleagues who reviewed and significantly contributed to various parts of our present work. These colleagues include Gary Kay, Jack Spector, Robert Kane, Joe Bleiberg, Michael Williams, Dave Spaulding, Bruce Becker, Gale Bach, Michael Franzen, Marvin Podd, Ray Corsini, Victoria Starbuck, and Mary Ann Kreihbel.

We especially want to note the efforts of our friend and colleague, Dr. Robert Kane. Robert coauthored the final chapter and contributed significantly to Chapter 4. We genuinely appreciate his friendship and collaboration.

We also appreciate the secretarial support provided by Vicki Eichhorn and Sue Vogt and the computer skills and assistance of Bruce Vieweg and Fred Hegge, who helped us pass the manuscript back and forth electronically via the Office of Military Performance Assessment Technology's Computer Bulletin Board System.

The Missouri Institute of Mental Health (MIMH) helped locate source documents and secured permissions for the various tables and charts we have included in our book.

Most of all we appreciate the goodnatured support of our families, who sacrificed numerous weekends and evenings with us so that we would have time to collaborate on this project.

## CHAPTER ONE

Theories of Memory

The new perishes before the old.
—Ribot's law (Ribot, 1882)

Memory is central to one's knowledge of the past, interpretation of the present, and prediction of the future. However, despite its central role in the lives of our clients, few clinicians have a good understanding of the structural organization of memory at either psychological or neurobiological levels.

Memory is in many ways our most precious asset. It determines our identity, influences how we perceive and interact with others, and provides the basis for everything from fundamental motor responses, such as walking, to complex intellectual acts such as comprehending and retaining the information that is now being read. Even a relatively mild impairment may interfere with multiple aspects of professional and personal life, and independent living becomes impossible in the absence of working memory.

Because it is so automatic and pervasive, we rarely notice or consciously consider the magnitude and the importance of memory. Nevertheless, memory guides our performance, shapes our behavior, and molds our personality. If one is robbed of the memory of one's past, a principal component of one's self-identity and personality has been destroyed.

THE CLINICAL ASSESSMENT OF MEMORY

THE CONCEPT OF MEMORY

Many categories for information processing and memory suggest themselves, and these provide a starting place for the important problem of classifying the kinds of learning and memory that can occur. Table 1.1 illustrates this point.

Memory is not a unitary entity but rather a mixture of complex functions. As a result, a variety of models have been developed to describe learning and memory. The situation is further complicated by the fact that the experimental and clinical literature have produced heuristic models of memory that are conceptually similar but that employ different and often diverse nomenclatures, as Squire (1987) illustrates. As a result, it is not surprising that the clinician encounters a problem in making sense of the contrasting terms used to describe various memory processes. Terminology is derived from different models found in the clinical, experimental psychology, and neuropsychology literature. Unfortunately, there is often no attempt to correlate various concepts. For example, if a memory study on a group of normal elderly individuals or demented patients has been performed by an experimental psychologist, we may find terms such as effortful versus automatic processing, or implicit versus explicit learning, but the relationship of these terms to familiar

Table 1.1. Two basic types of memory.

Fact Memory	Skill Memory
Declarative	Procedural
Memory	Habit
Explicit	Implicit
Knowing That	Knowing How
Cognitive Mediation	Semantic
Conscious Recollection	Skills
Elaboration	Integration
Memory with Record	Memory without Record
Autobiographical Memory	Perceptual Memory
Representational Memory	Dispositional Memory
Vertical Association	Horizontal Association
Locale	Taxon
Episodic	Semantic
Working	Reference

Source: Adapted from Squire (1987).

memory tasks, such as the Wechsler Memory Scale, or the Rey Auditory Verbal Learning Test, is rarely made clear.

Unfortunately, the majority of neuropsychological assessment tests were not derived from any particular theoretical model of memory. When a clinician without a background in experimental psychology attempts to read the memory literature, he or she often becomes discouraged because of the jargon and lack of correspondence between the experimental psychologist's terminology and that of the neuropsychologist.

We do not claim to resolve this dilemma, but we do attempt to present a framework for thinking about and assessing memory disorders, and where possible we relate experimental terminology to clinical terms.

Chunking
Short-term memory is thought to have a very small capacity of about 7 items and a duration of about 20 seconds. Using a method referred to as chunking, it is possible to work up to recalling an 80 digit number. For example, 1–9–7–3 can be condensed into a meaningful chunk (e.g., 1973).

THE VOCABULARY OF MEMORY

It is now appreciated that memory is not a single faculty but is composed instead of at least two distinct, separate systems, only one of which is impaired in amnesia. Specifically, memory functions in the brain seem to be differentially organized, depending on whether the information to be learned involves declarative or procedural knowledge.

DECLARATIVE MEMORY (KNOWING THAT)

Declarative memory refers to memory that is directly accessible to consciousness; that is, one can declare this memory. This type of memory deals with facts and data and is typically impaired when amnesia results from damage to medial temporal and diencephalic structures. Declarative memory in many ways can be seen as an amalgam of episodic and semantic memory, many aspects of which are affected by anterograde amnesia

3

(Aggleton, 1991). Declarative memory is directly accessible to conscious recollection and deals with those facts and data that are acquired through learning.

Declarative memory is believed to be "more cognitive," faster, and especially adapted for one-trial learning. It permits storage of information as single events that happened in particular times and places. The representation of experience in this manner affords a sense of familiarity about previous events. For example, whereas the ability to find a face that is hidden in a picture (and to perform this task very rapidly) is a perceptual skill, the ability to recognize a face as familiar after it is found depends on a declarative representation in memory.

Amnesia impairs the ability to acquire information about facts and events (declarative memory) but spares the capacity for skill learning and certain kinds of conditioning and habit learning. In addition, the phenomenon of priming still occurs in the amnestic patient. Declarative memory is accessible to conscious recollection and available to multiple response systems (Squire & Zola-Morgan, 1991).

Procedural Memory (Knowing How)

Procedural memory refers to learned skills or modifiable cognitive operations. This type of memory is often spared in amnesia, suggesting that structures other than those in the medial temporal and diencephalic regions mediate this type of memory. Both declarative and procedural memory refer to how material is represented in long-term memory.

Procedural memory is being used whenever one develops perceptual, motor, or cognitive skills. These usually require multiple learning trials and often allow little insight into *what* we have actually learned.

The claim that procedural abilities rely on a distinct neural system is supported by the finding that subjects with a variety of anterograde amnesias are able to learn procedural tasks. These tasks include mirror tracing, rotary pursuit tasks, mirror reading, and solving jigsaw puzzles, mathematical puzzles, and the Tower of Hanoi problem. Further support comes from classical conditioning: even patients with profound amnesic problems can still be classically conditioned. It is noteworthy that the amnesic patient may be able to master a particular skill but fail to remember where, when, and under what conditions the skill was acquired (i.e., the episodic aspects of the task). Procedural memory does not rely on medial temporal or diencephalic structures.

Procedural memory involves memory for skills and other cognitive operations. It is not accessible as facts, data, or time-and-place events but is demonstrated by learned skills or modifiable cognitive operations. Procedural memories are spared in amnesia, and amnestic patients show intact learning and retention of a variety of motor, perceptual, and cognitive skills, despite poor memory for the occurrence and parameters of the actual learning experience. Procedural memory is slow, more automatic, less cognitive, adapted for incremental learning, and not always accessible to information-processing systems other than the ones involved in its formation.

Procedural memory can be subdivided into several categories, such as motor skill learning, cognitive skill learning, priming, and simple forms of classical conditioning, and it is important to appreciate that procedural memory is not a single entity. It is a collection of different abilities, each dependent on its own specialized processing system. In addition to motor skill learning, cognitive skill learning, and priming, it includes perceptual learning, classical conditioning, and simpler examples of behavioral plasticity such as habituation, sensitization, and perceptual aftereffects. One therefore should not expect that a single lesion will affect all of procedural memory, at least not in the way that a single lesion in the hippocampus will affect all aspects of declarative memory. Declarative and procedural knowledge differ in their biological organization: Differences exist in the kind of information that is stored, how it is used, and what neural systems are required.

Squire and Cohen (1984) proposed that the medial-temporal cortex, which includes the hippocampus and other diencephalic structures, mediates declarative but not procedural memory. The medial temporal/midline diencephalic brain system is the area most commonly found to be damaged in cases of amnesia, and lesions in this region have a profound effect on declarative memory. Procedural memory is not affected by damage to these regions.

5

THE CLINICAL ASSESSMENT OF MEMORY

REFERENCE MEMORY

One will sometimes come across the term *reference memory*. Reference memory involves learning those aspects of a task that are consistent from trial to trial and require no updating or modification across trials. Reference memory is unaffected by hippocampal damage.

EXPLICIT MEMORY

Explicit memory refers to the conscious recollection of recent events and performance on recognition tests, such as that which occurs in laboratory learning exercises when a person is instructed to learn a list of words. This is similar to the concept of "intentional memory," whereby people are instructed to learn a body of material and they are aware of the goal and purpose of the exercise. This term is used to refer to processes operating at the time of retrieval. When a person is asked to remember "what occurred," the person will have to use explicit memory processes to recall the information. We are aware of explicit memory, and it is processed in our consciousness.

IMPLICIT MEMORY (INCIDENTAL MEMORY)

Implicit memory refers to the facilitation of performance on completion, identification, and other such tests that do not require conscious or intentional recollection of a specific prior episode. It is relatively easy to demonstrate that learning takes place, even when the person who is learning is unaware of having learned the information. This is similar to the concept of "incidental memory," whereby a person recalls more about a learning situation than is apparent to him or her. Implicit memory is inferred to have taken place when performance is facilitated by experience, despite the absence of conscious or intentional recollection of learning. It is important to appreciate that this refers primarily to a retrieval process, because someone can intentionally learn material but nonetheless years later be unable to remember the material unless given an implicit test of memory; that is, in spite of the intention at the time of learning, the memory may become manifest only when an appropriately structured implicit memory task is administered.

Implicit memory includes several kinds of abilities, all of which are nonconscious and expressed through performance.

These abilities provide for cumulative changes in perceptual or response systems and for the development of new skills and habits. The information is not accessible to conscious recollection and is inflexible, that is, it has limited access to systems not involved in the initial learning (Squire & Zola-Morgan, 1991).

The distinctions between implicit and explicit memory are descriptive and heuristic and do not necessarily imply the existence of two separate underlying systems. In fact, the major reason for advancing an implicit/explicit distinction stems from empirical observations of dissociations between performance on recall and recognition tests, on the one hand, and completion, identification, and similar tasks on the other. Neuropsychological investigations have shown that amnesic patients show intact performance on various implicit memory tests that do not require conscious recollection of previous learning episodes. A number of other studies have shown that amnesic patients can acquire various kinds of perceptual and motor skills in a normal or near normal manner, despite their inability to remember explicitly the episodes in which they acquired the skills. It has also been established that amnesic patients show normal priming effects on such implicit memory tasks as work completion, free association, and category instance production, as well as various other tests of implicit memory.

Figure 1.1 will help the reader appreciate the major classes of memory.

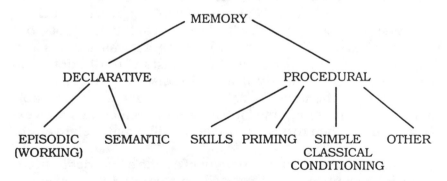

Figure 1.1. A schematic model of declarative and procedural memory. (*Source:* Squire, 1987.)

THE CLINICAL ASSESSMENT OF MEMORY

SUBDIVISIONS OF DECLARATIVE MEMORY

Declarative memory can be further subdivided into episodic and semantic memory. Although the neuroanatomy and neurophysiology of this model of brain organization remain unclear, some researchers have proposed that the frontal cortex is required to represent and use episodic memory effectively.

EPISODIC MEMORY

Episodic memory refers to autobiographical memory for events that are related to specific spatial or temporal contexts; the person not only remembers the event or information but also remembers when and where he learned it. There is no temporal dimension that necessarily underlies this type of memory. Episodic memory is severely affected by damage to the medial–temporal lobes and diencephalic structures.

Episodic memory is necessary to recall past events in an individual's life and is obviously important to the survival of the species. This system stores information related to temporally dated episodes that can later be recollected. Episodic memory stores the cumulated events of one's life; it is an individual's mental autobiography.

SEMANTIC MEMORY

Semantic memory refers to general knowledge of the world (e.g., facts, vocabulary, rules) that are independent of particular learning circumstances. For example, a person may have knowledge of an event but be uncertain as to when and where he learned that information. For example, almost every educated individual can identify Springfield as the capital of Illinois, but most of us have no idea when or where the fact was first learned. Semantic memory can be relatively resistant to disruption in many memory disorders until late in the disease process. For example, many patients with Alzheimer's disease will not be able to retain three or four items for 5 minutes on a mental status examination, yet their fund of information will remain relatively intact.

Semantic memory can be thought of as one's knowledge of the world and is contrasted with episodic memory, which is primarily one's knowledge of self. Semantic memory represents organized information such as facts, concepts, and vocabulary, and the content of semantic memory is explicitly known and available for recall. Unlike episodic memory, however, *semantic memory has no temporal landmarks*. It does not refer to particular events in a person's past.

Some investigators believe episodic memory is affected in amnesia, but semantic memory is spared. However, this tidy dichotomy is too simple to describe amnesia accurately, and many patients have lost significant portions of their semantic memory following brain injury. In addition, amnesic patients have difficulty both in learning new facts (semantic memory) and in acquiring information about specific events (episodic memory) (Shimamura & Squire, 1987). It now appears clear that the deficit associated with human amnesia, as well as that produced by hippocampal lesions in rats, involves both episodic and semantic memory, and both working and reference memory. This would be expected if the episodic/semantic distinctions represent a further subdivision of a general declarative memory system that is impaired in amnesia.

The idea that amnesia selectively affects episodic memory rests on the observation that amnesic patients almost always exhibit intact language functions and have available all of the semantic information they acquired in early life. Indeed, their IQ scores are routinely found to be normal. However, this intact semantic knowledge in amnesic patients stands in sharp contrast to their impaired capacity for acquiring new episodic information. Moreover, amnesic patients exhibit a pronounced impairment in semantic knowledge about the world when that knowledge is tied to events that occurred just before the onset of amnesia or during the years since the onset of amnesia.

Tulving (1983) initially developed the idea that episodic and semantic memory represent distinct memory systems. However, a good deal of controversy still exists concerning this theoretical distinction. The major problem with Tulving's position is that although many patients do experience difficulty remembering recent events (episodic recall) and have near normal retrieval capacity for vocabulary (semantic memory), this condition can be explained in terms of an impairment in new learning abilities together with intact access to old, premorbid knowledge acquired long before the onset of amnesia. One explanation seems as compelling as the other. In short, the distinction between episodic and semantic memory is confounded with the distinction between new and old learning.

Some patients who have recovered from encephalitis have extraordinary dense antero- and retrograde amnesias yet still show a highly accurate and sophisticated use of language (Aggelton, 1991). Such a division provides support for Tulving's proposal that long-term memories are either "episodic" (autobiographical information concerning events in our lives) or "semantic" (language, facts, general concepts, and rules about the world). An extreme version of this view is reflected in the position that all episodic memory may eventually become semantic memory.

It is tempting to transpose this distinction directly to the amnesic syndrome, but it is evident that there are shortcomings. It has been shown that amnesic subjects are impaired in learning new facts (semantic recall; e.g., geographical location of places), as well as new specific events (episodic recall). As a consequence, amnesic subjects show very clear impairments in semantic knowledge about the world when that knowledge is linked to events occurring after the onset of the amnesia. However, it has been found in a number of cases that the performance of the amnesic does not always parallel this semantic/episodic distinction.

GENERAL THEORIES OF MEMORY FROM A NEUROPSYCHOLOGICAL PERSPECTIVE

Developments in cognitive neuroscience have led to a concept of memory that posits multiple separable processes that can be differentially affected by neuropathological conditions. Memory processes can involve registration, encoding, storage, consolidation, or retrieval. In addition, memory tasks are often classified according to temporal demands into immediate memory, recent memory, and remote memory.

The use of clinical memory tests is generally based on the premise that memory consists of a known input, an observed output, and some objective way of determining the similarity of the output and the input. The operational definition of memory in clinical testing becomes the degree of correspondence between output and input. The formal assessment of memory provides the objective basis for measuring the closeness of this fit.

A popular experimental categorization of memory describes a *dual storage model* of memory and posits two fundamental types of memory: *short-term* and *long-term.* These two types of memory have fundamentally different characteristics. This model is congruent with the perspective of most clinical approaches and of this book.

Memory failure can result from a problem with retrieval or a true retention deficit. The retrieval deficit can be related to the inability to implement the correct retrieval cue. Alternatively, the memory might never have reached long-term storage in the first place or might have been subsequently lost through decay of the memory trace or interference from new memories. The permanence of long-term memory remains a topic of considerable debate.

Many memory theories have attempted to account for all aspects of amnesia by positing a defect in a single process. The most popular of these theories takes one of three forms and suggests that memory failure results from impairment in (a) the analysis or *encoding of information*, or the ability to attend to information delivery—processes that operate at the time of training; (b) the *maintenance or elaboration* of stored information—processes that operate during the retention interval; or (c) the *retrieval* of stored information—processes that operate at the time of testing. Each of these models will be discussed later in some detail.

SHORT-TERM MEMORY VERSUS LONG-TERM MEMORY

Short-term memory is a limited-capacity store with an extremely rapid decay period; that is, information is held for a brief period that ranges from seconds to about a minute.

Rehearsal or active thought is not required for short-term memory storage, which is heavily reliant on attentional processes. Its function is to "hold" information for further processing. Physicians frequently use the term *recent memory,* which can refer to memories for events that occurred hours or even days earlier. This terminology lacks precision, for it employs a single rubric to encompass at least two distinctly different types of memory.

Long-term memory refers to information that is characterized by almost unlimited capacity and a very slow rate of decay, that is, it lasts from minutes to years. Casual synonyms include delayed recall and *remote memory*.

Long-term memory is the type of memory that most people have in mind when they use the term *memory*, and it is also the entity that is most significantly impaired in most forms of amnesia.

> Memory and Infancy
> In ontogeny, declarative memory develops later than procedural memory. The late development of the declarative memory system may provide an explanation for infantile amnesia, the apparently universal inability to retrieve memories from the first year or two of life.

Evidence for a qualitative distinction between short-term memory and long-term memory is made all the stronger by the existence of a group of patients who have a severely limited auditory verbal short-term memory but who at the same time maintain near-normal long-term memory. For example, patients with damage in the supramarginal and angular gyri of the left hemisphere have been found to perform very poorly on Brown-Petersen learning tasks and show very reduced immediate memory spans for digits, words, or letters using auditory presentation. Similarly, in free recall tasks these patients may show a recency effect of only one item. In contrast, the same subjects show normal performance in tasks such as paired-associate learning, recall of stories, and the learning of word lists. It has been argued that these deficits reflect a specific loss of a temporary articulatory store which is an essential component of short-term memory storage.

These patients provide a *double dissociation* with amnesic subjects who fail tests of long-term memory yet perform normally on tests of short-term memory and vice versa. The critical anatomical foci in patients with reduced auditory verbal short-term memory are not known, but they appear to lie close to regions known to be important for auditory verbal reception.

PRIMARY MEMORY (WORKING MEMORY)

Primary memory is a type of short-term memory more related to active processing than actual memory storage. The term refers to the processes that support immediate retention and is similar to the notion of "attending to" material in consciousness. One of the most consistently observed features of the amnesic syndrome is that even the most profoundly amnesic patients exhibit normal immediate retention of various kinds of information, as assessed by such tasks as digit span (Schacter, Kaszniak, & Kihlstrom, 1991). If primary memory is equated with immediate retention, then amnesic patients possess intact primary memory. When primary memory is affected out of proportion to other cognitive functions, one needs to carefully assess the patient to determine if impaired performance results from an attention deficit rather than from a memory disorder.

The term *working memory* refers to one component of an elaborated model of primary memory. The model includes a limited capacity "processor" that is involved in selection and control functions, a temporary store for up to three items of speech-based information, and a "visuospatial scratchpad" that provides temporary storage of nonverbal information.

Stated another way, working memory can be defined as a limited-capacity system for short-term storage of those aspects of a task that change from trial to trial and that must be remembered to achieve success on any given trial.

The term *working memory* provides a richer dimension for the short-term memory concept. Working memory describes a work space or memory buffer in which one can maintain information while it is being processed. In one experiment, when subjects were required to remember a string of six digits at the same time that they performed other learning or reasoning tasks, their performance was disrupted less than might have been expected if short-term memory was a single common resource with limited capacity. A key aspect of the working-memory concept is that more than one component to working memory must exist. Thus, the digit-span task and at least some other aspects of working memory may not overlap at all.

It is possible to define working memory as a collection of temporary capacities intrinsic to information-processing subsystems. According to this view, the standard digit-span test assesses neither the span of consciousness nor the capacity of a single executive resource, but rather the span of just one working-memory system. Therefore, digit span is not a complete measure of short-term memory. This view posits that auditory-

13

verbal short-term memory is the temporary storage system only for phonologically coded speech sounds. Other information-processing systems have their own separate working-memory capacities.

SECONDARY MEMORY

Secondary memory refers to processes that support retention across long retention intervals. The emphasis is once again on the process rather than the storage concept. In general, secondary memory refers to material retained over long periods and relates to processes involved in storage and retrieval. The primary/secondary distinction receives support from studies of patients who exhibit normal long-term retention together with severely impaired immediate memory (Schacter et al., 1991).

AMNESIA

Amnesia refers to the partial or total loss of memory, that is, a profound inability to remember recent events against a background of relatively intact cognitive, linguistic, and perceptual abilities. Though observed as a consequence of multiple types of brain injury and disease, amnesia is usually attributable to damage in either the medial temporal and diencephalic brain regions.

The amnesic patient has an intact general fund of knowledge but a severe disability in learning new information. Thus, the traditional psychometric hallmark of the amnesic syndrome is a normal IQ, as typically measured by the WAIS-R, coupled with a memory quotient (MQ) at least 20 points lower as measured by the WMS-R (Albert & Lafleche, 1991).

ANTEROGRADE AMNESIA

Anterograde amnesia refers to the inability to learn new information such as people's names, events, and places, subsequent to some disturbance of the brain such as a head injury, electroconvulsive shock, or certain degenerative diseases.

Petersen and Weingartner (1991) report that anterograde amnesia is quite common, frequently resulting from head trauma, seizures, or drug exposure. It may be described as complete or incomplete, and typically occurs as a result of damage to medial temporal or diencephalic structures such as seen in herpes simplex encephalitis, Korsakoff's syndrome, temporal lobectomy, head trauma, or Alzheimer's disease. The anterograde feature refers to the timing of the amnesia, that is, from the time of trauma forward. Anterograde amnesia is likely to be present when an individual can't recall a particular new experience or piece of information a short time (e.g., minutes or hours) after it is first presented.

RETROGRADE AMNESIA

This term refers to the inability to recall material learned prior to a particular insult to the nervous system such as a head injury, seizure, or drug exposure. The two main features of the type of difficulty are its retrograde nature (i.e., the information that is lost occurred prior to the injury) and a time-dependent gradient. Memory loss is often incomplete and may have a temporal gradient, with events occurring immediately prior to the traumatic event being more difficult to remember. Retrograde amnesia is usually less severe than anterograde amnesia and may occur in cases of head trauma, Korsakoff's syndrome, and Alzheimer's disease.

POSTTRAUMATIC AMNESIA

Posttraumatic amnesia (PTA) can include both a period of retrograde amnesia and dense anterograde amnesia following a head injury. As a formal measure, PTA refers only to that period following head injury in which consciousness is severely clouded and the patient is unable to store and retrieve new information (Lezak, 1983). PTA is said to have ended when registration of information becomes continuous. Posttraumatic amnesia has become a standardized predictor of the magnitude of the deficits that will eventually result from a head injury, and it is a more powerful predictor than the total duration of a patient's coma.

THREE POSSIBLE EXPLANATIONS FOR AMNESIA

AMNESIA AS AN ENCODING DEFICIT

An encoding deficit is a disorder of processes operating at the time of training. The *Encoding Specificity Principle* (Tulving, 1983) states that specific encoding operations are performed on what is perceived and that these operations determine what is stored. What is stored in turn determines what retrieval cues are effective in providing access to what is stored.

The problem of failures in encoding can be illustrated by patients with Korsakoff's disease who appear to have difficulty engaging in deeper, more elaborate levels of information processing; as a result, they manage only an impoverished stimulus analysis. These patients exhibit tremendous difficulty distinguishing among unfamiliar faces, apparently limiting their analysis to the most superficial of facial features. As a result, they perform extremely poorly on tasks like the Diamond-Carey facial recognition task.

These patients also find it difficult to encode using semantic dimensions, even when instructed to use this strategy. This difficulty could result from frontal lobe dysfunction and may be independent of memory processes; support for this position can be found in proactive interference studies. If patients with dorsomedial nucleus damage (e.g., patients with Korsakoff's syndrome) are given four to eight extra practice trials to accomplish encoding, they exhibit an entirely normal rate of forgetting across at least 7 days. This is not true for electroconvulsive therapy (ECT) and medial temporal lobe patients, who exhibit a rapid rate of forgetting. This finding suggests that the deficit may be due primarily to an encoding deficit. However, retrievalists who are confronted with these findings argue that encoding and retrieval are too closely linked to draw such a conclusion.

Amnesia as a Storage Deficit

Amnesia also may result from a *storage deficit,* a disorder of processes operating during the retention interval, specifically, a disorder in postencoding processes (e.g., consolidation) such that memory is poorly maintained or elaborated with the passage of time. Support for this position comes from those forms of amnesia that are associated with an abnormally rapid rate of forgetting; patients with medial temporal lobe lesions, and those who have received ECT.

Consolidation (the process of transferring information from short-term memory to long-term memory) may underlie medial temporal lobe amnesia. The same forms of amnesia are associated with temporally limited retrograde amnesia, a disorder in which a patient loses only the months or years immediately preceding the onset of illness. This is hypothesized to be the result of a disorder of postencoding processes that ordinarily operate sometime after learning to maintain and elaborate memory. The postencoding (consolidation) process is believed to operate in long-term memory for years after learning initially occurs.

The *consolidation-block theory* holds that the basic deficit in amnesia is in the formation and storage of new long-term memories. This view easily captures the salient characteristics of amnesia (normal short-term memory, anterograde amnesia, lack of sense of familiarity), but it has trouble accounting for retrograde amnesia, priming, and skill acquisition. If no new memories are formed, how can performance be normal on priming and skill acquisition? If memories were consolidated long before the illness, why can't they be recalled?

AMNESIA AS A RETRIEVAL DEFICIT

A retrieval deficit is a disorder of processes operating at the time of retention testing. The retrieval failure theory illustrates yet another attempt to explain amnesia. This theory holds that new memories are formed normally (i.e., there is no consolidation block), but there is a specific deficit in the retrieval process. A defect in retrieval might explain why performance on priming tests and skill acquisition is normal. Both tasks provide the patient with extensive cues to retrieve memories that are available but temporarily inaccessible. Retrieval theory, however, cannot account for the patient's lost sense of familiarity, even when memory performance is normal, nor can it explain why some patients have only a very limited retrograde amnesia. If retrieval is deficient, then all past memories should be compromised. If one assumes that both consolidation and retrieval defects occur, it is still not possible to account for the pattern of retrograde amnesia or the existence of preserved skills.

Use of certain cuing and prompting techniques can elicit from amnesic patients information that otherwise seemed entirely absent from memory. These techniques include semantic prompting, cued recall, and recognition procedures. This finding implies that some information must have been adequately encoded and stored in order for it to be revealed when appropriate testing procedures are employed.

17

THE CLINICAL ASSESSMENT OF MEMORY

The word-completion method (e.g., using *mot* as a stimulus to elicit the word *motel*) demonstrates that amnestic patients can perform "normally" using this testing procedure only when they are instructed to respond with the first word that comes to mind when they are presented with the stimulus syllable. This suggests that information based on previous experience is stored normally in amnesia and can be retrieved under appropriate test conditions—that is, a retrieval deficit is present. Alternatively, it could simply mean that this test required use of only one memory subsystem rather than the entire integrated system.

All amnesic patients exhibit some form of retrograde amnesia, that is, apparent loss of memory from a period prior to the onset of amnesia. Information acquired during this period must have been encoded and stored in a normal way; that is, some information that must at some time have been adequately encoded and stored can't be expressed later. At the cellular-synaptic level, it appears that behavioral forgetting is accompanied by gradual disappearance of the relevant neural changes over a period of days and weeks (Kandel, 1976).

The failure of single or combined process theories to account for all aspects of amnesia has led to the conclusion that long-term memory is composed of different components or subsystems that mediate performance on different types of memory tests. Contemporary memory researchers emphasize the way in which defects are expressed in systems that handle particular types of memory.

PRESERVED CAPACITY FOR LEARNING IN AMNESIA

There are two broad classes of memory and memory tests: Explicit and implicit. Explicit tests present the patient with a series of recall and recognition tasks. Implicit tests never require the subject to reflect on the past; instead, he or she must perform a specified task (i.e., demonstrate procedural memory). Tests of priming and skill acquisition are implicit tests of memory. Amnesia primarily affects performance on explicit tests of long-term memory; that is, it is recognition, recall, and the sense of familiarity that is impaired in the amnesic patient.

Conscious recollection is *not* a necessary component of implicit tests such as priming or skill learning. In implicit tests, performance is driven by a retrieval cue that reactivates, without our awareness, only that portion of a stored event that fits with the cue, not the spatiotemporal context that locates the event in one's experience. As a result, the individual may emit the target word in response to a highly specific cue or perform a task faster or more efficiently with practice, but he or she may have no sense of familiarity or "pastness" in doing so.

This alternative explicit memory defect view can account for all of the basic features of the amnesic syndrome except the occurrence of extensive retrograde amnesia in some patients. Because it is virtually absent in some amnestic cases, retrograde amnesia probably involves structures and processes different from those of anterograde amnesia, which is the core of the amnesic syndrome.

PERCEPTUAL MOTOR SKILLS (SKILL ACQUISITION)

Skills like mirror reading are preserved in both antero- and retrograde amnesia. It is fascinating to note that amnesic patients can learn and retain pattern-analyzing operations and the encoding procedures required for motor tasks, such as mirror reading, but simultaneously demonstrate poor memory for the specific item information that would normally result from applying these operations or procedures. For example, H.M., a seizure patient famous in the history of neurology, who was treated surgically with bilateral ablation of the hippocampal gyri, learned a mirror-tracing task without any awareness of his prior experience with the task. He also demonstrated skill acquisition and retention on a rotary pursuit and bimanual tracking task. This ability to acquire skill without awareness on rotary pursuit tasks has been replicated in a variety of amnesic patients, including Korsakoff's syndrome patients and ECT patients. In every case, performance on this particular task was near normal and in marked contrast to the performance of these patients on verbal learning tasks and other explicit memory tasks.

This preserved capacity for learning in amnesia extends beyond perceptual-motor skills to perceptual and cognitive skills as well. For example, amnesic patients can improve at other cognitive tasks such as applying numerical rules, putting together jigsaw puzzles, and solving Tower of Hanoi and similar problems. Finally, previously acquired skills can survive amnesia.

For example, a mirror-reading skill was taught to depressed psychiatric patients just prior to ECT. After treatment the skill was retained at normal levels despite marked retrograde amnesia for the training experience itself.

In general "knowing how to" does not require active attention or conscious recall. Examples include the motor memories involved with recalling how to swing a golf club or computing a multiplication problem using a rule rather than rote memory (i.e, what is 3×3? A rule-based answer could involve the calculation $3 + 3 + 3 = 9$, whereas a rote answer would require recalling that $3 \times 3 = 9$). This "knowing how" (procedural) learning is not affected by medial temporal lobe or dorsomedial nucleus damage, but lesions in either area will selectively impair declarative memory (i.e., "knowing that").

PRIMING

Priming refers to facilitation of performance resulting from prior exposure to the information about which one is tested. This effect can be found even in the subject who shows dramatically impaired recall or recognition of the information, and the effect persists well beyond the span of short-term memory. Tests of priming usually involve showing a subject a set of words or pictures and then at a later stage providing that subject with the first few letters or a fragment of the picture. *Amnesic patients show normal priming effects.* When amnesic subjects are asked to form the first word or picture that comes into their mind on seeing the fragment they can perform like normal subjects; that is, they will often provide the original sample. In contrast, the amnesic subject may be impaired when he or she is told to use the fragment to recall a recently presented item.

The classification of priming with respect to other possible types of memory poses a problem. Although it fits more closely to an episodic/declarative type of division, it is unusual in that the subject is unaware that he or she possesses the knowledge that is being assessed. The presence of other characteristics that do not resemble declarative memory, coupled with its preservation in amnesia, have led some to argue that priming represents a further subcategory of procedural memory.

Picture- and word-completion performance is improved by priming. Amnesic patients perform better on word-recognition tasks if the words have been presented previously, though they can't remember the previous practice trials. However, instruction set has a marked effect on outcome in these studies, and normal performance is more likely to occur when the instructional set is to "complete the fragment to form the first word that comes to mind." This seems to direct the subject away from an intentional retrieval of memory for previously presented words. Amnesic patients perform like normal subjects if, and only if, both they and normal subjects are discouraged from treating the task as a memory test.

In both amnesic patients and control subjects, these priming effects tend to be transient and disappear after 2 hours. It is interesting to note that priming occurs for real words but not for pseudowords. In addition, when amnesic patients were cued with a particular homonym (e.g., "What is an example of a reed instrument?"), they would respond the cued response when later asked with a question that would permit use of either of the equivalent homonyms (e.g., "Spell "reed [read]"). There is conclusive evidence that prior exposure to stimuli can influence the performance of amnesic patients, even though these patients can not recall or recognize those same stimuli.

The performance levels achieved with priming in both normal subjects and amnesic patients falls short of the level that can be achieved by normal subjects when standard cued-recall techniques are used that instruct subjects to produce a previously presented word from declarative memory. Normal subjects can ultimately reach this higher level of performance, but amnestic patients can not.

Priming has never been shown to yield all of the information about previously presented words that is available in declarative memory (e.g., when and where genuine learning has occurred). We have very little information regarding the anatomy of priming effects, although a comparison of patients with matched memory problems but different degrees of cortical damage suggests that priming relies on the neocortex.

## CHAPTER TWO

The Neuroanatomy of Memory

There is abundant evidence that an anatomy of memory exists, and there is considerable agreement over many of its component parts. However, one anatomy will not suffice; there must be multiple anatomies reflecting multiple classes of learning and memory. Some of these "systems" are well established, whereas the existence of others has emerged only recently, and one can only speculate about their anatomical basis.

The best-understood system is that which enables us to learn new everyday information and events, and most of what we know about this system comes from studies of anterograde amnesia. Nevertheless, although we know an increasing amount about the *structures* involved in this process, we know far less about the actual *processes* involved in memory storage and retrieval.

The physical substrate of memory remains a fairly elusive neural network hidden in the "matted" interconnections of 100 billion or more nerve cells in the brain. Nonetheless, research has yielded enough information over the past several decades that tentative neuroanatomical models can be constructed and neuroanatomical components identified. The most important brain structures for memory are illustrated in Figure 2.1.

Neural structures and stations (cell assemblies) that contrib-

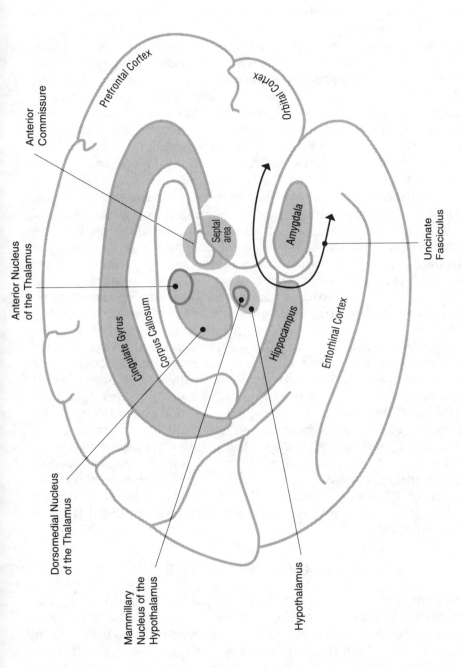

Figure 2.1. Major memory structures.

ute to memory have been identified, and an understanding of how their interconnections interact as memory is stored, retrieved, or linked with other experience is rapidly evolving. However, much of what we know about how memory is processed is derived from case studies of patients who have suffered injury, surgery, or diseases that have produced definable lesions and subsequent impairment of specific memory functions. In other words, most of what we know about how normal memory works is the byproduct of our study of pathological conditions and abnormal memory processes. An additional factor in our understanding of memory has been research involving lesion and stimulation studies of rats and macaque or rhesus monkeys. The macaque brain is about one-fourth the size of the brain of the chimpanzee, the nearest relative of human beings, and the chimpanzee brain in turn is only about one-fourth the size of the human brain. As a result, the models of memory that follow are somewhat limited because they were for, the most part, derived from research that studied the processing of damaged and infrahuman brains. Mishkin and Appenzeller (1987) summarized the situation as follows: "Our route to understanding human memory is an indirect one, with unavoidable drawbacks" (p. 80).

Increasing brain size has been accompanied by increasing brain complexity. The structures we study in the macaque all have counterparts in the human brain, but their functions may well have diverged in the course of evolution. In particular, the unique human capacity for language, and the cerebral specializations it has brought, limits the utility of comparisons with other species. In spite of these limitations to generalization, basic neural systems are likely to be common to monkeys and human beings, and research findings in animal studies have been consistent with what generally is known directly about human memory loss.

NEURAL NETWORKS

According to several theories, memory depends on the cooperative participation of assemblies of neurons that reside in cortical and subcortical brain systems and are specialized to process different kinds of information. Each specialized system has its own specific, short-term, working-memory capacity, as well as the capacity to retain in long-term memory specific features or dimensions of information. Each specialized system therefore stores the product of its own processing.

Long-term memory of even a single event depends on synaptic changes in a distributed ensemble of neurons, which themselves belong to many different processing systems. The ensemble, with all of its neurons acting together, constitutes memory for the whole event. Arguments by analogy from developmental neurobiology and sensory neurophysiology suggest that representations of events in memory are subject to competition and dynamic change. The strengthening of some connections within an ensemble occurs at the expense of other connections. These dynamic changes are the synaptic reflections of rehearsal, relearning, normal forgetting, and perhaps the passage of time alone; they result in a resculpting of the neural circuitry that originally represented the stored information (Squire, 1987).

Representations of experience continue to change and to be resculpted after learning occurs. One consequence of this process is normal forgetting. A second consequence is *consolidation*, the reorganization and stabilization of what remains. Consolidation allows at least some representations eventually to become independent of the brain system that is damaged in amnesia. Amnesic patients therefore often retain some remote, premorbid memory, despite their impaired new learning and despite loss of more recent, premorbid memory.

In short, the brain appears to integrate sensory input into a perceptual experience. This is true for all sensory modalities. The issue at hand, however, is how is this information translated from perception into memory.

Most often memories originate as sensory impressions (Mishkin & Appenzeller, 1987), and it is important to understand how the brain processes sensory information. However, such a digression is beyond the scope of this chapter and the reader is referred to any one of readily available texts on physiological psychology or behavioral neuroscience to supplement the following sections.

AMNESIA AND THE NEUROANATOMY OF MEMORY

Much of what is understood about the neuroanatomical correlates of memory has been derived from the study of amnesias and of anterograde amnesia in particular. Anterograde amnesia refers to the inability to learn new information, such as events, people's names, and places. It has been repeatedly shown that certain patterns of brain damage can produce a dramatic anterograde amnesia and yet spare a wide range of other cognitive abilities. This important finding leads to one inescapable conclusion: certain brain structures are necessary for the formation or retrieval of new memories and yet are not necessary for a wide range of other cognitive abilities. Thus, there must be a specific anatomy of memory mechanisms, and an obvious starting point is to define those regions responsible for anterograde amnesia. A second important feature of some anterograde amnesic syndromes is that memories prior to the onset of the impairment may be left intact. This, in turn, indicates that although those brain regions damaged may be crucial for normal memory function, they are unlikely to represent actual sites of memory storage.

Neuropathological studies have repeatedly shown that anterograde amnesia can be broadly defined as having either a temporal lobe or diencephalic origin. These two regions will initially be considered separately although, as will become apparent, they are almost certainly different components of the same system or systems.

NEUROANATOMICAL CORRELATES OF AMNESIA

Squire and Cohen (1984) proposed that there are at least two types of amnesia associated with neuroanatomical systems: medial temporal lobe amnesia (MTLA) & diencephalic amnesia (DCA).

MEDIAL TEMPORAL LOBE AMNESIA

The medial-temporal area can be conceptualized as a set of structures that permit storage and retrieval until consolidation is completed (perhaps by specifying the storage site or permitting consolidation via interaction with specific storage sites). This model presupposes that the temporal lobe establishes a relationship with distributed memory storage sites in the neocortex (and perhaps elsewhere). It then maintains the coherence of these ensembles until—as a result of consolidation— they can be maintained and can support retrieval on their own. The latter process could account for the rapid rate of forgetting and temporal gradient of amnesia associated with damage to this area.

Unilateral damage to the medial temporal lobes has different effects depending on which hemisphere is damaged. In general, left temporal lobe damage results in impaired memory for verbal material, and right temporal lobe damage leads to deficits in memory for visual and other nonverbal memories. However, this "localization rule" applies mainly to individuals who have experienced normal neurological development and are left-hemisphere-dominant for language.

MTLA involves two major limbic system structures: the amygdala and hippocampus. It can result from a variety of causes: the most common are listed in Table 2.1.

MTLA is associated with an abnormally rapid rate of forgetting and a temporally limited retrograde amnesia. It is believed to reflect a disorder of storage or postencoding processes that ordinarily operate during the time after learning to maintain and elaborate memory.

Scoville and Milner (1957) described a profound and selective impairment in human memory after bilateral surgical removal of the medial temporal lobe. Comprehensive neuropsychological evaluation of one patient from that series (patient H.M.), who underwent bilateral hippocampectomy, established the fundamental principle that the ability to acquire new memories is a distinct cerebral function, separable from other perceptual and

Table 2.1. Primary Causes of Medial Temporal Lobe Amnesia.

Extensive bilateral temporal lobe surgical resection, (e.g, to treat intractable seizures in epilepsy)

Encephalitis (e.g., herpes simplex)

Tumors (amnesia rarely occurs unless there was a loss of consciousness)

Trauma (mild to severe head injury)

Anoxia

Cerebral vascular accident (CVA of the posterior cerebral artery*)

*CVA of the Posterior Cerebral Artery causes loss of blood supply to the medial and inferior occipital lobes, and inferior surface of the temporal lobe. It also supplies portions of the thalamus, cerebral peduncle, internal capsule and choroid plexuses of the lateral and third ventricles.

cognitive abilities. Memory impairment has also been linked to medial temporal lobe damage in cases of viral encephalitis, posterior cerebral artery occlusion, and Alzheimer's disease. However, the medial temporal lobe is a large region that includes the hippocampal formation, the amygdaloid complex, and adjacent cortical areas, and it has been difficult to determine from human cases precisely which structures and connections within the medial temporal lobe are most clearly linked to memory.

Unilateral Temporal Lobe Amnesia

Unilateral damage can disrupt memory, although there appear to be clear differences between the effects of right and left hemispheric damage. Right temporal lobe damage disrupts tactile and visual maze learning, spatial position, facial recognition, and spatial memory; left temporal lobe damage impairs the recall of word lists, stories, nonsense syllables, and digit span performance.

> Many so-called "nonverbal tests" are more verbal than is intuitively obvious (e.g., the WMS-R visual-paired associates). In addition, there is some plasticity even in the adult central nervous system. Patients with significant right temporal lobe lesions can sometimes perform fairly well on some "nonverbal" tests because the brain is compensating or because the test isn't measuring purely "nonverbal" attributes.

Alzheimer's Disease and the Temporal Lobes

There is growing evidence that the most pervasive form of anterograde amnesia, Alzheimer's disease, is a consequence of medial temporal lobe damage. This disease produces widespread neuronal loss in a range of structures, including the temporal lobe, the prefrontal cortex, and basal forebrain regions such as the basal nucleus of Meynert. Although researchers have focused their attention on the basal nucleus of Meynert, there are good reasons for supposing that the medial temporal lobes are responsible for the loss of recent memory, which is so often the first symptom of Alzheimer's disease. First, those structures that suffer the greatest degree of cell loss as a consequence of the

28

disease include the amygdala and the hippocampus. The hippocampal pathology, which is primarily concentrated in the subiculum, field CA1, and entorhinal cortex, is of particular interest as it maps onto those regions described in the more circumscribed amnesias and would functionally isolate the hippocampus from nearly all of its afferent and efferent targets.

There is a second reason for associating Alzheimer's disease with medial temporal lobe damage. Longitudinal studies of Down's syndrome, which may be a heuristic model of Alzheimer's disease, strongly indicate that the plaques that are a characteristic of both diseases first form in the amygdala and hippocampus; whereas tangles are concentrated primarily in the entorhinal cortex. In light of the early and concomitant appearance of memory loss in Alzheimer's disease, these findings clearly implicate the medial temporal lobe, although they do not preclude a contributory effect from the basal forebrain.

THE HIPPOCAMPUS

The term *hippocampus* is derived from the Greek word for seahorse; the name was selected because the hippocampus is shaped much like a seahorse. The same structure is also referred to as Ammon's horn.

Since the 1950s the surgical removal of part of the temporal lobe has become a treatment reserved for patients with severe and intractable epileptic seizures focused in that part of the brain. This is because in the early days a handful of patients who received bilateral removal of the temporal lobes as a surgical intervention developed severe symptoms of amnesia. Patient H.M. is the best-known and best-studied case (summarized in a later section). Briefly, H.M.'s most striking symptom was a global amnesia, extending to memory for experience in every sensory modality. H.M.'s memory disturbance was primarily anterograde in nature—that is, he retained and could retrieve memories laid down prior to surgery, but could not form new memories postsurgery.

The organization of inputs to the hippocampus is slightly different in that the sensory (i.e., afferent) projections are first relayed through the parahippocampal, entorhinal, perirhinal, and prorhinal cortices. These cortical inputs then project through the perforant pathway to the hippocampus proper.

Many of their afferent projections terminate initially in the CA4 region of the hippocampus, from whence they pass, in a stepwise fashion, to CA2, CA1, and the subiculum.

The dense hippocampal projections to the mammillary bodies of the hypothalamus arise from all cell layers of the subiculum and presubiculum to pass exclusively through the fornix and terminate in the medial nuclei of the mammillary bodies, that part of the brain most consistently damaged by Korsakoff's disease. Additional projections terminate in the tuberomammillary nucleus. As in the case of the medial thalamus and amygdala, the medial mammillary nuclei do not project directly back upon the hippocampus. Instead, the mammillary body efferents to the hippocampus arise from the supra- and premammillary regions to terminate in the CA2 region of the hippocampus and the dentate gyrus.

The hippocampus also provides extensive thalamic inputs that may well be involved in mnemonic processes. In particular, dense projections arise from the subicular and entorhinal cortices to pass through the fornix to the anterior thalamic nuclei. In the case of the subiculum these projections terminate most heavily in the anterior medial and anterior ventral nuclei. Other subicular and entorhinal projections terminate in nucleus lateralis dorsalis, the medial pulvinar, and several of the more rostral midline nuclei. Some of the projections to the pulvinar and nucleus lateralis dorsalis appear to use nonfornical routes. The anterior medial and anterior ventral nuclei are of particular interest as they receive dense inputs from the hippocampus via the fornix and from the medial mammillary bodies via the mammillothalamic tract. These nuclei also project back upon the hippocampus and hence can provide an indirect route from the mammillary bodies to the hippocampus. The lateral dorsal thalamic nucleus, which is regarded as a member of the anterior complex, also has dense reciprocal hippocampal connections and hence should not be ignored in any consideration of diencephalic memory systems.

In summary, evidence for the involvement of the hippocampus in a wide range of amnesias of different etiologies appears to be incontrovertible. More precise localization of function within the hippocampal formation remains difficult, and indeed the anatomical organization of the structure makes it almost impossible to isolate one particular subfield. Nevertheless, the present pathological evidence suggests that there is a primary role for field CA1. As the hippocampus has both direct afferent and efferent connections with much of the temporal lobe cortex, it is also most likely that closely related regions such as the parahippocampal or entorhinal cortices will also prove to be associated with memory functions. The major connections between the hippocampus and other brain regions are illustrated in Figure 2.2.

The importance of the hippocampus in human memory was actually established from a case of amnesia. Patient R.B. developed memory impairment in 1978, at the age of 52, after an episode of global ischemia. He survived for 5 years, and during this time he exhibited significant memory impairment in the absence of other cognitive dysfunction. Upon his death, histological examination of the brain revealed a circumscribed bilateral lesion involving the entire rostrocaudal extent of the CA1 field of the hippocampus. Studies of animal models of global ischemia in the rodent have confirmed the vulnerability of CA1 neurons in the hippocampus to ischemia and implicated a mechanism for this selective lesion that involves the excitotoxic effects of a glutamate neurotransmitter. Findings from patient R.B. led inexorably to two conclusions. First, the hippocampus itself appeared to be a critical component of the medial temporal lobe memory system. This idea was later supported by an additional case in which memory impairment was associated with a bilateral lesion confined to the hippocampus. Second, because R.B. was not as severely amnesic as H.M., other hippocampal regions in addition to the CA1 field, or potentially structures outside the hippocampus, must be important for memory functions (Squire & Zola-Morgan, 1991).

THE AMYGDALA

Amygdala is the Greek word for almond. Here too the name is derived from the shape of the structure. The amygdala is a critical brain structure whose relevance to memory we are just beginning to understand.

According to Mishkin and Appenzeller (1987), it is impossible to reproduce a comparable global loss of memory in animals by removing the hippocampus alone. Through a series of experiments focusing on the amygdala rather than the hippocampus, Mishkin and his colleagues were able to demonstrate that it

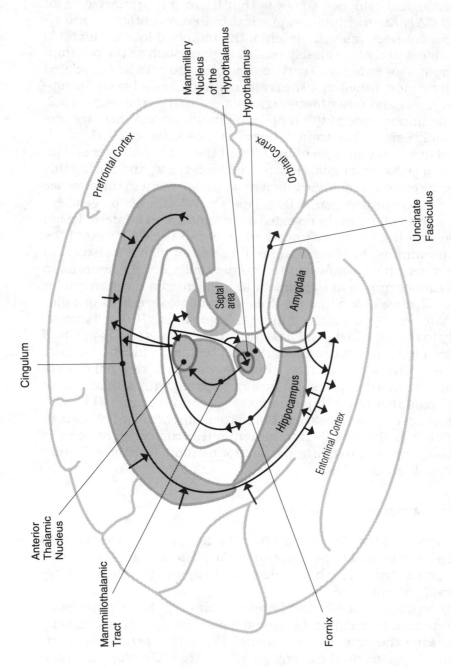

Figure 2.2. Hippocampal projections.

plays just as important a role in memory as the hippocampus. Simultaneous destruction of *both* the hippocampus and the amygdala, in both hemispheres of experimental monkeys, resulted in an extremely heuristic animal model of global anterograde amnesia. As a result of his research, Mishkin concluded that *severity of memory loss varies in proportion to the amount of damage sustained jointly by the amygdala and hippocampus.*

Sensory afferents to the amygdala arise directly from a number of cortical association areas such as the inferotemporal cortex, the superior temporal cortex, the insula, and the temporal sulcus. Some of these cortical regions provide sensory-specific information (e.g., the inferotemporal cortex, superior temporal cortex, and insula), and the other cortical inputs involve polysensory information. As a consequence, highly processed sensory information is allowed to converge upon the amygdala (Aggleton, 1991).

The amygdalothalamic projections arise primarily from the basal amygdaloid nuclei and terminate in characteristic patches in the rostral half of the medial magnocellular portion of the medial thalamus. Furthermore, both the entorhinal and perirhinal cortices project to the magnocellular medial thalamus, although there is little overlap with the amygdaloid projections. In spite of the substantial input from the amygdala to the medial thalamus, there are no direct reciprocal projections; in other words, the medial thalamus cannot influence the amygdala directly. This is clearly important when considering the relationship between temporal lobe and diencephalic amnesias.

The lack of reciprocal connections between the medial thalamus and the amygdala or temporal association cortex forces the researcher attempting to understand the structure of memory to turn his or her attention to the major efferent target of the medial thalamus—the prefrontal cortex. Researchers have been particularly interested in the caudal orbital cortex and caudal medial cortex as these adjacent areas receive inputs not only from the medial portion of the medial thalamus but also from the amygdala and the hippocampus. Parts of the rostral cingulate cortex, receive inputs from the amygdala and hippocampus, as well as the anterior thalamic nuclei, although most of the thalamic inputs terminate in the caudal cingulate cortex.

The Amygdala and Emotion

Mishkin and Appenzeller (1987) proposed that *the amygdala not only links sensory events and emotions, but also enables emotions to shape the perception and the storage of memories.* The amygdala, in its capacity as intermediary between the senses and the emotions, is the structure best suited to support such "selective attention," and its circuitry could give the amygdala this gatekeeping function. Sensory systems in the cortex not only send fibers to the amygdala but also receive projections from it—projections that, at least in the visual system, are densest in the highest processing stations. The amygdala is rich in neurotransmitters known as *endogenous opiates,* which in other parts of the nervous system are believed to regulate the transmission of nerve signals. In toto, the evidence suggests that opiate-containing fibers run from the amygdala to the sensory systems, where they may serve a gatekeeping function by releasing opiates in response to emotional states generated in the hypothalamus. In this way the amygdala may enable the emotions to influence what is perceived and learned. The amygdala's reciprocal effect on the cortex may explain why, in both monkeys and humans, emotionally charged events are easier to remember. One suspects the amygdala was directly involved when Marcel Proust dipped his cookie into his tea, triggering the flood of memories that led to the eventual publication of *Remembrance of Things Past.*

Both the amygdala and the hippocampus have afferent and efferent links with the neocortex. In the case of the hippocampus, many of these efferents are relayed via the entorhinal and parahippocampal cortices. Of particular interest is that the projections from the amygdala and the hippocampus, passing through the parahippocampal gyri, project to very widespread areas of cerebral association cortex; these reciprocal connections are at least as widespread as the inputs from the cortex to limbic structures (Aggleton, 1991). The major connections between the amygdala and other brain structures are illustrated in Figure 2.3.

It is interesting to examine the subcortical projections from the amygdala and hippocampus. Both structures project to diencephalic targets, which themselves have been implicated by studies of amnesia.

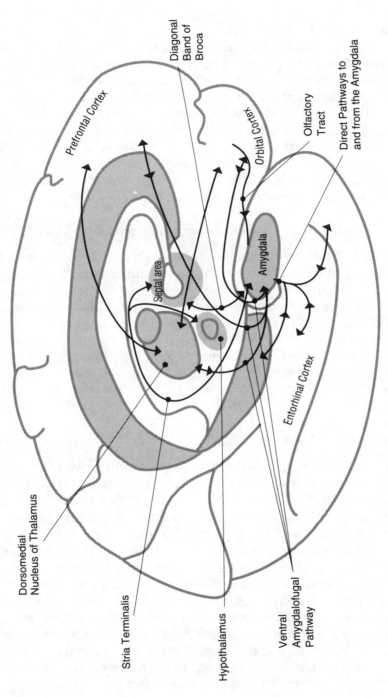

Figure 2.3. Amygdaloid connections.

The weight of the evidence suggests there may be two parallel limbic-diencephalic systems: one from the hippocampus via the fornix to the mammillary bodies and the anterior thalamic nuclei; the other from the amygdala to the magnocellular portion of the medial thalamus. The direct connections between the temporal and diencephalic regions are implicated in anterograde amnesia, and suggest that temporal lobe and diencephalic amnesias are different facets of the same underlying amnesic syndrome. although the structure and functions of the amygdala and hippocampus are clearly different, the two regions are reciprocally connected, and it is naive to consider these two limbic structures to be totally independent of one another.

The Amygdala, the Hippocampus, and Spatial Memory

The roles of the two memory circuits outlined above may differ in spatial learning. Although the hippocampus and the amygdala can substitute for each other in learning to recognize an object, *the hippocampus is particularly important for learning spatial relations.* There also appears to be a significant correlation between the extent of hippocampal damage and the degree of impairment in remembering the locations of objects. In contrast, there is little to no impairment of spatial memory associated with amygdaloid damage (Mishkin and Appenzeller, 1987).

DIENCEPHALIC AMNESIA (DCA)

Damage to the amygdala and the hippocampus, two major components of what is known as the limbic system, is not the only kind of neuropathology that can result in global amnesia. In other amnesic patients the site of the damage is the *diencephalon*, a cluster of nuclei at the center of the brain organized into two structures known as the thalamus and the hypothalamus. Parts of the diencephalon situated medially (near the midline of the brain) degenerate in Korsakoff's syndrome, producing the global amnesia seen in some chronic alcoholics. Diencephalic damage from strokes, injuries, infections, and tumors can cause the same amnesic syndrome. The clinical evidence that documents the importance of the diencephalic nuclei to memory is reinforced by the anatomical finding that the diencephalon receives fibers running from the hippocampus and the amygdala.

Much of what is known about diencephalic amnesia has been derived from study of the brains of patients with Korsakoff's syndrome, an amnesic and confabulatory syndrome described over 100 years ago and associated with vitamin B deficiencies and subsequent diencephalic damage due to chronic alcoholic abuse. The amnesic state associated with Korsakoff's syndrome results from damage in the hypothalamic and thalamic regions adjacent to the third ventricle. More detailed investigations have also emphasized the invariable damage to the mammillary bodies, which typically appear discolored and shrunken. It is common to find neuronal loss in the medial mammillary nucleus of patients with Korsakoff's syndrome.

The presumed key role of the mammillary bodies in diencephalic amnesia arose from descriptions of Korsakoff's syndrome in which the pathology appeared to be limited to the mammillary bodies. Additional evidence came from reports that colloid cysts and tumors located in the floor and walls of the third ventricle, and hence adjacent to the mammillary bodies, may produce an amnesic state. Furthermore, drainage or removal of the cyst has occasionally relieved the amnesia. The fact that one of the major inputs to the mammillary bodies is from the hippocampus seemed to provide the final confirmation of this structure's key mnemonic role (Aggleton, 1991).

The regions surrounding the third ventricle include the *dorsomedial nucleus* and the mammillary bodies, parts of the thalamus and hypothalamus, respectively. *Dorsomedial nucleus* connections include the prefrontal lobes (reciprocal connections), the amygdala, the ventral posterior nucleus of the thalamus, and the hypothalamus. The primary mammillary connections include the hippocampus (via the fornix) and the anterior nucleus of the thalamus (projecting to the cortex of the gyrus cinguli).

It is clear that a distinct diencephalic amnesia exists. Although few would argue that the mammillary bodies or their connections do not contribute to the syndrome, the status of other diencephalic regions remains unclear. The lack of confirmed, nearly complete lesions confined to particular diencephalic nuclei still precludes any unequivocal statement concerning the anatomical basis of diencephalic amnesia. Indeed, it may turn out that a combination of more than one structure or pathway is required to produce the full amnesic syndrome.

THE FRONTAL CORTEX

Mishkin and Appenzeller (1987) noted that nuclei in the thalamus that communicate with the limbic structures send fibers in turn to the ventromedial prefrontal cortex, a part of the cortex tucked under the front of the brain. Other researchers have found that surgical lesions in this region led to a profound loss of recognition memory.

Although the prefrontal cortex may well form an important further component in a medial temporal–medial diencephalic system, there is little evidence that prefrontal damage produces an amnesic syndrome comparable to that seen after damage to either the diencephalic or temporal regions. Some descriptions of prefrontal damage report the regular occurrence of anterograde memory problems, but many others do not. The latter cases include descriptions of the outcomes of prefrontal lobotomies and lobectomies, some of which involve damage to those orbital regions presumably most implicated by their anatomical connections. Furthermore, when memory disorders are observed in these patients, they most often relate to difficulties such as learning the temporal order of events, assessing the relative frequency and recency of stimuli, or learning conditional associations. Although it is the case that frontal damage may often be associated with memory problems, there are qualitative differences between these disorders and those associated with temporal or diencephalic damage.

An apparent exception has been the observation that rupture of the anterior cerebral artery or the anterior communicating artery can produce an anterograde amnesic state resembling Korsakoff's syndrome. Because such cases frequently involve the orbital cortex, they appear to strengthen the case for a prefrontal contribution to amnesia. Unfortunately, such vascular accidents also involve basal forebrain regions, and this subcortical damage is likely to be the real cause of the patient's amnesia.

In summary, a complex series of temporal-diencephalic connections has emerged that tightly links the amnesic syndromes observed after damage to these specific areas. This does not, however, mean that temporal lobe and diencephalic amnesias can be regarded as identical syndromes. Damage to different regions will result in different functional losses. Nevertheless, when the critical flow of information is from temporal regions to the diencephalon, the similarities will outweigh the differences. These similarities include comparable performance on a variety of neuropsychological measures, for example, difficulty in new learning, intact digit-span or immediate memory, and intact general intellectual ability.

Some researchers argue that temporal and diencephalic amnesias may be distinguished by different rates of forgetting, but recent studies have cast doubt on this distinction; at present there is no generally agreed qualitative difference between these amnesias. Given the apparent lack of appropriate back projections from some diencephalic regions to the temporal lobe, it is tempting to suppose that the major flow of information is to the prefrontal cortex, although the pathways involved in this transmission are not fully understood.

Warrington and Weiskrantz (1974) take another position and argue that amnesias reflect a disconnection of temporal-diencephalic-frontal structures in which different memory systems are isolated from one another. Whichever view proves nearer to the truth, it is becoming clear that the prefrontal cortex cannot be ignored and that a series of interrelated structures have been identified that form a complex anatomy of structures necessary for normal recent memory. Although vital to memory, these structures are unlikely to represent the sites of memory storage.

CLASSICAL CONDITIONING AND THE CEREBELLUM

R. F. Thompson (1987) and his colleagues have devoted the past 17 years to a search for memory traces, using classical conditioning of discrete behavioral responses. This search has led them to believe that the cerebellum plays a major role in the storage of memories related to associative "motor" learning.

The classical-conditioning paradigms that have been studied can be conceptualized as a type of procedural learning. In rats and rabbits, simple classically conditioned responses such as eye blink responses do not appear to be affected by hippocampal lesions. Further, excision of the neocortex in rats does not inhibit classical conditioning, providing that the stimuli are not too complex. On the strength of these data, Thompson (1987) and his colleagues have proposed that one subcortical site involved in classical conditioning is the cerebellum. They have found that selective lesions produce impairments in nictating membrane responses (i.e., conditioned eye blink responses in rabbits). Although this does not mean that cerebellar lesions disrupt all forms of classical conditioning, considerable advances have been made in mapping out the probable circuitry involved, including key roles for the interpositus nucleus of the cerebellum, the red nucleus of the midbrain, the inferior olive, and the fibers that interconnect them. In a *Science* article that captures the excitement of memory research, Thompson summarized his findings as follows:

> We believe that the memory traces for classical conditioning of discrete behavior responses learned associatively to neutral conditioned stimuli, with the use of aversive unconditioned stimuli, are stored in the cerebellum. . . . We have now succeeded in identifying key aspects of the essential memory trace circuit (which includes the cerebellum) for this category of learning and memory beyond reasonable doubt and are approaching the point when it will be possible to localize the essential memory traces themselves. (p. 1730)

CURRENT MODELS OF MEMORY

There are two prominent models of the neuroanatomy of memory, derived from the work of Mishkin and Appenzeller (1987) and that of Squire and Zola-Morgan (1991). We believe these two models are the most useful for the clinician, in part because they take into account the connections between the limbic and frontal cortical regions. The major difference between the two models concerns the role of the amygdala in memory processes. Mishkin and his colleagues believe that the amygdala plays a significant role; Squire and his colleagues do not.

MISHKIN'S MODEL

According to Mishkin, the crucial pathways for memory can be identified and are anchored in two structures located in the medial portion of the temporal lobe. Although they are structurally different, the amygdala and the hippocampus share at least one very important attribute. Both structures receive dense cortical inputs that allow sensory information for a range of modalities to gain access to these limbic structures. This would appear to be a prerequisite feature for structures involved in anterograde amnesia, as the deficits it produces are polysensory in nature; and yet, with the exception of olfaction, there is no specific sensory loss (Aggleton, 1991).

Mishkin (1982) proposed one way that medial temporal and diencephalic structures function together as a memory system. In this model, the critical structures are presumed to be the hippocampus, the amygdala, and their diencephalic targets, the anterior nucleus of the thalamus and the dorsomedial thalamic nucleus. This neuroanatomical perspective is compatible with the hypothesis that additional structures with strong links to these medial temporal and medial thalamic sites play a role in the same functional system. For example, the mammillary nuclei both project to the anterior nucleus and, in addition, receive substantial input from the hippocampal formation via the fornix. Also, the ventromedial frontal cortex receives projections from both the anterior nucleus and the dorsomedial thalamic nucleus. Consistent with these facts, lesions of the ventromedial (but not dorsolateral) prefrontal cortex in monkeys produce a recognition memory deficit. Recent radiographic data have also suggested that damage to the ventromedial prefrontal area can occur in those patients who develop amnesia following rupture and repair of anterior communicating artery aneurysms.

Finally, the basal forebrain (nucleus basalis, diagonal band of Broca, and septal nuclei) projects to both the amygdala and separately to the hippocampus (via the fornix). In the monkey, preliminary findings demonstrate that conjoint lesion of all three components of the basal forebrain — but not a lesion of two out of three components — will moderately impair performance on the delayed nonmatching-to-sample task. Basal forebrain pathology has also been hypothesized to contribute to the amnesia associated with rupture of the anterior communicating artery as a result of cerebral aneurysms.

The available data suggest that nucleus basalis lesions, or even larger lesions of the basal forebrain, do not cause severe amnesia in the absence of additional damage. Nevertheless, this idea became widely accepted following reports that patients suffering from Alzheimer's disease had selective neuronal loss in that region. More recent studies of the pathophysiology of Alzheimer's disease have found prominent pathology in the entorhinal cortex and in the subiculum of the hippocampal formation. Such damage effectively isolates the hippocampal formation from the neocortex. If medial temporal pathology were a typical early finding in Alzheimer's disease, it would explain why memory problems are so often the first significant symptom noted in with this disease.

Mishkin (1982) updated his theory in the Mishkin and Appenzeller article in *Scientific American* (1987) in which he argued that the visual system and other sensory systems as well, are linked with two parallel memory circuits including, at a minimum, the limbic structures of the temporal lobe, medial parts of the diencephalon, and the ventromedial prefrontal cortex. Although these circuits are critical to the function of memory, memories themselves are probably not stored there exclusively or even mainly.

Mishkin's position is supported by the clinical observation that damage to the limbic system in humans leaves old memories intact and accessible, suggesting they must be stored at an earlier station in the neural paths cited above. The likeliest repositories of memory, in fact, are the same areas of cortex where sensory impressions take shape.

The subcortical memory circuits must involve feedback loops with the cortex. After a processed sensory stimulus activates the amygdala and hippocampus, the memory circuits "play back" in the sensory area. That feedback presumably strengthens and possibly stores the neural representation of the sensory event that has just taken place. The neural representation itself probably takes the form of an assembly of many neurons, interconnected in a particular way.

As a result of feedback from the memory circuits, synapses (junctions between nerve cells) in the neural assembly must undergo changes that preserve the connection and transform the perception into a durable memory. Recognition takes place later, when the neural assembly is reactivated by the same sensory event that formed it.

Just how each structure in the memory circuits might contribute to the feedback is not known. There are already clues to the nature of the feedback as a whole, however. One clue lies in yet another structure that Mishkin's work has implicated in recognition memory. It is the basal forebrain cholinergic system, a cluster of neurons that provides the cortex and the limbic system with their major input of a neurotransmitter called acetylcholine.

Acetylcholine seems to play a vital role in memory. For one thing, it is depleted in Alzheimer's disease, and of course memory loss is the hallmark characteristic of Alzheimer's disease. Further, it was found that monkeys perform exceptionally well, relative to their own baseline performance, on tests of visual recognition memory when they are given *physostigmine,* a drug that enhances the action of acetylcholine. When they are given *scopolamine,* on the other hand, a substance that blocks the action of the neurotransmitter, their performance is impaired. Further support for the role of the forebrain in memory comes from ablation studies. Damaging the basal forebrain impairs recognition memory in monkeys, although the effect seen so far is not as severe or long-lasting as the effects of damaging the other structures, such as the temporal lobe and diencephalon.

Linking circuitry enables other structures to enlist the basal forebrain in memory formation. For example, the hippocampus and the amygdala have extensive projections to the basal forebrain, which in turn sends acetylcholine-containing fibers back not only to the limbic structures but also to the cortex. It is plausible to speculate that the activation of the subcortical memory circuits by a sensory stimulus triggers the release of acetylcholine from the basal forebrain into the sensory area. The acetylcholine (and probably other neurotransmitters whose release is triggered in the same way) would initiate a series of cellular steps that could modify synapses in sensory tissue, strengthening neural connections and transforming the sensory perception into a physical memory trace.

Results of recent biochemical studies suggest that possible mechanisms of synaptic modification are active in the areas believed to be likely sites of memory storage: the final stations of the visual system.

One of the most striking aspects of the anterograde amnesic syndrome is that premorbid memories may remain essentially intact. This suggests that those regions responsible for anterograde amnesia are not primary sites of memory storage, nor can they be necessary for the retrieval of old memories. In the case of H.M., it would appear that his event memory prior to the age of

16 years, when his first seizures occurred, is entirely normal. Because he has lost all of the medial temporal structures and the presumed initial flow of sensory information is from the temporal cortex to the subcortex, the storage of his premorbid memories must be "upstream" from the site of the lesion—namely, in the cortex. A similar logic dictates that diencephalic structures, which are "downstream," cannot be a site of memory storage, and as predicted, there are diencephalic amnesic cases with normal retrograde memory. Nevertheless, the existence of a diencephalic syndrome shows that a closed reciprocal temporal cortex–hippocampus–amygdala system is insufficient for the encoding, storage, and retrieval of memories.

Evidence for a cortical role in the storage of memory is seen in those diseases that produce a persistent retrograde amnesia. Although it may be logically impossible to distinguish a retrieval deficit from a storage deficit, certain diseases that produce extensive cortical damage (e.g., Alzheimer's disease or herpes encephalitis) may be accompanied by a severe, permanent retrograde amnesia. In both cases the cortical damage is typically most severe in the temporal and frontal lobes. Further evidence for the involvement of temporal association cortex has come from anatomical studies on the flow of visual information from the striate cortex to the parietal and temporal cortices and from the effects of inferotemporal damage upon complex visual learning tasks. These studies strongly suggest that the inferior temporal cortex acts as a storehouse for the central representation of visual stimuli.

SQUIRE AND ZOLA-MORGAN'S MODEL

Squire and Zola-Morgan (1991) have proposed that memory is not a single faculty but is composed instead of multiple separate systems, only one of which is impaired in amnesia. As support for their model, Squire and Zola-Morgan have marshaled the following arguments:

1. Coordinated and distributed activity in the neocortex is thought to underlie perception and immediate (short-term) memory.
2. These capacities are unaffected by medial temporal lobe damage.
3. However, if distributed cortical activity is to be trans-

formed into stable long-term memory, then the hippocampus and related structures must be engaged at the time of learning.

4. The hippocampus and related structures may serve as a device for forming connections between ordinarily unrelated events or stimulus features, which are processed and represented by distinct cortical sites.

5. In this sense, the hippocampal system is a storage site for a simple memory, a summary sketch, or an index. As long as a percept is in view or in mind, its representation remains coherent in short-term memory by virtue of mechanisms intrinsic to the neocortex. However, a problem potentially arises when attention shifts to a new percept or a new thought, and one then attempts to recover the original memory.

6. The capacity for later retrieval is achieved because the hippocampal system has "bound together" the relevant cortical sites that together represent memory for a whole event.

7. The role of this system can be further described in two important ways. First, the hippocampal system is crucial for the rapid acquisition of new information about facts and events, which are then available as conscious recollection. Long-term potentiation (LTP) in the hippocampus would be an appropriate mechanism for this specialized role of the hippocampus in rapidly forming conjunctions between unrelated events. In any case, many kinds of learning abilities (including skills, priming, habit learning, and simple forms of conditioning) lie outside the province of the medial temporal lobe memory system.

The role of the hippocampal system is only temporary, and its disturbance may not affect long-term memory. In humans, for example, very remote memory is unaffected by damage restricted to the medial temporal lobe. A prospective study of retrograde amnesia in the monkey showed that memories that initially depended on the integrity of the hippocampal formation gradually became reorganized (consolidated) so that after a period of several weeks they became independent of the hippocampal formation. Thus, as time passes after learning, more permanent memory develops, presumably as a result of slow synaptic change and in concert with normal forgetting. Remembering eventually becomes possible without the participation of the medial temporal lobe memory system.

Cumulative and systematic research with monkeys and related research with humans has identified the components of this medial temporal lobe memory system: the hippocampus, together with adjacent, anatomically related cortex (i.e., the entorhinal, perirhinal, and parahippocampal cortex). This system is fast, has limited capacity, and performs a crucial function at the time of learning by establishing long-term declarative memory. Its role continues after learning, through a lengthy period of reorganization and consolidation, during which memories stored in the neocortex eventually become independent of the medial temporal lobe memory system. This process, by which the burden of long-term (permanent) memory storage is gradually assumed by the neocortex, assures that the medial temporal lobe system is always available for the acquisition of new information. The anatomy and function of the system, and its relation to neocortex, are becoming well enough understood that computational modeling should provide a fruitful way to make these ideas more formal and quantitative.

RELEVANT ANIMAL RESEARCH

Animal research, especially work with monkeys, has demonstrated the relevance of the hippocampus and amygdala to memory. For example, Zola-Morgan, Squire and Mishkin (1982) compared groups of monkeys with ablations in the hippocampal–amygdala region with monkeys with dorsomedial nucleus lesions. On delayed nonmatching-to-sample tasks (which involved reinforcement for selection of the novel stimulus items) these investigators found rapid forgetting in monkeys with hippocampal-amygdala lesions but relatively normal curves of forgetting in monkeys with dorsomedial nucleus lesions.

Similar experiments have demonstrated that monkeys with medial temporal lobe lesions can learn a visual pattern discrimination task at a normal rate because this procedure is similar to motor learning in humans (Iverson, 1976). Mishkin (1978) studied monkeys with discrete and separate lesions of amygdala and hippocampus and found that these lesions resulted in only mild (and roughly equivalent) impairment on nonmatching-to-sample tasks (such as getting food from under the novel nonmatching object). In contrast, combined hippocampal and amygdala lesions caused severe impairment. In addition, these lesions caused impairment in the tactile modality, suggesting that the impairment resulting from injury in this region is modality-general in the monkey, just as it is in the human (Murray & Mishkin, 1981).

The fornix itself does not appear critical to memory because damage to that organ does not result in significant impairment (Gaffan, 1974).

SELECTED CASE STUDIES

Theories about the neuroanatomical structures associated with memory have by and large come from case reports and clinical and laboratory studies that involve the loss of or damage to one or more structures in the brain. Several classic case studies have resulted in the development of specific models for the neuroanatomical basis of memory. The individuals involved in these studies incurred substantial damage to or removal of neuroanatomical structures that are presently considered to be memory-processing centers.

The most famous and longest-studied case in the history of memory research is that of H.M., a patient who experienced severe epileptic seizures for about 11 years. At age 27, he underwent bilateral resection of the anterior portion of his temporal lobes in a desperate attempt to treat his seizure disorder. In fact, his seizures stopped after the operation; unfortunately, he also lost the ability to register and consolidate memories. Subsequent research has supported the importance of the medial termporal lobes for memory. However, the specific roles and functions of medial temporal lobe structures such as the amygdala and hippocampus are still not fully understood.

Another case study that suggests that structures bordering the third ventricle are involved in memory was more recently reported by Brown, Kieran, and Patel (1989). The patient in this report, J.E., suffered from a left medial thalamic hematoma that resulted in mild figural memory deficits and the loss of the ability to retain verbal memories. J.E. was a 69-year-old, right-handed black male with 12 years of education. He was a retired postal clerk. J.E. experienced a "sudden onset of confusion" on January 3, 1986. He was subsequently diagnosed as having a discrete left thalamic lesion, specifically a dorsal medical nucleus (DMN) hematoma. The lesion resulted in a severe anterograde amnesia. The memory deficit was most apparent with verbal materials, but J.E. also performed poorly on tests of figural memory. A formal neuropsychological evaluation was performed on January 28, 3½ weeks after the onset of symptoms. The primary finding of this evaluation was that J.E. demonstrated an anterograde memory deficit for verbal and geometric material when the amount of material recalled was large relative to his short-term memory capacity or when he had to recall the material after the elapse of several minutes. In contrast, his verbal short-term memory functioning was intact. He had *no* consistent remote memory deficit.

The importance of J.E.'s case is that it clearly demonstrates that isolated thalamic damage can cause memory deficits. Brown, Kieran, and Suresh (1989) maintain that the lesions in most cases of "so-called" amnesia also involve cortical structures. For example, in one celebrated case (Squire, 1987) that involved a fencing foil injury to the left DMN, the orbital-frontal cortex, the neostriatum, the rostrum of the corpus callosum, and white matter near the thalamus were also involved. Patients with alcoholic Korsakoff's syndrome also frequently have lesions outside the medial thalamus, and postmortem studies of these patients have nearly always found extensive bilateral nerve cell loss and gliosis of the mammillary bodies, in addition to involvement of the DMN.

CHAPTER THREE

The Neuropathology of Memory

NEUROLOGICAL DISORDERS AFFECTING MEMORY

DEMENTIA

Dementia is a generic term referring to progressive loss of a variety of higher mental functions, usually occurring in old age. About 15% of adults over age 65 suffer from one specific cause of dementia—Alzheimer's disease or senile dementia of the Alzheimer's type (SDAT). About one half of all patients with dementia have Alzheimer's disease.

Alzheimer's Disease

Alzheimer's disease already has affected over 4 million Americans, and it claims 100,000 lives each year. However, despite the magnitude of the current dilemma, these statistics pale beside the looming public health problem that faces the country as the baby boomers turn into the Geritol® generation. It is predicted that Alzheimer's disease alone will affect 14 million Americans by the year 2040.

Alzheimer's disease has a gradual and insidious onset. Its initial symptoms include loss of initiative, forgetfulness, naming difficulties, difficulty with concentrating and calculating, and

49

spatial disorientation. In many patients, an amnesic syndrome will be the most prominent symptom; in other patients, naming or spatial disorders are the primary symptoms. It is common for the patient with early symptoms of Alzheimer's disease to be all too aware of his or her failing mental prowess and for symptoms to be exacerbated by the patient's anxiety over loss of cognitive skills.

As the disease progresses, more severe deficits appear, and more body systems are affected. Over a period that can vary from a few months to as much as 10 years, Alzheimer's disease leads to severe deterioration of intellectual functions and eventually to death, usually as a result of pneumonia or some other complication.

At this time there is no accepted or available treatment that will arrest or slow down the degeneration of neurons that causes the amnesias associated with senile dementia and dementia of the Alzheimer's type. However, there is active research investigating palliative drugs that restore acetylcholine in the brain, as well as studies of the potential for treatment of dementia-producing diseases with nerve growth factor and transplantation of neural tissue. Protein abnormalities and degeneration of the hippocampus may serve as early markers for the disease, permitting earlier intervention.

Relatives of patients often ask if the fact that a family member has Alzheimer's disease increases the risk of the disease for other members of the family. Unfortunately, the answer is yes, *if the patient develops the disease before the age of 70.* In those cases in which the disease develops after the age of 70, the risk is no greater than that for the general public (Strub & Black, 1988). Although the precise genetic basis for Alzheimer's disease is not well understood, almost all people with Down's syndrome who live past 45 years of age will develop Alzheimer's disease, and a genetic marker for a hereditary form of Alzheimer's disease has been identified on chromosome 21. About 43% of monozygotic twins are concordant for dementia, in contrast to only 8% of dizygotic twins (Lishman, 1978).

Alzheimer's disease is selective with respect to areas of degeneration and with respect to neurotransmitter systems that are affected, and the severity of degeneration in the cerebral cortex varies from one region to another. However, the earliest symptoms of Alzheimer's disease almost always include memory loss and construction dyspraxia, suggesting hippocampus and parietal lobe damage. Specific language impairment is rare in the earliest stages of the disease, but patients often develop what Darley (1964) referred to as the "language of confusion." In addition, mild dysnomia and diminished verbal fluency are common, although their presence may not be noted in patients with good social skills and the ability to "camouflage" their verbal problems.

In Alzheimer's disease, minimal neuronal loss occurs in the frontal lobes and moderate loss in the temporal and parietal neocortex; the most severe deterioration is found in medial temporal lobe structures, specifically the hippocampus and amygdala. Alzheimer's disease directly affects the *nucleus basalis of Meinert* in the basal forebrain. This a major source of cholinergic projections to the cerebral cortex. Another subcortical nucleus, the *locus ceruleus*, is affected in some patients but not in others. The locus ceruleus has the greatest concentration of noradrenergic neurons in the central nervous system, and axons from the locus ceruleus project throughout the cortex to other subcortical structures and the spinal cord. In almost all patients with Alzheimer's disease, one finds accumulations of *neurofibrillary tangles, neuritic plaques*, and deposits of *amyloid protein.*

At a minimum, the assessment of a patient suspected of having Alzheimer's disease or a related dementia must include a survey of the following abilities: attention, memory, language, visual perception, and praxis. The clinician will have to be especially sensitive to the needs of the elderly patient and must tailor instructions to fit the existing abilities of the patient. For example, word-finding difficulty is common in Alzheimer's disease, and this can confound performance on some tests. Instructions must be simple and repeated often enough so that you know that the patient understands what he or she is being asked to do. It can be difficult for even mildly demented patients to make the transition from task instruction to task performance, so we encourage our students to embellish task instructions. Although a nonstandard presentation is not optimal, it is preferable to working with a confused patient who cannot recall exactly what is being requested by the examiner.

The relationship between specific brain areas and specific neurotransmitters is presented in Table 3.1.

Table 3.1. Relationship between brain regions, neurotransmitters and behavior.

BRAIN REGIONS	ASSOCIATED BEHAVIORS
Frontal lobe	Problem solving, fluency, temporal ordering
Temporal lobe	Visual and auditory perception, language
Parietal lobe	Language, praxis, spatial abilities
Hippocampus & amygdala	Memory, affect, spatial abilities
Basal forebrain	Memory and other cognitive functions
Locus coeruleus	Attention, arousal, spatial memory
NEUROTRANSMITTERS	**ASSOCIATED BEHAVIORS**
Acetylcholine	Memory, perhaps other cognitive functions
Somatostatin	Motor functions
Dopamine	Motor functions, mood, memory, cognition
Norepinephrine	Attention, arousal, mood, memory, spatial abilities
Serotonin	Arousal, circadian rhythms
Vasopressin	Cognition (via ANS)

Source: Adapted from Corkin et al. (1986).

Pick's Disease

Pick's disease involves selective degeneration of neurons in the frontal and temporal lobes, and patients frequently present with initial symptoms of personality change, inappropriate social behavior, disinhibition, and sometimes apathy. They typically lack insight into their problems, and in contrast to patients with either pseudodementia or Alzheimer's disease, they are more likely to deny the existence of behavioral change or personal problems.

Patients with Pick's disease show variable memory deficits and little or no visuospatial impairment. Some patients have a progressive aphasia caused by degenerative damage to the left temporal lobe; however, the more common presentation includes marked changes in personality, disinhibition, unconcern, and socially inappropriate behaviors caused by frontal lobe degeneration.

Pick's disease patients may be fully oriented and display pre-served memory for day-to-day events. They can recall six to seven digits, and they can retain six to seven items and recall them after a 2 minute delay. They usually will not be able to summarize a short story immediately after reading it aloud; however, they may perform well if presented with a multiple-choice questionnaire about the story. Delayed recall perfor-mance after 1 hour is performed well in the early stages of the illness. However, these patients are apt to become increasingly rigid and inflexible as their disease progresses, and they may be prone to violent outbursts.

The Pick's disease patient may be disinhibited, and may talk loudly and laugh frequently and inappropriately. In the early stages of the disease, it is unusual to see word-finding difficulty, and comprehension and speech are normal. Mental subtraction and completion of two-figure written sums are likely to be im-paired. Stereotyped mannerisms and lack of initiative are early signs that the illness is progressing rapidly, as is perseveration of previous responses on repetition tasks.

Unlike Alzheimer's disease, which is about twice as common in women, Pick's disease appears to have approximately equal prevalence in men and women. However, the disease is far less common than Alzheimers disease: 50 to 100 cases of Alzheim-er's disease will occur in the United States for every case of Pick's disease. Therefore, *Baye's theorem should guide the astute clini-cian to diagnose Alzheimer's disease when he or she can not de-cide between the two diagnoses or even in cases in which the data are equivocal but seem to tilt in favor of a diagnosis of Pick's disease.*

Multi-Infarct Dementia

Multiple small cerebral infarcts can result in memory distur-bance, although for most patients the magnitude of memory dysfunction will not be as great as with other dementias, and it is unusual for a multi-infarct patient to present with memory disturbance as an isolated complaint (as is common in Alzheim-er's disease). In addition, the clinical presentation, most often characterized by a stepwise history of deteriorating mental func-tion, should help differentiate this disorder from both Alzheim-er's and Pick's diseases. It is also common for multi-infarct

53

patients to have a well-documented history of hypertension or cerebrovascular disease (e.g., transient ischemic attacks), and specific neurological signs (e.g., abnormal reflexes) are far more common.

Emotional lability is common and occurs early in cases of multiinfarct dementia. Some patients will present with a *pseudobulbar syndrome*, resulting from bilateral subcortical damage to the corticobulbar tracts and the striatum. Patients will display strong emotional outbursts such as laughing or crying, and these outbursts will be totally unrelated to the patient's environment and circumstances. These emotional displays are totally involuntary, and family members need to be counseled to appreciate that their loved one's behavior is out of his or her control, and that the family member's presence is not the cause of the seemingly deep affective responses that may occur.

Patients with multiinfarct disorders (and occasionally other multiple lesion disorders as well) sometimes exhibit a fascinating phenomenon known as *reduplicative paramnesia*. The disorder is characterized by the deep conviction that one is actually in another place or setting, despite overwhelming evidence to the contrary. For example, patients will become convinced that their hospital room is in fact their living room and the room will continue to *feel* like their living room; although with enough persuasion and argument, patients will come to concede that the room really is not their living room. We know of a nurse in her early 40s with a serious history of multiple infarcts; she awoke one night in her room at the Rehabilitation Hospital of Chicago convinced that the skyscrapers outside her window were the homes that were once outside her house in the little suburb in which she formerly lived and that the prints on the wall were the ones that had once graced the walls of her own home. Knowing full well that she had gone to bed in the Rehabilitation Hospital the night before, she became convinced that she had died and was now a ghost haunting her own house. Being a pragmatic woman, she solved the dilemma by calling her sister to ask if she had died while in the hospital. Both her sister and most of the hospital staff were sure she was psychotic; an astute psychologist identified the phenomenon as reduplicative paramnesia resulting from a stroke she had experienced the night before. Although patients will eventually come to accept the staff's explanations, the subjective feelings associated with reduplicative paramnesia tend to remain strong.

HIPPOCAMPAL INFARCTIONS

In a series of classic studies in the 1950s, Scoville and Milner (1957) demonstrated the critical role of the hippocampus for memory, and specifically documented that bilateral damage to the hippocampus significantly disrupted the ability to acquire new information. Patients with surgical ablation of the hippocampus or those who experience bilateral damage secondary to vascular or neoplastic disease or trauma lose the ability to *consolidate* new memories (however, the actual storage of memory must reside in other parts of the brain because these patients retain the ability to retrieve old, previously learned information).

There is good evidence that memory deficits are less severe if only one hippocampal gyrus is lesioned. Loss of the left hippocampal gyrus decreases verbal memory, whereas the removal of the right hippocampal gyrus interferes with memory for nonverbal stimuli such as maze learning.

Memory problems often persist in patients who have made an otherwise good recovery from cerebrovascular accidents involving the hippocampus. However, despite their problems with learning new material, patients with damage to the hippocampus are able to regulate their behavior according to specific rules. This stands in marked contrast to patients with frontal lobe damage who tend to break rules frequently and make repetitive errors (Stuss & Benson, 1983).

TRANSIENT GLOBAL AMNESIA

Transient global amnesia (TGA) can be easily confused with dissociative disorders. By definition, transient global amnesias have a neurological basis, most commonly vascular, and are often related to ischemia in the posterior cerebral arteries. Acute memory deficits are present, but they are limited to the period of the ischemic episode. Nonvascular causes of TGAs include seizures, migraines, benzodiazepine intoxication, hypoglycemia, and neoplasms (Cummings, 1985).

TGAs can be triggered by sexual intercourse or other forms of exertion. They are almost always of short duration (less than 24 hours) and are characterized by confusion as well as amnesia.

Individuals experiencing TGA will often repeat the same question over and over. They are agitated and troubled by their loss of memory; in contrast, patients experiencing dissociative disorders are seemingly untroubled by their loss of memory. The amnesic episode is typically a one-time event; however, patients with serious cerebrovascular disease may experience multiple TGA episodes before infarctions actually occur. Retrograde amnesia is common after an attack; however, this problem usually abates over time.

Individuals experiencing TGAs typically retain their personal identities and recognize familiar faces, although they may be confused about their current circumstances and unable to retain what they are told during the acute episode. Depression is relatively rare in these patients, although they are troubled by their amnesia. In contrast, patients with psychogenic amnesias lose their identity, are able to retain new learning that occurs during the amnesic episode, frequently have a history of depression, and are often indifferent to their condition. Age of onset is another characteristic one can use to differentiate between TGAs and psychogenic amnesias: TGAs are far more common in older male patients (who are more likely to develop vascular disease), whereas psychogenic amnesias are rare in the elderly and most common in adolescents and young adult females. Finally, psychogenic amnesias are more likely to be triggered by an emotional experience or a threatening situation, often do not have a clearly definable onset, and are more likely to cease abruptly.

ALCOHOLIC AMNESTIC DISORDER (KORSAKOFF'S SYNDROME)

Patients who chronically abuse alcohol are at high risk to develop an acute neurological disorder referred to as *Wernicke's encephalopathy*, characterized by marked confusion, gait ataxia, and ocular abnormalities. The Wernicke's encephalopathy patient has a gait that is wide-based and unsteady, and ocular abnormalities may include weakness or paralysis of congegate gaze, nystagmus, or rotation abnormalities. This triad of symptoms develops as a result of thiamine deficiencies, and treatment is straightforward, with rapid relief from the more dramatic symptoms. However, the majority of patients will be found to have a residual memory deficit, and the ability to learn new information will be significantly impaired (Victor, Adams, & Collins, 1971).

Wernicke's encephalopathy is an acute problem, but it leads to and results in Korsakoff's syndrome (sometimes referred to as Wernicke-Korsakoff's), a far more serious and chronic condition defined by dramatic anterograde amnesia and memory failure markedly greater than any other cognitive limitation. These deficits are permanent and result from symmetrical lesions found along the walls of the third and fourth ventricles, in the mammillary bodies and the dorsomedial nucleus of the thalamus, and in the cerebellum and cerebral cortex.

The memory impairment in Korsakoff's syndrome is circumscribed, and patients typically continue to perform well on the WAIS-R Information and Vocabulary subtests. However, they cannot recall three words after 10 seconds, and neither rote rehearsal nor the use of verbal or visual mnemonics is effective in facilitating recall (Ryan & Butters, 1986).

Anyone who has interviewed a patient with Korsakoff's syndrome will never forget the experience. These patients remain suspended in time: they are able to relate to the past but are totally unable to integrate memories of the present into their experiential world. Sometimes they are friendly and garrulous, and students may be amazed by the contrast between their relatively good presentation during an initial interview and the magnitude of memory impairment that becomes apparent with appropriate testing. We have prepared a videotape for teaching medical students that shows a patient with Korsakoff's syndrome being asked on four different occasions what he had for breakfast. Each time the patient forgot the previous response and reported an entirely different menu.

Although it is fascinating when it is present, confabulation is neither necessary nor sufficient for a diagnosis of Korsakoff's syndrome. Patients may be taciturn and withdrawn, and confabulation is more apt to occur in response to specific questions than as a spontaneous remark.

Ryan and Butters (1986) operationally define Korsakoff's syndrome as (a) a WAIS Verbal IQ of 90 or more, (b) a Wechsler Memory Scale (WMS) Memory Quotient at least 20 points lower than the Verbal IQ, and (c) a history of chronic alcoholism. Table 3.2 presents comparative WAIS and WMS data for patients with Korsakoff's disorder, alcoholics, and nonalcoholic controls.

THE CLINICAL ASSESSMENT OF MEMORY

Table 3.2. Mean scores (± SD) of Alcoholic Korsakoff Patients, Neurologically Intact Alcoholics, and Nonalcoholic Control Subjects on Selected Scales.

	Alcoholic Korsakoffs	Alcoholics	Nonalcoholic Controls
Mean age	55	54	55
Years of education	12.2 ± 2.1	11.3 ± 2.3	12.1 ± 1.4
WAIS Verbal IQ	106.1 ± 12.2	115.2 ± 6.7	116.7 ± 9.4
WMS Memory Quotient	76.2 ± 10.9	108.7 ± 19.9	116.9 ± 15.1
WMS Raw Scores			
Information	2.7 ± 1.3	5.6 ± 0.9	5.9 ± 0.3
Orientation	2.2 ± 1.3	4.9 ± 0.3	4.9 ± 0.3
Mental Control	6.4 ± 2.7	7.2 ± 1.7	7.5 ± 1.8
Memory Passages	4.8 ± 3.2	8.7 ± 2.3	9.4 ± 2.1
Digits Total	11.6 ± 2.1	11.5 ± 1.5	11.7 ± 2.2
Visual Reproductions	3.5 ± 1.9	7.7 ± 3.4	8.1 ± 2.4
Associate Learning	6.1 ± 1.3	13.1 ± 2.8	13.8 ± 3.5

Source: Ryan & Butters (1986).

POSTTRAUMATIC AMNESIA

Posttraumatic amnesia is a common phenomenon, and Arthur Benton (1979) maintains that it is the single most common complaint of patients who have experienced traumatic brain injuries. This corresponds exactly with our own experience with numerous patients who became well enough to return to work but who continued to complain of problems with the memory requirements of their jobs. Unfortunately, employers, coworkers, and family may note the absence of obvious neurological symptoms and interpret the continuing problems as malingering or an attempt to "work the system" to ensure higher legal settlements or worker's compensation awards.

The effects of head injury on memory functions can vary dramatically, depending on the severity and site of the injury. However, on occasion even mild injuries will result in dramatic disturbance of memory, even in those cases where there is no loss of consciousness. Following minor head injuries (which often have major effects), there is typically a period of brief anterograde amnesia and a somewhat longer period of retrograde amnesia. For example, a head-injured football player may continue to play the game but have limited recollection of the plays immediately before his injury and no recollection at all of what

58

happened in the rest of the game, following his concussion. With major head injuries, dramatic loss of personal identity may occur, similar to that portrayed in Madonna's popular film *Desperately Seeking Susan.*

The anterograde amnesia that follows head injury is most often not complete but typically involves pockets of dim memory surrounded by the darker gloom of total amnesia. Although this complicates assessment, *the clinician must make an attempt to estimate the total duration of posttraumatic amnesia, because it is a far more useful predictor of severity of injury and likelihood of recovery than either duration of retrograde amnesia or the length of time a patient was comatose following a head injury.*

Problems with memory and attention also characterize the patient who develops chronic traumatic encephalopathy, or *dementia pugilistica* as a result of repeated concussions. Sometimes known as the punch-drunk syndrome and vividly portrayed in the boxing movie *Raging Bull*, dementia pugilistica patients present with dysarthric speech, paranoia, emotional lability, and impaired learning ability. These problems tend to be dramatically exacerbated by the effects of alcohol. A study by Casson et al. (1984) demonstrated that 87% of professional boxers had definite evidence of brain damage. The damage was most notable on tests of short-term memory, presumably because of the effects of boxing on deep, midline brain structures. Although not every boxer will develop these problems, most will, and the likelihood appears to be directly related to the total number of fights in a boxer's career. Strub and Black (1988) have attempted to correlate the duration of a fighter's career with the likelihood of brain injury, and maintain that "a ten year career with 150 fights results in a 50 percent chance of dementia developing, whereas a shorter fighting career with fewer than 50 fights results in only a 5 to 10 percent risk" (p. 327).

PSYCHOGENIC AMNESIA

Psychogenic amnesia is characterized by the sudden inability to recall important personal information, in the absence of intoxication or organic mental disorders that could account for the memory failure. When the amnesic syndrome is accompanied by travel to a distant location and assumption of a new identity, the diagnosis of *psychogenic fugue* is appropriate. Both of these

59

conditions are classified as dissociative disorders, and sometimes referred to as hysterical neuroses.

Patients with psychogenic fugue often assume a new identity that is far more interesting than their formerly staid and proper life. They are aware of their loss of personal identity but are typically unconcerned about the loss. Alcohol abuse may predispose individuals to develop fugue states, and it is common to find that severe psychological stress preceded the development of the fugue state (e.g., divorce, loss of a child). Most patients recover rapidly, and it is rare for the disorder to reoccur. Occasionally, a single event will trigger the return of personal memories (one of our fugue patients suddenly "came to" after seeing a newscast of his hometown and recognizing a neighborhood that he used to visit on a regular basis); however, it is more common for memories to return gradually over a period of weeks or months.

Psychogenic amnesia can take four basic shapes. Most patients with psychogenic amnesia will experience *localized* amnesia, most commonly loss of memory for a period of time surrounding an especially salient (and negative) event, such as the drowning death of a child. Patients with *selective* amnesia will recall some events during the amnesic period but not all. Somewhat less common are patients who experience *generalized* amnesia, in which all personal memories are lost, and *continuous* amnesia, which involves loss of all memories after a specified event or point in time.

The patient with psychogenic amnesia retains motor and cognitive skills that were possessed prior to the amnesic episode. For example, patients who knew shorthand, could ride a bike, and had memorized the capitals of all states retain these skills during the period of psychogenic amnesia or the fugue state. These skills are more likely to be impaired when there is an organic basis for memory disturbance. In addition, patients can actively learn new information and acquire new skills during a dissociative episode; patients whose memory disorders are linked to brain disease or trauma find it much more difficult to perform well on tests of new learning.

Despite these differences, it is sometimes difficult to discriminate between posttraumatic amnesia and psychogenic amnesia, as is illustrated by the following case.

PATIENT J.B.

J.B. was a 33-year–old white female with 13 years of education. She was right-handed, married, and the mother of three children; however, she had been separated from her husband for some months, partially as a consequence of a major head injury she experienced following an athletic injury. She had a good work history and no evidence of significant psychopathology prior to her accident.

This patient had been knocked unconscious and taken to a local hospital where she remained in a coma for 3 weeks following her injury. There was evidence of a right frontal hemorrhage with considerable right-sided cerebral edema.

When she came out of her coma, J.B. was totally unable to recognize or recall any memories of her husband, children, friends, marriage, parents, or any of the details of her past life. She retained basic motor and academic skills (e.g., she could still type and recite the Pledge of Allegiance); however, there was absolute total loss of all personal identity. With time and patience, J.B. came to recall tiny bits of her own history, triggered most often by pictures of her family in photo albums. However, she was never able to recall any of her history prior to her teenage years, and much of her personal life had to be recreated for her. She reported: "I spent two years relearning the past thirty years of my life." This dense personal amnesia resulted in considerable distress for her family: for example, she was initially quite uncomfortable sleeping with the man who claimed to be her husband, and she did not feel any maternal love for her children after her accident. Her husband, apparently unable to cope with the stress of the situation, eventually left town, and J.B. had to become reacquainted with her children and raise them on her own.

A fascinating aspect of this patient's symptom pattern was her total loss of the ability to relate emotions and memories. She also experienced periodic depression (although she reported mild euphoria for the first 6 months after her injury). There was mild expressive aphasia immediately after her release from the hospital, and J.B. never regained her sense of smell and taste. She also reported that she became a "cajun food junkie" because everything else tasted bland, and she lost the ability to use smell to determine when meat or milk had spoiled.

J.B. was concerned because she had lost the ability to distinguish right from wrong behavior, according to the standards and mores under which she had been raised. To determine "how to behave properly in social situations," J.B. watched daytime soap operas during her convalescence and attempted to model her behavior in accordance with soap opera standards. She was actively looking for someone with whom to have an affair when her husband realized what was happening and smashed the family television. J.B. did not understand her husband's consternation and could not see why he had become so upset. She subsequently became pregnant by another man, ostensibly forgetting that pregnancy was a potential consequence of intercourse. J.B., who had already had two children, was pregnant for 5 months before she realized what had caused the cessation of her menses.

This patient was involved in litigation related to her accident, so the question of malingering was critical to differential diagnosis. However, J.B. performed quite well on all neuropsychological tests that were administered, and there was no significant evidence of cerebral impairment on the Halstead-Reitan Battery. Tapping speed and grip strength were mildly depressed on the nondominant (left) side. J.B. earned a full scale IQ of 107, and there was no suggestion of malingering on any of the tests that were administered. It is particularly significant that this patient was able to perform well on all memory tasks administered. She scored above the 80th percentile on the Wechsler Memory Scale subtests, and she was able to recall all 15 of the Rey Auditory Verbal Learning Test items by the fifth trial, with full recall after a brief interruption and again after a 30 minute delay.

One would be hard-pressed to argue that a patient who performed so consistently and so well was malingering or that a psychogenic amnesia coincided perfectly with recovery from 3 weeks in a coma. However, while the patient's amnesia for family and friends, as well as her loss of personal moral standards, appear genuine and the result of her head injury, current models of memory are totally inadequate to explain the patient's behavior.

DEPRESSION AND MEMORY

Herbert Weingartner (1986) has argued that cognitive impairment in depression is the result of effort-demanding cognitive processes that are linked to alterations in the reward-reinforcement system of the brain. This position is supported by the clinical observation that those processes which require effort and sustained concentration are the ones most severely impaired in depression. Weingartner also points out that the "standard" tests clinicians often use in the assessment of depressed patients may be measuring altered motivation rather than mood-related changes in memory.

In depression, cognitive changes are evident on effort-demanding tasks, but are not present on those tasks that can be accomplished automatically. An effortful, cognitive capacity-demanding process is one that is sensitive to motivation and reinforcement, set, attention, intention, and alertness. When attention is shared with another activity in executing an effort-demanding task, performance suffers. In contrast, automatic cognitive operations are hypothesized to be cognitively "easy" to perform and require little sustained effort; that is, they can be accomplished almost automatically. Tasks, procedures, and processing conditions that can be accomplished automatically are those that are performed with almost equal effectiveness under incidental processing conditions, in contrast to circumstances in which subjects are directed to focus on some task. One type of automatic task may involve executing overlearned habits in which performance is almost errorless. Effort-demanding and automatic processes may be mediated by different psychobiological mechanisms.

A series of studies have supported this hypothesis. For example, in one experiment, 10 depressed and 10 control subjects were tested on recall of lists of words and compared on effort–demanding versus superficial processing conditions (e.g., unrelated words vs. categorically related words such as the names of vegetables). The researchers concluded that depressed patients reliably learn and remember less information than do normal controls only under effort-demanding processing conditions.

THE CLINICAL ASSESSMENT OF MEMORY

Memory for events that have been superficially processed does not distinguish patients from control subjects, nor does recall of highly related, easily encoded information distinguish depressed patients from normal control subjects.

In another experiment subjects underwent a similar procedure, but this time the presence of cues was used as the independent variable. Depressed patients did poorly in the effort-demanding, free-recall procedure but were indistinguishable from normals on the cued-recall condition. This study also demonstrated that administration of 20 mg of amphetamine significantly increased memory for depressed patients in the effort-demanding condition.

In the last series of studies, patients with senile dementia of the Alzheimer's type (SDAT), depressed patients, and normal subjects were compared on a simple memory task that required recollection of stimulus words presented one to seven times. The patients were then simply asked how often each word was presented. Patients in the normal control group remembered more words (effort-demanding) and were reasonably accurate at guessing the frequency of presentation of each word. Depressed patients could not recall the words but were about as accurate as normals in guessing the frequency of presentation for each stimulus item. Patients with Alzheimer's disease performed poorly on both tasks (i.e., both effort-demanding and automatic processing tasks).

The following conclusions can be drawn from this series of studies:

1. Effort-demanding cognitive processes are differentially impaired in depression.
2. Treatments that improve depression appear to facilitate memory and related cognitive processes in depressed patients.
3. In patients with Alzheimer's disease, memory-learning impairments are equally evident on effort-demanding and automatic processing tasks.
4. The cognitive processes associated with incidental memory are modulated by brain systems that are extrinsic to those directly involved in the storage and maintenance of memories.

This extrinsic system is tied to those brain regions that regulate arousal and activation; these, in turn, are linked to subcortical regions and neurochemical events that regulate the appreciation of reinforcing properties of events (self-stimulation reward systems). The regions involved include limbic system structures, but other systems are also implicated. Neurochemically, the noradrenergic-dopaminergic system appears to play an important role in defining the biology of extrinsic, effort-related cognitive processing.

In contrast, the types of cognitive processes that are involved in some automatic operations, particularly those that are required for the storage and retrieval of knowledge, are dependent upon neocortical structures. These structures are the ones compromised in Alzheimer's disease. Neurochemically, this system is linked to cholinergic processes.

PARTIALING OUT THE EFFECTS OF DEPRESSION AND AGE ON COGNITIVE FUNCTIONS

Depression is frequently seen in individuals with senile dementia, particularly in the early stages of this illness, and deRosiers (1992) estimates that major depression will develop as a prodromal symptom in 15 – 20% of patients who later develop Alzheimer's disease. However, research examining the relationship between depression and memory is beset with methodological pitfalls. Some of these pitfalls will be discussed below.

Patients with high IQs and high educational levels tend to moderate or narrow the effects of both aging and depression on cognitive tests, making it important that researchers not attenuate their effects by drawing samples from highly educated or extremely intelligent populations (e.g., college professors).

Both patients with right-hemisphere lesions and depressed patients exhibit conceptual rigidity and tend to retain untenable hypotheses. They have difficulty with tests like the Stroop and Gorham Proverbs test. One study demonstrated essentially equivalent performance on a variety of measures between younger and older subjects. However, *the older patients who were depressed perceived themselves as performing far more poorly than they really were.* These problems may be compounded by the fact that institutionalization and hospitalization are known to exacerbate mental deterioration and confusion in some elderly persons.

A high degree of mental deterioration, coupled with low to moderate educational background, is associated with evidence of mental deterioration on relatively simple measures of cognitive functioning, but the presence of depression in such patients is not a significant factor in further lowering their ability to perform.

In subjects from high-socioeconomic-status backgrounds and high-education backgrounds, who are just beginning to show signs of senility and cognitive impairment, the presence of clinical depression can be detected in a further lowering of their levels of cognitive functioning. To demonstrate cognitive deficits secondary to depression in such subjects, however, it may be necessary to use highly technical or conceptually difficult cognitive tests.

Raskin (1986) points out a common methodological flaw in studies of "aged depression": most subjects in these studies do not meet established scientific or professional criteria for the diagnosis of depression and can be characterized most accurately as suffering from mild to moderate dysphoria. Such people *complain* of memory problems but generally do not show evidence of memory impairment on objective tests.

The effects of aging in moderately to severely depressed patients are more likely to appear on tests measuring the ability to shift cognitive sets and on problems requiring skills in reasoning ability than on simple measures of recall and recognition.

The astute clinician often can detect the presence of depression in persons with early signs of senile dementia. On tests sampling both immediate and delayed recall, depressed senile patients could be differentiated from nondepressed senile patients only when the tests were made more difficult. For example, in one study significant differences were present between two groups engaged in a task requiring them to repeat 10 digits but were not present on a task requiring simple repetitions of five to seven digits. These findings suggest that there may be a syndrome of depressive pseudodementia in persons who are in the early stages of senile dementia and that treating depression in these persons may result in at least a temporary improvement in their cognitive skills.

The tendency to complain or to manifest the "sick set" (i.e., complaints about memory, and psychic and somatic distress on a wide range of symptoms) is more prominent in persons with acute as opposed to chronic depression. It is not entirely clear whether these persons have problems with their memory or to what extent such problems impair daily functioning.

THE DIAGNOSIS OF DEMENTIA

In the case of dementia, clinicians will wish to know (a) if the dementia is reversible and (b) if it is caused by physical agents, disease, or psychiatric disturbance (e.g., depression). In addition, it will be important to assess persistence of the memory disturbance, the particular disease most likely to account for the problem, and the potential long-term outcomes.

Perhaps most important, the clinician should be able to evaluate a patient's ability to function independently, assess his or her ability to work and make independent decisions, and determine a baseline of ability on which to build an intervention strategy.

Clinicians should always be looking for the functional value of test data. What is the "real-world" significance of a given test profile? Does it help determine the functions that can be performed at work or at home? Can we use it to develop intervention strategies for cognitive support or identify deficits in "day-to-day" functions so that we can alert the family of the patient? What is the value of testing in addressing crucial functional questions such as the ability to drive a car, consent to or reject surgery, maintain financial control of one's assets, change a will, and so on?

ASSESSING TREATMENT

Measures used to assess effects of treatment for cognitive impairment often differ in one important respect from the standardized tests typically used for diagnosing patients and selecting subjects: normative data are not essential for measures used to assess treatment because change in performance is the critical variable, not performance relative to preexisting population norms.

THE CLINICAL ASSESSMENT OF MEMORY

Availability of equivalent forms is one of the most important considerations for selection for inclusion of a test in a treatment assessment battery. Length is also a consideration, especially for the elderly. Patients become bored and tired after an hour or so of testing. We recommend limiting testing to 1 hour or scheduling frequent breaks, especially when working with elderly patients.

Some elderly people will not perform tasks that they view as trivial or ridiculous. Some probably have a need to escape from a situation they view as threatening, but others are simply being assertive. Thus, measures of clinical memory do need some reasonable degree of face validity. We cannot emphasize this too strongly. The four tests described below are all interesting, have face validity, and are sensitive to aging and drug effects.

The telephone task (Crook, Ferris, McCarthy, & Rae, 1980) involves presentation of 3-digit area codes, 7-digit phone numbers, and 10-digit combinations of the two, presented in random order. Immediately following each presentation, the subject must dial the number on a standard telephone dial. Accuracy of recall on a 7- and 10-digit number recall task is sensitive to the effects of aging and dementia.

The shopping list is similar to the California Verbal Learning Test (CVLT) (see Chapter 4). The misplaced-objects task (Crook, Ferris, & McCarthy, 1979) is a visuospatial memory task based on the common complaint of putting something away and not remembering where it was placed. The subject places representations of 10 common household objects (keys, glasses, book, etc.) in the various rooms of a representation of a 10-room house. The subject later must recall where each object was placed. This task is sensitive to both normal aging and senile dementia.

Finally, in the facial recognition task (Ferris, Crook, Clark, McCarthy, & Rae, 1980), the subject views a continuous sequence of unfamiliar faces and must indicate whether each face is "new" (first presentation) or has been shown earlier in the sequence (second presentation). The interval between the first and second presentations is varied. This task may also be administered as a series of three learning trials, followed by a delayed recognition trial.

DIFFERENTIATING DEPRESSION AND DEMENTIA IN THE ELDERLY

Depression is an insidious but commonplace illness that can result in diminished motivation, difficulty in concentration, and marked impairment of memory. Of course, all of these symptoms can also be found in demented patients. However, relatively simple tests of memory ability often can be surprisingly helpful for the differential diagnosis of depression and dementia. For example, Table 3.3 lists neuropsychological test performance on selected measures for two patients of approximately the same age and with very similar presenting complaints—concern by family members because of the patient's apparent loss of memory. Can you use these data to determine which of the two patients had a genuine dementia?

Table 3.3. Comparison of test data for a patient with Alzheimer's disease and a patient with a pseudodementia secondary to depression. Both patients presented with virtually identical complaints and referral notes.

Test	Patient A.M.	Patient B.L.
Trails A	39 sec.	36 sec.
Trails B	88 sec.	141 sec. (3 errors)
VIQ	120	96
PIQ	95	87
FSI	109	92
Digit Span	7	11
Digit Symbol	5	6
Controlled Word Association Test	47th Percentile	82nd Percentile
Halstead's Impairment Index	.86	.70
Category Errors	101	98
Finger Tapping Speed	40 Right; 36 Left	52 Right; 32 Left
Ingles Memory Task	5 trials	Discontinued after 45 trials
Rey Auditory Verbal Learning Test		
First 5 Trials:	5–7–10–12–13	3–5–7–8–6
Trial B:	3	4
Delayed Recall:	8	0
Education	17 years	16 years

THE CLINICAL ASSESSMENT OF MEMORY

PATIENT A. M.

A 61-year-old white female retired schoolteacher had a history of marked weight loss, somatic delusions, complaints of marked memory loss, constipation, and phobic avoidance of social situations. The patient was taking a complex medication regimen that included Serax, Bentyl, Antivert, Reglan, Restoril, ibuprofen, Carafate, and L-tryptophan. She had taken tricyclics in the past with poor response. There was a long history of smoking two packs of cigarettes per day, and she was a social drinker. There was no obvious psychomotor history and no significant prior psychiatry history.

PATIENT B. L.

Patient B. L. was a 63-year-old white female retired schoolteacher, widowed, with a history of bipolar disorder. She was referred by a local psychiatrist for evaluation of memory complaints that were believed to be related to her history of psychiatric illness. There was a history of ulcers, and the patient was taking lithium and doxepin. There was no history of alcohol or tobacco use. B.L. remained active in the community, and she presented as socially skilled and poised. She lived alone and resisted the attempts of her children to get her to live with one of them. The patient was articulate and attractive and minimized the significance of her memory problems.

EVALUATION

It is clear that traditional neuropsychological screening measures can be misleading in cases like those presented here. Both patients appear to be markedly impaired on the Halstead-Reitan Neuropsychological Battery, and global performance measures like the Category Test fail to discriminate between the two patients. Both patients also have difficulty with tasks that require effortful responding (e.g., Digit Symbol). However, the performance of the two patients on the Rey Auditory Verbal Learning Test (AVLT) is different and highly significant. Patient A.M. can and does learn and retain what she learns across time (her delayed recall is adequate if not stellar); in contrast, patient B.L. had a great deal of difficulty with this simple learning task, and there was absolutely no retention after a brief delay. Likewise, A.M. could learn three simple paired associates without particular difficulty; in B.L.'s case, this simple test had to be discontinued after 45 trials. These differences are especially salient when one realizes that both patients displayed essentially equivalent performance on the Halstead-Reitan Battery.

On the basis of strong paired-associate learning and the AVLT, A.M. was diagnosed as being depressed, with a concomitant pseudodementia, whereas B.L. was diagnosed as presenting with early Alzheimer's disease. A. M. was treated with a different antidepressant and responded positively; after 1 year she had recovered completely, and there was no evidence of memory disturbance. Patient B.L. did in fact have Alzheimer's disease; she reluctantly moved in with one of her daughters and died in a nursing home several years later. At autopsy, her brain was found to have the high concentration of plaques and neurofibrillary tangles characteristic of the disease that prompted her referral.

CHAPTER FOUR

Psychological Tests for the Assessment of Memory

The assessment of memory is complex and requires considerable clinical judgment. The clinician must ensure that the patient is motivated to perform well, has sufficient language ability to comprehend the instructions that accompany the test, and has the motor skills necessary to respond appropriately. In addition, the clinician must choose from a daunting number of potential measures of memory ability. The test(s) chosen must be comprehensive enough to assess a full range of memory abilities while at the same time not so time-consuming and demanding that completing the test(s) becomes onerous for the patient.

This chapter reviews the most popular and widely used tests of memory ability. In addition, we have included some fairly obscure memory measures because we have found them valuable clinically. Whenever possible, we have included detailed instructions about administration of each test. However, we cannot underscore strongly enough that this book is designed only to *introduce* the reader to these measures. There is no substitute for detailed study of the manuals that were developed for most of these tests, and *it is unethical to administer and interpret tests without the type of in-depth knowledge that comes from studying the manual.* With this caveat in mind, we hope you will profit from reading about the major memory tests discussed in this chapter.

THE WECHSLER MEMORY SCALE-REVISED (WMS-R)

In 1945, David Wechsler developed the Wechsler Memory Scale (WMS) to supplement his well-known measures of intelligence. However, there was widespread dissatisfaction with the WMS almost from its introduction, and most clinicians agreed that the test failed to provide a comprehensive overview of memory functions. In fact, many neuropsychologists did not use the entire test, but adapted the modification introduced by Russell (1975), who factor-analyzed the WMS and selected/retained only those memory subtests that were most sensitive to brain damage and differentiated verbal from figural memory (i.e., Logical Memory and Visual Reproduction). In addition, a delayed-recall condition was included for both of the remaining subtests, to evaluate retention over a 30-minute interval. The Russell revision compensates for some of the inadequacies of the original WMS; however, it is often supplemented with other measures of memory functioning (Russell, 1988).

The Boston revision of the WMS retained all of the elements of the original WMS but added items to the scale to improve its utility for routine neuropsychological assessment (Milberg, Hebben, & Kaplan, 1986). The most important changes from a memory assessment standpoint relate to the Logical Memory, Visual Reproduction, and Paired Associate subtests. Not only were delayed-recall conditions added, but direct questioning and recognition were also included (Loring & Papanicolaou, 1987).

Many of the original problems with the WMS were corrected with the 1987 publication of the Wechsler Memory Scale-Revised (WMS-R) (Wechsler, 1987). The revised test requires 45 to 60 minutes to administer and comes with normative data for ages 16 through 74. It assesses memory for verbal and figural stimuli, meaningful and abstract material, and delayed as well as immediate recall. The subtests are outlined in Table 4.1. The test is set up to produce mean scores of 100, with standard devi-

73

Table 4.1. Subtests from the Wechsler Memory Scale-Revised.

Attention and Short-Term Recall	Delayed Recall
Mental Control	
Logical Memory I	Logical Memory II
Verbal Paired Associates I	Verbal Paired Associates II
Digit Span	
Figural Memory	
Visual Paired Associates I	Visual Paired Associates II
Visual Reproduction I	Visual Reproduction II
Visual Memory Span	

ations of 15 points, much like the familiar Wechsler Adult Intelligence Scale IQ scores.

The major advantages to using the WMS-R are (1) it was standardized with age-based norms, (2) the nonverbal subset includes nonconstructional items, (3) summary scores include measures of immediate and delayed recall of verbal and nonverbal memory, and (4) it provides an assessment of attention/concentration independent of memory.

Despite the improvements reflected in the WMS-R, problems still exist. For example, the standardization sample consists of only 316 subjects, and some caution is necessary insofar as interpolated estimates were made for the age ranges 18–19, 25–34, and 45–54. This limited standardization is inadequate, given the broad range of the target population, and it is particularly striking to compare this sample with the 2,000 subjects used in the development of norms for the WAIS-R (Elwood, 1991). In addition, Butters et al. (1988) demonstrated that a normal group of 51-year-olds had a mean difference of more than a standard deviation (i.e., 17 points) between General Memory and their scores on the Attention/Concentration subscales—not the difference of zero that one would expect. In addition, there are substantial practice effects on the test (Wechsler, 1987).

The omission of normal subjects in the age range of 45–54 in the standardization sample is especially troubling, for this is the age at which many patients begin to experience the first signs of benign senescent forgetfulness and present for neuropsychological evaluation of memory functions.

Reliability coefficients for the WMS-R are disappointingly low, ranging from .41 to .88, with a mean reliability of .61. Most of the subtest scores do not meet the basic level of .80, generally considered the minimal acceptable level for subtest scales (Anastasia, 1988). In contrast, the average WAIS-R subtest has a reliability coefficient of .83.

Elwood (1991) argues for the use of confidence intervals rather than absolute values when reporting WMS-R findings. Calculation of confidence intervals requires knowledge of the standard error of measurement and simple arithmetic. The supplemental work sheet recommended by Elwood is presented in Table 4.2. which provides a convenient way to calculate both true score

Table 4.2. WMS-R Supplemental Worksheet.

1. WMS-R Confidence Intervals

Index	Obtained Score (X)	Estimated True Score (T)	Margin of Error	Confidence Interval ___%
Verbal Memory	0.77 X ___	+ 23 = ___	+/– (5.61 z = ___)	= ___ – ___
Visual Memory	0.70 X ___	+ 30 = ___	+/– (5.93 z = ___)	= ___ – ___
General Memory	0.81 X ___	+ 19 = ___	+/– (5.52 z = ___)	= ___ – ___
Atten/Concen	0.90 X ___	+ 10 = ___	+/– (4.37 z = ___)	= ___ – ___
Delayed Memory	0.77 X ___	+ 23 = ___	+/– (5.74 z = ___)	= ___ – ___

Confidence Level

	68%	85%	90%	95%	99%
Z =	1.00	1.44	1.64	1.96	2.58

2. Significance of Pairwise Index Comparisons

Index Comparison	True Scores T_1	T_2	Score Difference	Z Score	Significance Level
General with Attn/Con	___ – ___ =		[ ]	+ 7.05 = ___	___
Verbal with Visual	___ – ___ =		[ ]	+ 8.15 = ___	___
General with Delayed	___ – ___ =		[ ]	+ 7.95 = ___	___

Source: Elwood (1991). Adapted with permission of the Plenum Publishing Corp.

confidence intervals and significance tests. It also permits the clinician to make pairwise comparisons between individual tests.

VALIDITY STUDIES OF THE WMS-R

Recent studies that have focused on issues of validity and diagnostic potential of the WMS-R have shown the battery to be useful in the assessment of the cognitive effects of a variety of conditions, including amnesic disorders, Alzheimer's disease, and Huntington's disease (Butters et al., 1988). However, the WMS-R did not adequately reflect the severity of memory impairment in profoundly amnesic patients. Variability of performance was more characteristic of amnesic patients than demented patients. However, WMS-R data could not be used to discriminate between cortical and subcortical dementias.

Ryan and Lewis (1988) demonstrated memory deficits in chronic alcoholics using the WMS-R. Previous research indicated that chronic alcoholics have subtle memory deficits that require sensitive measures for detection. The original WMS did not have the sensitivity to detect deficits in this group. The results of the Ryan and Lewis study suggest that the WMS-R is more sensitive than its predecessor. Fischer (1988) used the WMS-R to study patients with multiple sclerosis (MS). Results indicated that the WMS-R was sensitive to memory problems experienced by these patients. The authors also used the WMS-R to show differences in the type and severity of impairment in MS patients.

In summary, the WMS-R is superior to the original WMS. However, recognition and remote memory are not assessed, and the measurement of nonverbal memory is deficient. In addition, the WMS-R fails to differentiate between patients with left and right temporal lobe lesions.

FACTOR STRUCTURE OF THE WMS-R

A number of researchers have factor-analyzed the WMS-R measures, sometimes with different results. However, in general it appears that there are two major factors and three minor factors. The major factors are General Memory and Attention/Concentration. The minor factors are Verbal Memory, Visual Memory, and Delayed Recall.

The *General Memory* factor is defined by the following subtests: figural memory, logical memory I, visual paired associates I, verbal paired associates I, and visual reproduction. It is clearly more heavily dependent upon verbal memory functions than on visual memory functions. Of the possible 193 points after weighting, 124 are from the verbal subtests, and 69 are from the visual subtests (64% vs. 36%).

The *Attention/Concentration Composite* factor is made up of mental control, digit span, and visual memory span. The *Verbal Memory Composite* is associated with logical memory and verbal paired-associate recall; the *Visual Memory Composite* is loaded by the figural memory, visual paired-associate, and visual reproduction subtests. It is interesting to note that figural memory appears to be a measure of higher-order visual attention span. This subtest also loads heavily on the attention/concentration factor. Likewise, visual paired associates contains a significant verbal component, and patients will often spontaneously employ verbal labeling to match the colors and designs. Given this verbal mediation, it is clear that visual paired associates is not a selectively sensitive measure of visual learning. In addition, Brown, Sawyer, Nathan, and Shatz (1987) reported that paired-associate learning of geometric figures that could not be easily verbalized was not selectively sensitive to right cerebral dysfunction. Similar results have been found for the WMS-R "visual" subtests.

The visual reproduction subtest of the WMS-R is a significant component of the Visual Memory Composite factor. Loring and Papanicolaou (1987) conducted factor-analytic studies of this single subtest and identified a strong visual-perceptual-motor ability factor, and only secondarily a memory factor, mainly involving immediate recall. Delayed visual-reproduction performance is more closely related to memory than it is to perceptual motor skills in normal subjects. It has also been shown to be helpful in discrimination of right unilateral temporal lobe seizure activity.

The *Delayed Recall Composite* factor is composed of those tests that are repeated after a brief delay: logical memory II, visual paired associates II, verbal paired associates II, and visual reproduction II. The contrast between general memory factor scores and delayed memory factor scores is a meaningful measure that can be very useful for diagnostic purposes.

THE CLINICAL ASSESSMENT OF MEMORY

Interpretation of the WMS-R

Gender is not correlated with WMS-R performance. However, performance is highly correlated with educational level, and the test provides separate norms for subjects with less than a high school education (mean range of scores, 93–94), high school graduates (99–100), and subjects with more than 12 years of education (105–108).

The information and orientation subtests include items similar to those found in most formal mental status examinations. Scores on the information and orientation questions are intended primarily to identify persons for whom the meaning of scores on the rest of the scale may be questionable. It is rare for a patient to miss more than two of these items; if he or she misses more than three, there is no point in continuing the test. Making more than two errors on the information and orientation subtests suggests disorientation, resistance, inattention, preoccupation, aphasia, dementia, delusional thinking, or questionable validity of responses. Psychiatric patients generally score in normal range on the orientation and information scales.

Recall of the past president may be the most sensitive question on the orientation section. The most commonly missed items are the past president, day of month, name of place, name of city, and age.

The pattern of performance of the WMS-R can sometimes be a basis for diagnostic inferences. For example, patients with temporal lobe dysfunction display rapid rate of forgetting of newly learned information, whereas patients with diencephalic lesions display a normal rate of forgetting. Comparison of the General Memory Index to the Delayed Recall Index provides an estimate of whether there is a disproportionate decline in the patient's ability to retain newly learned information. If the WMS-R results suggest a delayed-recall deficit is present, the CVLT and/or BVRT can be used to determine whether the problem is one of storage or retrieval.

Delayed recall is very sensitive to cerebral pathology. Immediate recall is less sensitive and not very helpful in discriminating brain damage from depression. As a general rule, *normal subjects being tested for delayed recall on the WMS-R should be able to remember about two-thirds of the material they were able to recall on the immediate recall trial.* Whereas depressed patients will average 1 point less on their delayed-recall score, neurologic patients score an average of 5 points less.

LATERALIZATION AND THE WMS-R

Verbal memory is relatively lateralized to the left hemisphere, and pictorial (e.g., facial recognition) memory is associated with right hemisphere function. Because the WMS-R is primarily a verbal test (i.e., most of the "visual tests" are verbally mediated), it may not be especially helpful in lateralizing dysfunction. *Differences between verbal and visual subtests have to be fairly substantial to be really helpful in diagnosing cerebral pathology and should not be used by themselves for the purpose of lateralizing deficits.* As noted in the WMS-R manual, summary index contrasts were unable to differentiate patients with left temporal lobe epilepsy from patients whose temporal lobe seizures originated in the right hemisphere.

The reasons for the poor specificity of the WMS-R in lateralizing dysfunction are complex. For example, Loring, Lee, Martin, and Meador (1989) note that because many patients begin experiencing seizures relatively early in life, functional reorganization of cognitive systems within the brain is likely to occur. Patients with unilateral seizure onset may also have bilateral mesial temporal lobe sclerosis resulting from the spread of seizures across the interhemispheric commissures. Either of these conditions can decrease the likelihood of finding material-specific differences as a function of temporal lobectomy laterality.

Loring et al. (1989) reported results from patients who had previously undergone temporal lobe resection. He found that the summary indexes failed to correctly predict unilateral temporal dysfunction and also incorrectly suggested lateralized dysfunction. Using a 15 point discrepancy between verbal and visual memory scores as their criterion, only two out of ten right hemisphere patients were correctly classified, and eight out of ten right temporal lobectomy patients were incorrectly classified (i.e., their Visual Memory Indices were greater than their Verbal Memory scores). Loring et al. concluded that the Visual Memory/Verbal Memory comparison contributed little to the diagnostic utility of the WMS-R.

Errors such as those noted above can have serious repercussions. For example, many neurosurgeons require an absence of evidence of significant temporal lobe dysfunction contralateral to the side of proposed surgery. Thus, if a patient is otherwise a good surgical candidate for temporal lobectomy (e.g., unilateral interictal EEG abnormalities, unilateral ictal seizure onset) but has apparent neuropsychological evidence of contralateral dysfunction, the patient may be required to undergo invasive procedures prior to surgery (e.g., depth electrode implantation), undergo a less extensive temporal lobe resection that includes the amygdala but spares the hippocampus, or undergo special memory testing at the time of surgery.

PSYCHOPATHOLOGY AND WMS-R PERFORMANCE

Depressed patients tend to obtain normal scores on the Attention/Concentration measures, but perform poorly on measures of general memory, visual memory, and delayed recall. They also tend to have verbal memory scores that exceed their visual memory scores. Schizophrenic patients perform poorly on all memory indices, but do not differ from other groups across specific contrasts. These patients will typically perform worse than depressed patients on all measures of memory other than visual memory. In contrast, patients with posttraumatic stress disorders (PTSD) have particular problems with visual memory.

Alcoholics perform adequately on measures of orientation and information, but poorly on almost all other memory measures. Performance on measures of verbal memory are likely to be somewhat better than performance on tasks requiring visual memory.

Patients with dementia are likely to perform poorly on all WMS-R measures, including information and orientation. Patients who have Senile Dementia of the Alzheimer's Type (SDAT) tend to have more memory dysfunction than patients with other dementing illnesses, and are likely to obtain their highest scores on the Attention/Concentration subtest. Intrusion errors are commonly produced by patients with Alzheimer's disease,, and have been shown to be correlated with a reduction in choline acetyltransferase (ChAT) levels and with large numbers of cortical senile plaques. Patients with Korsakoff's syndrome also perform quite poorly on the WMS-R, but are apt to have fewer intrusion errors. This most likely is related to the greater involvement of association corticies and/or basal forebrain structures in Alzheimers.

Alzheimer's patients are impaired on problem solving and some visuoperceptual tasks. Similarly, patients with frontal lobe pathology are highly sensitive to proactive interference and produce numerous intrusion errors on tests such as the CVLT and AVLT. Since hemorrhagic lesions in the medial diencephalon can interrupt the major thalamic input to the prefrontal region, patients with either Alzheimer's or Korsakoff's syndromes may display frontal symptoms either due to direct damage to the frontal cortices or to a disconnection of the frontal region from a major source of afferent input. Also, there is evidence that patients with Korsakoff's have significant deterioration of the basal forebrain structures that provide the prefrontal region with its major cholinergic input.

Patients with both cerebrovascular accidents and brain tumors tend to show impaired memory performance on the WMS-R, and verbal memory skills are likely to be better preserved than visual memory skills. Patients with MS tend to have less marked but still impaired memory ability and also tend to score better on verbal memory tests. However, the specific level of impairment will depend on the severity of the disorder and its stage. For example, Fischer (1988) studied 45 MS patients and compared them with 25 matched controls. He found that although the MS patients as a group performed more poorly on all five indexes, 20% exhibited marked global impairment in attention/concentration, learning, and delayed memory; 56% had intact attention and concentration but displayed mild deficits in learning and delayed memory; and 24% displayed no memory deficits at all.

Patients exposed to work site toxins tend to perform poorly on all measures except information/orientation and do not exhibit a consistent pattern of performance on the WMS-R. Head-injured patients show similar poor performance across measures, with especially salient deficits on measures of delayed recall. However, the attention/concentration measures from the WMS-R may not be sensitive enough to identify genuine impairment in patients with mild head injury, and the PASAT is recommended for this population. The PASAT produces "attention overload," dramatically increasing its sensitivity in cases of mild impairment.

NORMAL AGING AND FORGETTING RATES

The relationship between age and memory impairment is complex and controversial. However, it appears that genuine deficits in memory occur as a normal result of the aging process, even in healthy adults. These deficits are far more apparent on visuospatial tasks than on verbal tasks. For our purposes, it is important simply to note that *there are no norms in the WMS-R manual for persons above the age of 74. If you extrapolate or use the 70–74 norms for adults older than 74, you run the risk of underestimating their true abilities.*

Cullum, Butters, Troster, and Salmon, (1990) have provided helpful normative data for elderly subjects that expand the initial WMS-R norms. Their subjects were drawn from the San Diego area and were highly educated (mean education level, 14.5 years). If these limitations are kept in mind, the data reported in Table 4.3 may be helpful.

These same authors calculated "savings scores" for both younger (age 50–75) and older (age 75–95) groups. The savings scores were defined as (Delayed Recall/Immediate Recall) × 100. As illustrated in Table 4.4, the last learning trials score was used to produce contrasts between the visual and verbal paired associate scores.

Several findings from this study are significant. One especially important observation is that 75–95-year-old subjects demonstrated significantly lower savings scores (i.e., more rapid rate of forgetting). However, the two groups were quite similar on both Logical Memory and on the Attention/Concentration score, and it was only on the Visual Reproduction score that the very elderly failed to achieve at least a 70% savings score. A similar finding was reported by Huppert and Kopelman (1989) using a picture-recognition task. They reported a mild acquisition and a somewhat faster rate of forgetting of visuospatial material in normal aging. In comparison, dementia gives rise to a severe acquisition deficit while producing no further effect on the forgetting rate.

The hippocampal complex may be particularly susceptible to histological changes in normal aging (and to a greater degree in dementia). In normal aging, histological abnormalities such as neurofibrillary tangles and senile plaques tend to be confined to the hippocampus and the immediately adjacent anteromedial temporal structures. These anatomical correlates could account

Table 4.3. Normal aging and forgetting rates on the Wechsler Memory Scale-Revised.

SUBTEST AGE:	Cullum 50–70		WMS–R STD 55–64	Cullum 75–95		WMS–R STD 70–74	WMS–R Max.
	M	SD	M	M	SD	M	SCORE
Digit Span	14.9	(3.7)	14.9	15.3	(3.7)	13.8	24
VIS. SPAN	14.7	(2.4)	15.0	14.1	(2.5)	13.8	26
Log. Mem. I	29.2	(7.7)	22.5	25.0	(7.5)	20.9	50
Log. Mem. II	25.6	(7.9)	18.1	20.9	(8.4)	14.7	50
Verb. Pair. Assoc.I	18.7	(2.9)	18.0	18.3	(2.8)	16.8	24
Verb. Pair. Assoc.II	7.6	(0.7)	6.9	6.9	(1.2)	6.7	8
Vis. Repro. I	34.3	(3.9)	29.0	29.1	(7.3)	24.2	41
Vis. Repro. II	29.1	(6.1)	25.4	20.1	(9.1)	16.5	41
Vis. Pair. Assoc.I	14.2	(3.7)	11.2	12.7	(3.5)	8.4	18
Vis. Pair. Assoc. II	5.6	(0.9)	4.6	4.8	(1.4)	4.0	6
Fig. Mem.	6.5	(1.7)	6.2	6.5	(1.5)	5.8	10
RAW SUMMARY SCORES							
Attn/Concen.	64.7	(9.3)	64.8	64.5	(11.2)	59.9	102
Verb. Mem	78.0	(16.3)	62.9	68.3	(16.8)	58.7	124
Vis. Mem.	55.0	(7.1)	46.4	48.3	(9.7)	38.5	69
Gen. Mem	133.0	(2.7)	109.3	116.6	(22.0)	97.2	193
Delay. Mem.	81.1	(12.8)	66.6	64.5	(17.4)	52.6	119

Source: Cullum et al. (1990). Reprinted with permission from *Archives of Clinical Neuropsychology*, 5, 23–30. Copyright 1990, Pergamon Press.

Table 4.4. WMS–R savings scores for younger and older age group and Alzheimer's dementia group.

Savings Score	Age 50–75		Age 75–95		DAT
	M%	SD	M%	SD	M%
Logical Memory	87	13	83	18	15
Verbal Pair. Assoc.	96	8	88	13	
Visual Repro.	85	15	68	25	20
Vis. Pair. Assoc.	97	20	84	23	

for the mild acquisition and rapid rate of forgetting reported above.

A FINAL NOTE ON THE ADMINISTRATION OF THE WMS-R

During the initial presentation of the visual paired associates, each pair of stimuli is shown for only 3 seconds, with the verbal instruction, "Look at this pair." This is supposed to interfere with verbal encoding of the designs and thus makes it more of a *visual* task. In addition, we also have the examinee *point to* (not say) the color. This helps keep the memory trial from being verbally mediated. It is also important to remember to close Folder B when going through the 3-second exposure (learning) trials.

THE MEMORY ASSESSMENT SCALE (MAS)

J. Michael Williams (1990) of Hahnemann University School of Medicine developed a memory battery that corrects many of the deficiencies of the WMS-R: the Memory Assessment Scale (MAS). In brief, Williams has argued that (a) the WMS-R has incomplete norms; (b) some tasks are invalid (e.g., visual paired associates is verbally mediated); (c) many of the subscale tasks and scoring methods are poorly designed on the WMS-R (e.g., it is difficult to compare subtest scores with each other or with WAIS-R subscale scores); and (d) many validity studies of the WMS-R have produced negative findings. Many of these deficiencies have been addressed with the MAS.

The major functions assessed by the MAS include verbal and nonverbal attention, concentration, and short-term memory; verbal and nonverbal learning and immediate memory; and memory for verbal and nonverbal material following delay. The test also provides measures of recognition, assesses intrusions during verbal learning recall, and provides for an analysis of retrieval strategies. The test was designed to be practical for clinicians to administer quickly and conveniently, and extensive normative data are provided in the MAS manual. The entire test takes about 1 hour to administer.

There are 12 specific subtests on the MAS (listed in Table 4.5). In addition to scores for these 12 scales, the MAS yields a global memory score and three summary scores: short-term memory, verbal memory, and visual memory. Summary score results for four neuropathological groups are presented in Figure 4.1.

Normative data for the MAS were collected from 843 neurologically intact adults in the age range from 18 to 90 years. Subjects were recruited through newspaper advertisements and by soliciting local community groups. A subset of the larger group was stratified to provide a sample representative of the total U.S. population norms for age, education, and gender as reflected in census data.

An initial validation study compared scores from 110 neurological patients with those obtained from the normative sample. Comparisons were based upon scale and standard scores from age- and education-normative tables. All neurological groups had significantly lower scores on all MAS subtests and summary scores. Subtest scores from CVA patients showed the expected

Table 4.5. Brief descriptions of the twelve MAS Subtests.

List Learning. An auditory verbal learning test requiring recall of 12 common words from four semantic categories: countries, colors, birds, and cities. The test involves free recall, cued recall, clustering, and recognition procedures.

Prose memory. An auditory prose recall task. Subjects recall the story from memory and then are questioned about details.

List Recall. The subject is required to recall the 12 words presented on the initial list learning subtest. After free recall testing, categorical prompts are used, followed by a trial in which the subject selects the appropriate stimulus words from a list of 24 words.

Verbal Span. A variation of Digit Span forward and backward.

Visual Span. A nonverbal analogue of the verbal span subtest which requires pointing to a set of stars in the same order as the examiner. Similar to Corsi's block tapping test; however, stimuli are presented on a page and the test is easier to administer than the Corsi test.

Visual Recognition. A recognition task for geometric and nonverbal designs.

Visual Reproduction. This subtest requires reproduction of a geometric design after a brief interruption. Scoring principles are derived from analysis of the differential performance of 100 normal and brain-damaged subjects.

Names–Faces. A measure of the subjects ability to associate verbal and nonverbal stimuli. The test employs high-school yearbook photographs of people in natural settings.

Delayed Recall. A delayed memory task using the stimulus words learned in the first subtest.

Delayed Prose Memory. Assesses recollection of details from a story. Free recall is followed by a series of nine structured questions.

Delayed Visual Recognition. This subtest requires recognition of 10 previously presented designs from an array of 20 designs.

Delayed Names–Faces Recall. Requires recognition of the correct names of individuals previously portrayed in the Names–Faces subtest.

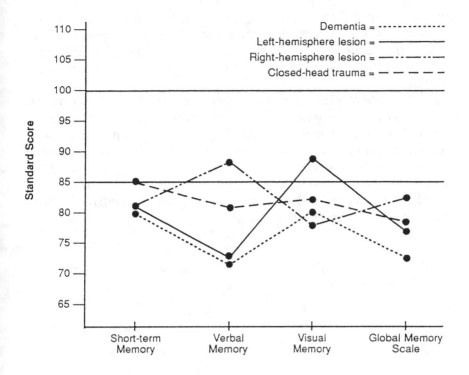

FIGURE 4.1. Mean MAS Summary Scale scores and Global Memory Scale scores by diagnostic group.

verbal/nonverbal memory discrepancy pattern consistent with lesion localization. Patients with left-hemisphere lesions did worse than patients with right-hemisphere lesions on MAS verbal memory subtests. Conversely, patients with right-hemisphere lesions did less well on tests of nonverbal memory. Differences in scores for patients with lateralized lesions were statistically significant for the MAS Verbal and Global Memory summary scores.

The MAS can be distinguished from other tests of memory by its close links to amnesia research and cognitive psychology. The test is specifically built around four basic principles of memory: (a) the separation of verbal and visual/spatial memory, (b) the distinction between immediate and delayed recall, (c) the principle of interference during recall, and (d) the difference between recall and recognition memory. The comparison of MAS verbal and visual summary scores can be used to generate hypotheses and make initial inferences about possible lateralization effects.

The MAS is a relatively new memory battery and has not yet been employed in independent investigations with different neurological patient groups. Nevertheless, the MAS appears to be a promising general memory assessment battery. As Larrabee (1991) noted in his review of the MAS, the battery's normative sample is over twice the size of that used in developing the WMS-R. Unlike the WMS-R, the MAS manual provides both age- and education-based normative tables.

REY AUDITORY VERBAL LEARNING TEST (AVLT)

GENERAL INFORMATION AND HISTORY

The original source of the Auditory Verbal Learning Test (AVLT) was published by Rey in French in 1964. The version presented here is Lezak's (1983) English version. It consists of 15 concrete nouns, read aloud to the subject at the rate of 1 per second. The subject is presented with five learning trials followed by an interference trial with a new list. Finally, immediate recall and later a 30-minute recall is tested. The free-recall responses are recorded after each learning trial.

The AVLT measures immediate (short-term) recall, long-term recall, 30-minute delayed recall, and learning over repeated trials. Common errors include *confabulation* (recalling an unrelated word not on either list), *phonemic association* (inserting a word that sounds similar to one of the stimuli), and *semantic association* (substituting a word with a similar meaning for one of the stimuli).

The structure of the AVLT permits an analysis of both learning and retention. The use of a list-learning technique yields a learning curve. Recording order of recall allows for assessing both primacy and recency effects. Use of the interference list permits assessment of both proactive and retroactive interference.

Recognition memory on the AVLT may be measured in two ways. The subject may be presented with a 50-word list and asked to identify the words on the original list (Lezak, 1983). An alternative method is to present the subject with a written paragraph containing words from the AVLT list (Query & Megran, 1983).

ADMINISTRATION

Prior to beginning the first list, patients are told that they will be read a word list and then asked to repeat as many words as they can remember, in any order (see Table 4.6). During the first trial, the examiner reads a list of 15 words (i.e., List A) at the rate of 1 per second. The examiner then writes down the words recalled by the patient in the order recalled. In this way the patient's pattern of recall can be tracked, noting how the patient associates words and whether he or she proceeds systematically or recalls words in a hit-or-miss manner. If the patient asks the examiner whether a word has already been said, the patient is told;

89

Table 4.6. Instructions for the Rey Auditory Verbal Learning Test.

LIST A

"I am going to read a list of words. Listen carefully and when I stop, you are to say back as many words as you can remember. It doesn't matter in what order you repeat them. Just try to remember as many as you can."

"Now I'm going to read the same list again, and once again when I stop I want you to tell me as many words as you can remember, including words you said the first time. It doesn't matter in what order you say them. Just say as many words as you can remember whether or not you said them before."

LIST B

"Now I'm going to read a second list of words. This time, you are to say back as many words of this second list as you can remember. Again, the order in which you say the words does not matter. Just try to remember as many as you can."

A 30-minute delayed recall follows the short delay recall of List A. Reques the patient to say all the words can be remembered from List A.

If the number of words missed on the recall trial is >2, administer the 50-word recognition list. Ask the individual to circle all the words they recognize from List A.

however, this information is not volunteered, because it may distract the patient and interfere with performance (Lezak, 1983).

When the patient indicates that no additional words can be recalled, the examiner gives a second set of instructions and rereads the list. The patient is told that the same list will be read again and that, when it is completed, the patient is to say back as many words as can be remembered. The patient is also asked to repeat the words said the first time and told that the order is not important. The second set of instructions must emphasize the inclusion of the previously said words so that the patient does not think that the test is one of elimination (Lezak, 1983).

The instructions and list are repeated for trials 3–5. Praise may be given as words are recalled, and the patient may be told the number of words recalled, especially if the patient is able to use the information for reassurance or as a challenge. On the completion of the last trial, the second word list (List B) is read, with instructions similar to those for the first word list. Following the second-list trial, the patient is asked to recall as many words from the first list as he or she can (Trial 7). Should either the first- or second-list presentation be spoiled by interruptions, improper administration, confusion, or premature response on the patient's part, a third word list (List C) is available (Lezak, 1983). According to Ryan, Geisser, Randall, & Georgemiller, (1986), the reliability of this list as an alternative form ranges from .60 to .77. Lists A, B, and C are included in Table 4.7.

A recognition list (see Table 4.7) of 50 words (List A, List B, and new words) should be included to help discern whether deficient performance is due to poor retention or poor retrieval. This is recommended especially in those cases where there is more than a two-word decline on the 30-minute delayed-recall trial. If the subject has actually retained the stimuli but cannot retrieve them easily, he or she will probably perform well on the recognition task. However, if the problem is simply difficulty in retaining new information, performance will be as poor on the recognition task as on the delayed free-recall trial.

A recognition list of 50 words is presented in Table 4.8. This list includes words from lists A and B and words that are seman-

Table 4.7. Rey Auditory Verbal Learning Test stimulus words.

LIST A	LIST B	LIST C
drum	desk	book
curtain	range	flower
bell	bird	train
coffee	shoe	meadow
school	stove	rug
parent	mountain	harp
moon	glasses	salt
garden	towel	finger
hat	cloud	apple
farmer	boat	chimney
nose	lamb	button
turkey	gun	key
color	pencil	dog
house	church	glass
river	fish	rattle

THE CLINICAL ASSESSMENT OF MEMORY

Table 4.8. (A) Words from list A; (B) words from list B: (S) words with a semantic association to a word on list A or B as indicated; (P) words phonemically similar to a word on list A or B.

Word List for Testing AVLT Recognition				
Bell (A)	Home (SA)	Towel (B)	Boat (B)	Glasses (B)
Window (SA)	Fish (B)	Curtain (A)	Hot (PA)	Stocking (SB)
Hat (A)	Moon (A)	Flower (SA)	Parent (A)	Shoe (B)
Barn (SA)	Tree (PA)	Color (A)	Water (Sa)	Teacher (SA)
Ranger (B)	Balloon (PA)	Desk (B)	Farmer (A)	Stove (B)
Nose (A)	Bird (B)	Gun (B)	Rose (SPA)	Nest (SPB)
Weather (SB)	Mountain (B)	Crayon (SA)	Cloud (B)	Children (SA)
School (A)	Coffee (A)	Church (B)	House (A)	Drum (A)
Hand (PA)	Mouse (PA)	Turkey (A)	Stranger (PB)	Toffee (PA)
Pencil (B)	River (A)	Fountain (PB)	Garden (A)	Lamb (B)

Source: Lezak (1983).

tically associated (S) or phonemically similar (P) to words on lists A or B. This list can be used to identify evidence of disordered recall (like that which troubles patients with impaired frontal lobe functions who can learn readily enough but can't keep track or make order out of what they have learned).

SCORING THE AVLT

The score for each trial is the number of words correctly recalled. A total score, the sum of trials 1 through 5, should also be calculated. Words that are repeated can be noted, as can words that were not on the list (errors or confabulations) (Lezak, 1983).

Norms from Weins, McMinn, and Crossen (1988) are presented in Tables 4.9a–4.9c. Subjects in this study included 222 healthy applicants for civil service positions in the Pacific Northwest. Ages ranged from 19 to 51 years. The sample was composed of 193 males and 29 females and included a small representation of 12 racial-minority subjects. It should be noted that the recognition trial in this study immediately followed the List A recall trial; that is, there was no 30–minute delayed recall or recognition trial. Note that the norms in Table 4.9 are generally lower than Rey's 1964 data (reported in Lezak, 1983) and may be considered most appropriate when testing "contemporary" Americans (Weins et al., 1988).

Table 4.9a. Rey Auditory Verbal Learning Test Scores by WAIS-R Full Scale IQ.

WAIS-R FISQ	n	I Mean	SD	II Mean	SD	III Mean	SD	IV Mean	SD	V Mean	SD	Recall Mean	SD	Recognition Mean	SD
80–89	5	8.0	2.5	10.4	1.7	10.8	2.2	11.0	2.1	11.0	3.0	10.6	2.4	14.0	0.7
90–99	29	7.1	1.6	9.7	1.8	11.4	2.1	12.2	1.8	13.0	2.0	11.2	2.2	14.0	1.1
100–109	81	7.2	1.8	9.9	2.5	11.8	2.0	12.4	1.9	12.9	1.8	11.6	2.3	14.2	0.9
110–119	55	7.5	1.7	10.4	2.2	11.9	1.9	13.1	1.4	13.2	1.6	12.1	2.3	14.0	1.2
120–129	38	7.7	1.8	10.7	2.2	12.7	1.7	13.3	1.5	13.7	1.7	12.6	1.9	14.4	0.8
130–139	3	10.0	2.6	12.3	2.5	13.7	1.5	15.0	0	14.7	0.6	14.3	1.2	15.0	0

WAIS-R FISQ	n	Distractor Trial (List B) Mean	SD	Words Learned (Trials V–I) Mean	SD	Percentage Recall Mean	SD	Error Mean	SD	Repetitions Mean	SD	Total Words (Trials I–V) Mean	SD
80–89	5	6.6	2.6	3.0	1.7	99.5	22.0	2.2	1.8	2.6	3.2	51.2	10.9
90–99	29	6.0	1.6	5.9	2.2	86.7	14.5	3.2	3.9	5.6	5.7	53.4	7.4
100–109	81	6.5	1.5	5.7	1.9	90.1	12.0	2.2	2.9	5.2	5.8	54.2	8.2
110–119	55	6.8	1.5	5.7	2.1	91.8	12.1	2.1	2.4	7.0	6.9	56.1	7.0
120–129	38	7.2	1.9	6.0	1.8	92.5	9.9	2.0	2.3	5.4	6.3	58.1	7.2
130–139	3	7.7	1.5	4.7	2.5	97.9	10.4	2.0	1.7	.7	1.2	65.7	6.7

Table 4.9b. Rey Auditory-Verbal Learning Test Scores by Age.

Age	n	I		II		III		IV		V		Recall		Recognition	
		Mean	SD	Mean	SD	Mean	SD	Mean	SD	Mean	SD	Mean	SD	Mean	SD
20–29	126	7.4	1.7	10.4	2.2	12.2	1.9	13.0	1.7	13.4	1.7	12.1	2.2	14.2	1.0
30–39	71	7.4	1.9	9.9	2.5	11.7	2.0	12.4	1.8	12.7	1.8	11.7	2.2	14.2	1.1
40–49	12	7.3	2.2	9.8	2.7	11.4	2.6	12.3	1.8	12.5	2.5	11.2	3.1	13.8	9

Age	n	Distractor Trial (List B)		Words Learned (Trials V–I)		Perentage Recall		Total Words (Trials I–V)		Error		Repetitions	
		Mean	SD	Mean	SD	Mean	SD	Mean	SD	Mean	SD	Mean	SD
20–29	126	6.8	1.6	6.0	2.0	90.4	12.4	56.3	7.4	2.2	3.0	5.8	6.1
30–39	71	6.5	1.7	5.3	1.9	92.0	12.7	54.2	8.3	2.3	2.5	5.0	5.5
40–49	12	6.6	1.8	5.2	2.6	88.9	10.11	53.3	10.3	2.7	2.3	7.3	10.1

Table 4.9c. Rey Auditory-Verbal Learning Test Scores by Education.

Years of Education	n	I Mean	I SD	II Mean	II SD	III Mean	III SD	IV Mean	IV SD	V Mean	V SD	Recall Mean	Recall SD	Recognition Mean	Recognition SD
12	34	7.0	1.6	9.9	3.5	11.7	2.0	11.9	3.5	12.4	2.3	11.4	2.4	13.9	1.2
13	25	7.5	1.2	10.1	2.4	11.9	2.4	12.7	1.7	13.2	1.6	12.1	2.1	13.9	1.2
14	50	7.2	1.9	9.9	2.3	11.8	2.1	13.0	1.9	13.2	2.0	12.3	2.2	14.4	.8
15	19	7.4	2.2	10.3	2.9	12.4	2.0	12.6	2.1	13.2	1.9	11.4	2.7	14.3	.7
16	80	7.6	1.9	10.5	2.2	12.1	1.8	13.0	1.4	13.3	1.5	12.0	2.1	14.2	.9
17+	5	7.8	2.6	10.4	3.0	12.4	1.1	13.8	1.3	13.4	1.7	11.2	3.1	13.4	1.8

Years of Education	n	Distractor Trial (List B) Mean	SD	Words Learned (Trials V-I) Mean	SD	Percentage Recall Mean	SD	Error Mean	SD	Repetitions Mean	SD	Total Words (Trials I-V) Mean	SD
12	34	6.6	1.8	5.3	2.0	93.1	13.5	1.9	1.9	6.6	6.7	52.9	7.9
13	25	6.0	1.6	5.7	1.6	91.4	10.4	1.4	1.7	7.1	7.3	55.3	7.7
14	50	6.7	1.8	6.0	2.2	93.3	11.0	2.5	3.2	6.5	6.9	55.2	8.4
15	19	6.6	.9	5.7	2.1	86.0	15.7	2.3	3.5	2.6	2.7	55.8	9.5
16	80	6.8	1.7	5.7	2.0	90.0	11.8	2.6	3.0	5.0	5.6	56.5	7.2
17+	5	7.8	1.1	5.6	3.0	83.0	16.6	1.2	1.6	4.2	1.6	57.8	7.7

Table 4.10a: AVLT Scales by Age: Males.

Age	n	30-Minute Delayed Recall		30-Minute Recognition	
		Mean	SD	Mean	SD
20–29	10	10.6	2.4	14.2	0.8
30–39	10	10.4	2.3	13.5	1.5
40–49	11	10.5	2.7	14.2	1.0

Table 4.10b: AVLT Scores by Age: Females.

Age	n	30-Minute Delayed Recall		30-Minute Recognition	
		Mean	SD	Mean	SD
20–29	10	11.0	2.0	14.4	0.8
30–39	10	12.2	2.5	14.2	1.7
40–49	11	11.1	2.3	14.4	0.8

Source: Adapted from Geffen et al. (1990).

Normative data for a comparable sample has been compiled by Geffen et al. (Geffen, Hoor, O'Hanlon, Clark, & Geffen, 1990). Norms for the 30-minute delated recall and delayed recognition for males and females are presented in Table 4.10. Subjects in the Geffen et al. study included healthy adults with above-average IQs. Additional norms for a broader sample are provided in the original publication.

INTERPRETATION OF THE AVLT

Performance on the Rey AVLT is correlated with age and IQ, and interpretations should be adjusted accordingly. However, with this caveat in mind, the following rules should be helpful.

There is normally an improvement of about five or six words over the initial five learning trials. Most normal individuals come close to perfect recall by the fifth trial (mean, 13.1; range, 12.5 to 13.4 for ages up to 49); however, performance can decline dramatically with older groups, decreasing to nine or fewer words for the 70+ age category.

It is sometimes instructive to compare Trial 5 with Trial 7 (short-delay free recall of List 1). A decline of more than three words recalled is abnormal and probably reflects a retention or retrieval problem.

The 30-minute delayed recall should show little decline in healthy adults (providing no other verbal tasks intervened during the delay interval). Any decline of more than three words should be a red flag for the clinician, suggesting the need for more extensive assessment of memory functions.

Ordinarily, the immediate memory span for digits (from the WAIS-R or WMS-R digits forward) and the number of words recalled on Trial 1 will be within 1 or 2 points of each other, providing supporting evidence regarding the length of span. Hence, Trial 1 may be considered an index of immediate memory. The average person can recall seven words on Trial 1. Larger differences usually favor the digit span and seem to occur in patients with intact immediate memory and concentration who become confused by too much stimulation. These patients tend to have difficulty with complex material or situations and perform better when confronted with simplified, highly structured tasks. When the difference favors the more difficult word list retention task, the lower digit-span score is usually due to inattention, lack of concentration, or psychiatric difficulties (Lezak, 1983).

Slowness in shifting from one response to another can show up in a low score on Trial 1. When this occurs in a person whose immediate verbal memory span is within normal limits, recall B will be at least two or three words longer than that of Trial 1 and usually within normal limits. In these cases, recall for Trial 2 will often show a much greater rate of acquisition than the rate found for patients whose initial recall is abnormally low. Occasionally, a large jump in score will not take place until Trial 3. When this phenomenon is observed, the examiner should review the pattern of the patient's performance on other tests in which slowness in establishing a response set might show up, such as Block Design (e.g., a patient may get 2 points at most on each of the first two designs and complete designs 4, 5, and 6 accurately and faster than the first two). In a situation such as this, it is often helpful to check performance on the FAS test to see if marked improvement occurs on the S trial (Lezak, 1983). A patient who performs much more poorly on presentation of List B than on the first trial of List A is demonstrating *proactive interference.*

Most brain-damaged patients show a learning curve over the five trials. The appearance of a curve, even at a low level (e.g., from three or four words to eight over trials 1–5), demonstrates some ability to learn, especially if the gain is maintained on the delayed-recall trial. Demonstration of learning ability may be important in determining if a client is capable of benefiting from rehabilitation training and formal schooling (Lezak, 1983).

Interpretation of the recognition list of 50 words (Lists A and B and new words) should help determine whether deficient performance is due to poor retention or poor retrieval. If the subject has actually retained the stimuli but cannot retrieve them easily, he or she will probably perform well on the recognition task. However, if the problem is simply difficulty in retaining new information, performance will be as poor on the recognition task as on the delayed free-recall trial.

John Crossen and Art Wiens (1988) have provided useful data on the effects of head injury on Rey AVLT performance. Their norms are reproduced in Table 4.11. Subjects in their study consisted of individuals with a mean age of 33.2 years (SD = 8.9 years), mean education level of 12.1 years (SD = 1.5 years), and FSIQ mean of 90.2 (SD = 10.0). The head-injury subjects were 3.7 years posthead trauma on the average. The severity of head injury was rated moderate to severe, and the sample included patients with both closed-head injuries and fractures. All patients had a loss of consciousness of at least 1 hour. The "healthy normal" group was of similar age and education levels.

Table 4.11. Residual neuropsychological deficits following head injury. *n = 10; **n = 34.

Test Score	Head Injured*		Healthy Normals**	
	Mean	SD	Mean	SD
Trails 1–5	35.0	7.7	52.9	7.9
Trial 5	8.2	2.0	13.4	2.3
Recall	5.3	3.0	11.4	2.4
Recognition	11.5	3.5	13.9	1.2
Intrusions	5.0	6.4	1.9	1.9

Source: Crossen & Wiens (1988).

Table 4.12. Four alternate forms for the AVLT.

A	B	C	D	E	F	G	H
Drum	Desk	Book	Bowl	Street	Baby	Tower	Sky
Curtain	Ranger	Flower	Dawn	Grass	Ocean	Wheat	Dollar
Bell	Bird	Train	Judge	Door	Palace	Queen	Valley
Coffee	Shoe	Rug	Grant	Arm	Lip	Sugar	Butter
School	Stove	Meadow	Insect	Star	Bar	Home	Hall
Parent	Mountain	Harp	Plane	Wife	Dress	Boy	Diamond
Moon	Glasses	Salt	County	Window	Steam	Doctor	Winter
Garden	Towel	Finger	Pool	City	Coin	Camp	Mother
Hat	Cloud	Apple	Seed	Pupil	Rock	Flag	Christmas
Farmer	Boat	Chimney	Sheep	Cabin	Army	Letter	Meat
Nose	Lamb	Button	Meal	Lake	Building	Corn	Forest
Turkey	Gum	Key	Coat	Pipe	Friend	Nail	Gold
Color	Pencil	Dog	Bottle	Skin	Storm	Cattle	Plant
House	Church	Glass	Peach	Fire	Village	Shore	Money
River	Fish	Rattle	Chair	Clock	Cell	Body	Hotel

Source: Shapiro and Harrison (1990).

As mentioned earlier, the version presented by Lezak (1983) includes an alternate form C, and Shapiro and Harrison (1990) constructed a set of additional alternate forms. These additional forms permit expansion of the AVLT from a screening test to a repeated-measures test that can be used for evaluation of progressive changes across time, e.g., decline or recovery of function during serial testing procedures for dementia or with head injured patients. The four versions of the AVLT presented in Table 4.12 yielded comparable mean recall scores for each trial with a difference of less than one point across forms. Further, correlation coefficients derived from comparisons of each trial of each alternate form with the original AVLT averaged 0.80. These results suggest that norms for the original version of the AVLT can be used with these alternate forms.

VALIDITY STUDIES OF THE AVLT

Several investigators used the AVLT to study patterns of memory impairment associated with different clinical populations. Butters, Wolfe, Granholm, & Martone (1986) used the AVLT to demonstrate differences in memory impairment in patients with Huntington's disease or Korsakoff's syndrome. Recognition memory was superior in the Huntington's disease patients. The alcoholic Korsakoff's syndrome patients showed greater sensitivity to proactive interference. Mungus (1983) administered the AVLT to amnesics, head trauma patients, individuals with attention deficit disorder, schizophrenics, and nonpsychotic psychiatric patients. Amnesics and head trauma patients were differentiated from the other patient groups by difficulty in recalling the original items following presentation of the interference list. Amnesics differed from all other groups by the total number of words recalled. Amnesics showed a marked recency effect and a diminished primacy effect. Query and Megran (1983) added to the normative base of the AVLT by publishing a set of age-related norms based on 677 medically hospitalized male patients.

Sex differences appear to play a role in verbal learning, and females consistently perform better on these tests. This is reflected in norms for the Selective Reminding Verbal Learning Test (Larrabee, Trahan, Custiss, & Levin, 1988; Ruff, Quayhagen, & Light, 1988), the California Verbal Learning test (Delis, Kramer, Kaplan, & Ober, 1987), and the AVLT. Bolla-Wilson and Bleecker (1986) studied the influences of age, sex, education, and IQ on AVLT performance. Verbal intelligence and sex accounted for a significant proportion of the variance on every learning trial of the AVLT. Higher verbal intelligence correlated with better performance, and women performed better than men. Age was a significant factor on the first two trials only. Bolla-Wilson and Bleecker found no relationship between AVLT performance and education. Further normative studies with the AVLT should provide separate norms for males and females and should further subdivide norms based on an individual's measured verbal intelligence. A factor-analytic study of the AVLT (Ryan, Rosenbert, & Mittenberg, 1984) demonstrated it to be primarily a test of verbal learning.

Ryan, Geisser, Randall, and Georgemiller (1986) provided validation of an alternative form of the AVLT. In an initial study they provided data supporting alternative form reliability. In a follow-up study, Ryan and his colleagues (1986) demonstrated equivalent diagnostic sensitivity of the two forms. Shapiro and Harrison (1990) provided word lists for four alternative and equivalent forms of the AVLT.

CALIFORNIA VERBAL LEARNING TEST (CVLT)

The California Verbal Learning Test (CVLT) was patterned after Rey's AVLT and is designed to provide diagnosis and treatment planning for patients with memory impairment. The test's authors provide satisfactory normative data and a readable test manual. The original sample for the CVLT was composed of 273 neurologically intact, geographically distributed adults with a mean age of 58.9 years and an average of 13.8 years of education. The educational background of the normative sample is highly skewed toward the upper end of the scale.

The CVLT measures both recall and recognition of word lists over a number of trials. In addition, it measures multiple aspects of *how* verbal learning occurs, or fails to occur, in addition to measuring the *amount* of verbal material learned. It does this in the context of an everyday memory task (a shopping list) that allows the creation of direct inferences about how an examinee uses memory in the context of day-to-day life.

The CVLT requires the subject to learn a list of 16 words (i.e., the Monday Shopping list) over five trials in a standard free-recall procedure. The words are from four different semantic categories (i.e., spices and herbs, fruits, tools, and clothing). After the fifth trial, a second shopping list (the Tuesday Shopping List) is administered, and following its free recall, the subject is asked for spontaneous recall of the initial Monday list. This is followed by cued-recall trials (e.g., "Tell me all the words that are tools"). The test concludes with a 20-minute delayed free- and cued-recall trial and a recognition trial.

In addition to more traditional measures of memory, the CVLT has incorporated techniques and concepts derived from cognitive psychology (e.g., proactive and retroactive interference, semantic cuing, and prototypic response distractors for recognition memory). The use of a distractor list (i.e., the Tuesday list) allows for the examination of prior list intrusion errors, which may be an important aspect of a patient's neuropsychological status. For example, *both alcoholic Korsakoff's syndrome and Alzheimer's disease patients can be distinguished from those with Huntington's disease by the presence of a higher number of intrusion errors.*

The CVLT has good test-retest reliability. The average improvement on the second testing in the total immediate recall of

Table 4.13. Variables derived from quantitive analysis of CVLT.

1. Levels of total recall and recognition on all trials
2. Semantic and serial learning strategies
3. Serial position effects
4. Learning rate across trials
5. Consistency of item recall across trials
6. Degree of vulnerability to proactive and retroactive interference
7. Retention of information over short and longer delays
8. Enhancement of recall performance by category cuing and recognition testing
9. Indices of recognition performance (discriminability and response bias) derived from signal-detection theory
10. Perseverations and intrusions in recall
11. False positive in recognition

List A across five trials is about two words (i.e., less than one-half word per trial). The average improvement on short- and long-delay recall trials and on recognition hits is about 1 word.

Despite major similarities, there are a number of important differences between the CVLT and the AVLT. Rey's test involves use of 15 unrelated words. The CVLT entails the learning of categorized lists. The CVLT words include (a) higher-frequency, well-established categories (e.g., "clothing") to minimize floor effects in brain-damaged populations and (b) lower-frequency "fuzzy" categories (e.g., "spices and herbs") to minimize ceiling effects in normal examinees. Word frequencies of items within each category were also varied systematically for the same reasons.

Computer scoring of the CVLT generates an impressive (and at first intimidating) amount of quantitative information. Some of the variables generated by the CVLT are listed in Table 4.13.

INTERPRETATION OF THE CVLT

This section has been in part derived from the CVLT manual (Delis et al., 1987) and organized to follow the outline structure of the summary and standard score output from page 3 of the

CVLT computer-scored printout. An example of this printout is illustrated in Table 4.14.

Recall Measures (Number Correct)

List A: Immediate Free Recall (trials 1–5 total; Trial 1; Trial 5). Scores on immediate free recall trials provide global measures of learning performance. Specific interpretation of low scores on these trials requires an evaluation of the examinee's learning characteristics and recall errors.

List B: Immediate Free Recall. Performance on List B may be adversely affected by the five previous List A trials. A low score on immediate free recall of List B relative to Trial 1 of List A may be related to an unusually high degree of proactive interference. List B serves as an interference list and is administered once immediately following the fifth trial of List A. List B words were selected to be as comparable to List A as possible. Two of the categories on List B are the same as categories on List A (i.e., herbs and spices and fruits). A shared-nonshared category recall contrast enables an assessment of proactive interference.

Proactive interference refers to the decremental effect of prior learning on retention of subsequently learned material. Proactive interference can be manifested in two ways on the CVLT: (a) immediate recall of List B may be worse than immediate recall on the first trial of List A due to interference from the learning of List A over the five trials, or (b) recall of shared categories items from List B may be worse than from the nonshared categories due to their semantic similarity to words on List A. Recall of words from the nonshared categories that is superior to recall of shared words on List B is referred to as *release from proactive inhibition*. Failure to release from proactive interference is frequently found in patients with frontal lobe pathology as well as in patients with Korsakoff's syndrome.

Retroactive interference refers to the decremental effect of subsequent learning on the retention of previously learned material. Formal procedures for measuring proactive and retroactive interference are presented in Appendix D of the CVLT manual.

List A: Short-Delay Free Recall. After the single presentation and free recall of List B, free recall of List A is elicited. Recall on this short-delay trial may show a decrement relative to recall on Trial 5 of List A. A low score on the Short-Delay Free Recall trial

Table 4.14. Summary data from CVLT computer-scored printout, raw and standard for CVLT indices.

	Raw Score		Standard Score	
RECALL MEASURES (Number Correct)				← Scaled to T-Score
List A Trials 1–5 Total:	52	>	39	
List A Trial 1:	6		–1	
List A Trail 5:	12		–2	
List B:	6	∨	–1	
List A Short-Delay Free Recall:	11	∨	–1	
List A Short-Delay Cued Recall:	10	∨	–2	
List A Long-Delay Free Recall:	10	∨	–2	
List A Long-Delay Cued Recall:	9	∨	–3	
LEARNING CHARACTERISTICS, LIST A TRIALS 1–5				
Semantic Cluster Ratio (Observed/Expected):	2.4		0	
Serial Cluster Ratio (Observed/Expected):	2.3		0	
Percent of Correct Recall from Primary Region:	33	%	+1	
Percent of Correct Recall from Middle Region:	37	%	–1	
Percent of Correct Recall from Recency Region:	31	%	0	
Slope (Increment in Words Recalled/Trial):	+1.4		0	
Percent Recall Consistency Across Trials 1–5:	85	%	0	

RECALL ERRORS (LISTS A and B)

Perseverations (Free and Cued Recall Total):	12	+2
Free Recall Intrusions (Total):	1	0
Cued Recall Intrusions (Total):	1	0
Intrusions (Free and Cued Recall Total):	2	Not Normed

RECOGNITION MEASURES

Recognition Hits:	>	13 <	-4
Discriminability:	>	91 %<	-1
False Positives:		1	0
Response Bias:		-.5	-1

	Percent Change	Difference Score
CONTRAST MEASURES		
List B Compared To List A Trial 1:	0 %	0
Short-Delay Free Recall Compared To List A Trial 5:	-8.33 %	+1
Long-Delay Free Recall Compared to Short-Delay Free Recall:	-9.09 %	-1
Recognition (Hits) Compared to Long-Delay Free Recall:	30 %	-2
Discriminability Compared To Long-Delay Free Recall:	–	+1

Source: Reprinted with permission from the Psychological Corporation.

of List A relative to Trial 5 of List A may be related to the combination of unusually high degrees of forgetting during the delay interval and retroactive interference (i.e., the decremental effect of attempting to learn List B on short-delay free recall of List A).

List A: Cued Recall. After the short-delay recall trial of List A, a cued-recall trial for List A is administered, and the patient is asked to recall words from each of the four categories in turn. This trial permits a comparison of free recall to category-cued recall. If a patient shows *impaired free recall* but significantly *better cued recall*, then deficits in retrieval may be present. (This type of performance is characteristic of patients with recently diagnosed Huntington's disease.) If free recall and cued recall are both impaired, then problems in encoding may contribute significantly to the examinee's memory dysfunction (e.g., as in Korsakoff's syndrome, where a distraction interval will elicit poor delayed recall. Patients with Korsakoff's syndrome perform poorly on CVLT measures of delayed recall primarily because of the distraction factor, not because of a rapid rate of forgetting.)

Sometimes patients who are trying to use a semantic recall strategy give semantically related "intrusion" responses (i.e., words that were not on the list). These responses are often prototypical of one of the list's categories. For this reason, in the original selection of words for both lists, the four most frequent exemplars of a particular category were excluded.

List A: Long-Delay Free Recall. Long-delay testing on the CVLT requires 20 minutes of nonverbal activity (to minimize interference) and then a free-recall trial for List A. Performance on long-delay testing reflects the examinee's ability to retain verbal information over time. However, *poor performance on the long delay recall trial does not necessarily imply rapid rates of forgetting.* This point is demonstrated by the performance of patients such as those with Korsakoff's syndrome, in whom the severity of the memory problem is particularly evident after a distraction interval has been imposed between learning and recall. This problem is related to frontal symptomatology and does not result from a rapid rate of forgetting. When patients with Korsakoff's syndrome are allowed to rehearse, they display a normal rate of forgetting because their deficit is primarily due to an encoding deficit.

List A Long-Delay Cued Recall. Categorical cuing interposed between short-delay and long-delay free recall enables the examiner to determine the extent to which the presentation of category names on a previous trial enhances semantic clustering on a later free-recall trial. This has implications for cognitive rehabilitation of memory processes because it may indicate whether a patient with impoverished semantic clustering can adopt a semantic strategy provided by the examiner.

Learning Characteristics, List A, Trials 1–5

Semantic Clustering. The CVLT words allow the patient to use semantic clustering strategies. The ability to exploit these strategies appears to decline in the normal elderly and is markedly deficient in amnesic patients such as those with Korsakoff's syndrome.

The *semantic clustering ratio* (Observed/Expected) indicates the degree to which the examinee uses the active learning strategy of reorganizing the target words into categorical groups. Semantic clustering can be a highly effective learning strategy because the 16 words can be categorized into four higher-order semantic units for more efficient encoding and retrieval. Low semantic-clustering scores correlate with poor performance on many of the other CVLT parameters and suggest that the examinee is using less effective learning strategies (e.g., serial clustering).

Serial-Order Clustering. A common but less efficient alternative strategy is the recall of items in the same order as they were presented. Use of a serial-order clustering strategy correlates with poor performance on many of the other CVLT parameters.

The *serial clustering ratio* (Observed/Expected) indicates the degree to which the examinee recalls target words in the same order as they are presented. High serial-clustering scores correlate with poor performance on many of the other CVLT parameters. Serial clustering may reflect a "stimulus-bound" response style in which the examinee adheres rigidly to the temporal order of the list when recalling the words. Occasionally, an examinee with superior memory skills will recall all 16 target items after the first two or three trials by using semantic clustering and then switch to serial clustering as a way of making the task more challenging. For such an examinee, a high serial-cluster score is ac-

107

tually a reflection of superior learning ability and cognitive flexibility.

Pooled Serial-Position Recall Data. Examinees frequently favor recall of items from the beginning (a *primacy effect*) and the end (a *recency effect*) of a list. The primacy-recency effect indicates that some information is being encoded into long-term storage (primacy effect) and some is being processed in short-term storage (recency effect). Patients who are impaired in encoding information into long-term storage would be expected to recall words primarily from the recency region, suggesting that they are using a predominantly passive recall strategy of simply echoing back the last words presented.

Technically, the "primacy = long-term" and "recency = short-term" storage pertains to only the first presentation of List 1. As a result, one must be cautious about making conclusions about the integrity of a patient's long- and short-term storage based on recall from the primacy and recency regions.

Examinees typically recall a larger percentage of the words that are in the primacy and recency regions of a list than of the words in the middle region. Poor recall of primacy-region words may indicate a passive learning style.

Slope (Increment in Words Recalled per Trial). A slope value of near 0 may indicate that the examinee quickly reaches a learning plateau; a slope of >1.00 reflects sizable increases in recall from trial to trial (see reference group norms for specific values for each age and sex group).

Learning across trials can vary greatly because of the impact of psychological variables such as anxiety. However, patients who are highly anxious or have problems acquiring the set of a task often perform poorly on the first trial but improve considerably on subsequent trials. In contrast, patients with limited learning capacity may achieve a normal or close to normal score on the first trial but quickly reach a learning plateau on subsequent trials. The slope of the regression line indicates the amount of new learning over the first five trials.

Percent Consistency Across Trials. This index measures the percentage of target words recalled on one of the first four trials that are also recalled on the very next trial (i.e., trials 2–5). Low recall consistency reflects haphazard or disorganized styles of learning and may indicate that the examinee has difficulty formulating or maintaining a learning plan.

Percent Recall Consistency Across Trials. Inconsistent recall may occur when a patient with limited learning capacity abandons one recall strategy for another (i.e., recalling words from the primacy region on one trial and the recency region on another trial). *Inconsistent recall is more prominent in amnesic patients, particularly those with frontal-system pathology.* These patients respond to each repeated presentation of each list as though it were a new list. Luria (1981) attributed this problem in recall to an "inability to retain the plan of memorizing."

Recall Errors (Lists A and B)

The CVLT measures two types of recall errors: (a) perseverations, which are repetitions of responses previously given on the same trial; and (b) intrusions, which are responses not on the target list.

Perseverations (Free- and Cued-Recall Total). A high number of perseverations can occur for at least two reasons. Problems in response inhibition may cause the reporting of a word shortly after it was originally reported on a trial; this is called a *proximal perseveration*. These errors are often associated with frontal-system pathology. Examinees with this type of impairment are unable to inhibit repeating their most recent responses. In contrast, a patient may repeat a response a considerable time after it was originally used; this is referred to as a *distal perseveration*. Distal perseverations are common in patients with attention or amnesic deficits. Patients who give distal perseverations often have forgotten that they reported the response earlier on that trial, and they most often believe they are making the perseverative response for the first time.

Free-Recall Intrusions (Total). High rates of intrusions may reflect problems in discriminating relevant from irrelevant responses. Intrusions have been found to be characteristic of patients with dementia of the Alzheimer type and those with Korsakoff's syndrome.

If an examinee tends to report intrusions that are in the same category as the preceding responses (i.e., when the intrusions are semantically clustered), it may indicate that some semantic processing is occurring but there is impairment in the ability to discriminate previously studied items from other category members.

Cued-Recall Intrusions (Total). If intrusions are given primarily on cued-recall rather than free-recall trials, external prompting by the examiner may be responsible for triggering problems in response discrimination. However, if the intrusions reported either on the List B trial or the delayed trials of List A are primarily items from the other CVLT list (e.g., List A items are recalled on the List B trial), or if they belong to the shared categories represented in lists A and B, the difficulties observed in response discrimination are most likely related to an unusually high degree of proactive or retroactive interference.

Recognition Measures

In testing recognition memory, the CVLT utilizes an auditory presentation of a list containing the target words and 28 distractor words in a yes/no recognition paradigm. All items are names of objects that could be on a shopping list. This test yields hits, misses, false positives ("yes" on a distractor item), and correct rejections ("no" on a distractor item).

Recognition Hits. Accurate recognition generally indicates that the target item was encoded. However, a high hit rate does not necessarily indicate accurate performance on a recognition test because a high false-positive rate may occur concurrently. The astute clinician will watch for patterns of response bias (e.g., the patient who says yes to everything).

Discriminability. Discriminability refers to the ability to distinguish target items from distractor items (i.e., "signal" from "noise"). Scores on this scale range from 0% (all responses are false-positive) to 100% (all responses are hits or correct rejections). The index takes into account both hits and false positives, and it provides the single best measure of overall recognition performance.

A low discriminability score may indicate an impairment in differentiating target items from distractor items, suggesting that problems in encoding contribute significantly to the examinee's memory deficits.

False Positives. False-positive responses may indicate one or both of the following: (a) a deficit in discriminating target items from distractor items, and/or (b) a significant response bias (i.e., the tendency to favor "yes" or "no" responses regardless of stimulus type).

Response Biases. A perfect score on the recognition trial (16 hits, 0 false positives) yields a response bias score of 0 and indicates a "neutral" response tendency. In contrast, scores approaching +1 or −1 reflect a "yes" or "no" response bias, regardless of the type of recognition item. However, Corwin (1993) recommended that appropriate transformations be employed to eliminate rates of 0 and 1. She also recommended that all measures of discrimination and bias be calculated so as to produce rates rather than raw numbers.

There are five types of distractors on the recognition list:

List B categorically shared items (e.g., fruits and herbs and spices)
List B nonshared category items (fish and utensils)
Neither list but prototypical items (apples for fruit)
Neither list but phonemically similar (drums for plums)
Neither list and unrelated (e.g., aspirin or rug)

On this recognition test, the semantically or phonemically related distractors permit an assessment of "depth of processing" of the target items. Deficits in the ability to process verbal information at a semantic level have been well documented as a consequence of normal aging.

The extent to which phonemically related as opposed to semantically related distractors are endorsed as List A items may reflect the degree to which the List A items were initially processed at a higher (semantic) or lower (phonemic) level.

A high number of "neither list—unrelated" false positives represents the most impaired performance because these items should be the most conspicuous distractors; that is, they are never presented on the learning trials of the test, and they do not share obvious semantic or phonemic features with the target items. In contrast, a few "List B-shared" false positive represent the least impaired performance, because these words have the potential to be the most confusing distractors; that is, they were previously presented on the test and are semantically related to the target items.

A high number of "Neither List—Phonemically Similar" false positive may reflect either a superficial processing strategy (more phonemic than semantic), or a hearing problem (e.g., reduced auditory acuity may cause an examinee to perceive "chimes" as "chives").

Contrast Measures (Between Trial Contrasts)

Comparing an examinee's recognition performance with free-recall and cued recall performance may also address the issue of whether memory problems reflect predominantly encoding or retrieval difficulties. Recognition testing maximally aids retrieval, whereas cued-recall testing provides a lesser degree of assistance. Free-recall testing provides no assistance. As with cued recall, markedly better performance on recognition than on free recall may indicate more of a retrieval than an encoding problem.

List B Compared to List A, Trial 1. A large negative difference in standard scores between the List B trial and Trial 1 of List A may reflect an unusually high degree of proactive interference.

Short-Delay Free Recall Compared to List A, Trial 5. A large negative difference in standard scores between Short-Delay Free Recall and Trial 5 of List A may indicate unusually high degrees of forgetting during the short delay and of retroactive interference.

Long-Delay Free Recall Compared to Short-Delay Free Recall. A large negative difference in standard scores between these two trials may indicate an impairment in retention after a period of approximately 20 minutes.

Recognition Hits Compared to Long-Delay Free Recall. A large positive difference in standard scores between recognition hits and long-delay free recall may indicate that recognition performance is considerably better than free-recall performance (provided there are few false positives on recognition). Such scores invite the interpretation that problems in retrieval contribute significantly to lower memory performance on the free-recall trial.

Discriminability Compared to Long-Delay Free Recall. The difference in standard scores between recognition discriminability and long-delay free recall provides the best contrast measure of

112

performance on these two trials because the discriminability index takes into account both hits and false positives. A large positive difference may suggest that problems in retrieval contribute significantly to lower memory performance on long-delay free recall.

THE ALTERNATIVE CVLT FORM II

An alternative form exists for the CVLT. The stimulus words for CVLT Forms I and II were derived from a study by Delis and his colleagues (1987) involving 41 normal volunteer subjects from San Diego, California. Subjects ranged in age from 19 to 79 years (mean, 38 years), with an average education level of 12.5 years. Subjects were tested in a counterbalanced order, with an average test–retest interval of 8 days (range, 6–15).

The two forms yielded equivalent mean scores for all 19 learning and memory variables. However, the primacy–recency effect was weaker on the second testing session, probably because of the semantic cuing conducted during the first session. The two forms yielded almost identical relationships between overall memory performance and age and education. Sixteen of the CVLT variables resulted in significant alternative-form reliability coefficients (range, .84–.54; p. <.001).

VALIDITY OF THE CVLT

Despite the relatively recent release of the CVLT, numerous studies have been conducted to clarify its factor structure and demonstrate patterns of performance associated with different neurological conditions.

Chronic Alcoholism

The CVLT manual reports one study of 25 males with a history of heavy drinking for an average of 10 years. These subjects had been sober for 20–120 days. The average patient was 54 years old and had a high school education. Patient deficits included mild immediate-recall problems on Trial 1 of List A, which became more pronounced on Trial 5 of List A. They were relatively inconsistent in their recall across trials 1–5. They had a high false-positive error rate on recognition testing and a low hit rate on target items (possibly due to encoding problems associated with a frontal syndrome). Finally, they displayed a normal rate of forgetting on short and delayed recall and normal primacy-recency effects.

In another study reported by Kane (1991), the CVLT was used to study memory impairments associated with chronic alcohol abuse. With age- and education-matched controls, alcoholics demonstrated poorer free recall, less semantic organization in recall, and an increased number of intrusion errors. The groups did not differ with respect to rate of forgetting of learned verbal material.

Parkinson's Disease

Another study reported in the manual involved 30 patients with an average age of 65 and about 13 years of education on average. These patients displayed multiple deficits, including below-average performance on all immediate- and delayed-recall trials. However, these same patients showed a normal decrement in recall after both short- and long-delay intervals. High intrusion rates were present but fewer than normal perseverations. Recognition scores fell in the normal range; however, high false-positive scores (related to a "yes" response bias) were noted, resulting in a low discriminability index. There was also a high recency effect, suggesting a passive learning style. The patients tended to avoid semantic clustering, and their recall across trials 1–5 was inconsistent. They were not prone to proactive interference (although recall of List B was mildly impaired). Delis et al. (1987) found that the degree of CVLT learning impairment was correlated with the level of motor dysfunction present in these patients.

Multiple Sclerosis

The CVLT manual describes a study of 56 MS patients with an average age of 43 and a high school education. Forty-six patients had the chronic, progressive form of the disease, and 10 had a remitting-relapsing form.

The deficits observed in these patients included mild problems with immediate recall on Trial 1 of List A, which became more pronounced on Trial 5 of List A. Performance on List B was mildly impaired, but this was not due to proactive interference. Normal rates of forgetting were present, with above-average perseverations and intrusions. Recognition performance as measured by the discriminability index was better than long-delay free-recall performance, possibly due to a retrieval versus encoding problem.

In a different study, Kessler, Lauer, and Kausch (1985) demonstrated that CVLT recall impairment was related to level of motor dysfunction. Impairment on the CVLT correlated with overall disease severity measured by degree of physical disability. Patients with severe MS demonstrated impaired learning, greater susceptibility to the effects of interference, and a greater number of false positive errors following a 1-week delay.

Huntington's Disease

One study reported in the CVLT manual examined 14 patients with Huntington's disease. These patients had an average age of 48 and an average educational level of 12 years. All had choreiform movements and/or impaired voluntary movement.

These patients displayed below-average free recall on List A, which had become more prominent by the fifth trial and persisted across the delayed-recall trials. Almost one-half of List A items recalled on trials 1–5 were from the recency region of the list, indicating a passive learning style. Also, an unusually small percentage of the words recalled were from the middle region. Little semantic clustering was present, but there was a high number of intrusions and relatively few perseverations. Recall across trials 1–5 was moderately inconsistent.

The subjects identified more target items than were produced on free recall, but performance was still below normal. Because they made a moderately high number of false-positive errors, their recognition performance, as measured by the discriminability index, was equivalent to their impaired long-delay free-recall performance. However, subsequent analyses suggested that those Huntington's disease patients in the earlier stages of the disease showed improvement on recognition discriminability relative to free recall.

Alzheimer's Disease

The CVLT manual documents profound memory disturbance in patients with Alzheimer's disease. This is clearly seen in highly impaired recall on the first trial of List A, with progressive deterioration of performance across trials. Patients with Alzheimer's disease do not use semantic clustering and are very recency-oriented. They are severely impaired on all delayed free- and

115

cued-recall trials. They display an exceptionally high number of intrusions and have a marked "yes" bias, resulting in a discriminability index far worse than their long-delay free-recall performance (Delis et al., 1987).

Head Injury

Crossen, Novack, Trenerry, and Craig (1988) have reported CVLT findings for 33 head-injured and 33 neurologically normal adult males. The head-injured patients had spent an average of 20 days in coma and had experienced an average of 83 days of posttraumatic amnesia. The average age of the sample was 34, and subjects averaged a high school education.

The head-injured patients appeared to have a retrieval deficit caused by use of an inefficient encoding strategy. When they used semantic clustering, their scores improved, as demonstrated by the higher cued-recall scores. They also had encoding problems that could be improved. Teaching behavioral techniques such as clustering, subjective organization, and category searching may provide helpful rehabilitation tools; however, the clinician must ensure that these techniques do not lead to greater intrusion rates without significant gains in encoding efficiency.

When compared to matched controls, head-injured persons exhibited less recall of material over learning trials 1–5 (i.e., recall of 8 versus 13 list items on trial 5), failed to employ semantic-clustering strategies, exhibited a greater number of intrusion errors, and demonstrated decreased recognition of list items. In addition deficits in long-term verbal memory (as measured by delayed-recall trials) were found. For example, the head injured group recalled only 61% of the items from their highest learning trial, whereas normal controls were able to freely recall 94%.

THE HOPKINS VERBAL LEARNING TEST (HVLT)

The Hopkins Verbal Learning Test (HVLT) was developed by Brandt (1991) and represents a variation to the list-learning approach to memory assessment. Its structure and presentation are similar to the approach presented in the AVLT and CVLT sections of this chapter. However, the HVLT is shorter, requires only about 10 minutes to administer, and has six alternative forms. It appears to be a suitable alternative to the CVLT and AVLT when patients are too impaired for more comprehensive tests (i.e., when brevity is a practical and necessary consideration) and when repeated testing is required.

The test requires presentation of a 12-item list of semantically categorized words over three free-recall trials. This is followed by oral presentation of 24 items to test recognition memory. Each word list includes words that are from three specified semantic categories. Word categories were selected from those reported by Battig and Montague (1969). Four words that represent frequent responses to each of the three selected categories are included in each list of 12 words. An exception occurs in that the two highest-frequency responses per category are presented only in the recognition list, as semantic distractors. The recognition list consists of 24 words; 12 target and 12 distractor words. Half of the recognition items were derived from the same semantic categories as the target words, and the other half were drawn from unrelated categories.

PROCEDURE

The following procedure for the administration of the HVLT was derived from that reported by Brandt (1991) during development of the normative data presented later in this section. The patient is instructed to (a) listen carefully as the examiner reads the word list and (b) attempt to memorize the words. The word list is then read to the patient at the approximate rate of one word every 2 seconds. The patients' free recall of the list is recorded. The same procedure is repeated for two more trials. After the third learning trial, the patient is read 24 words from the recognition word list and is asked to say "yes" in response to each word that was on the original list and "no" to each word that was not.

NORMS

Brandt (1991) presented validity and normative data for the six HVLT forms. Subjects in his study consisted of 129 healthy individuals (64 males and 65 females). Ages ranged from 19 to 77, and all subjects had at least a 12th-grade education.

Results of this study indicated that the six HVLT forms are equivalent. Further, recognition performance for normals was near perfect on all of the forms. The number of true positives (hits) was either 11 or 12 in every case. Finally, there was no relationship between age and accuracy of recall or recognition for the normative sample. However, it should be noted that in this particular sample only seven subjects were over 70 years of age. Normative data from this study are presented in Table 4.15.

Brandt (1991) also compared performance of 45 Alzheimer's disease patients with that of 18 normal control subjects who were 65 and older. He found that the Alzheimer's disease group scored significantly below the normal elderly group on both total recall and discrimination tasks. A cutting score between 19 and 20 for total recall correctly identified 42 of the 45 Alzheimer's disease patients (sensitivity, 94%) and all 18 normal control subjects as unimpaired (specificity, 100%). A cutting score between 10 and 11 for the discrimination score had identical sensitivity and specificity.

Table 4.15. HVLT performance for 129 normal subjects. Means (+/– SD).

	Form 1	Form 2	Form 3	Form 4	Form 5	Form 6
Recall						
Trial 1	7.17 (2.18)	8.09 (1.48)	7.26 (1.29)	7.25 (1.59)	7.85 (2.07)	8.10 (1.64)
Trial 2	9.17 (2.07)	9.86 (1.75)	9.70 (1.18)	9.75 (1.83)	9.96 (1.51)	9.90 (1.55)
Trial 3	9.88 (1.90)	11.09 (1.15)	10.43 (1.12)	10.55 (1.43)	10.54 (1.55)	10.71 (1.10)
TOTAL	26.24 (5.54)	29.05 (3.42)	27.39 (3.17)	27.55 (4.41)	28.35 (4.55)	28.71 (3.61)
Recognition						
True–Pos.	11.88 (0.33)	11.68 (0.65)	11.95 (0.21)	11.80 (0.41)	12.00 (0.00)	11.86 (0.35)
False–Pos. Related	0.59 (0.71)	0.41 (0.73)	0.00 (0.00)	0.60 (0.60)	0.23 (0.43)	0.10 (0.30)
Unrelated	0.00 (0.00)	0.00 (0.00)	0.04 (0.21)	0.00 (0.00)	0.00 (0.00)	0.05 (0.21)
DISCRIMINATION	11.29 (0.92)	11.27 (1.16)	11.91 (0.29)	11.20 (0.70)	11.77 (0.43)	11.71 (0.56)

Source: Adapted from Brandt (1991).

Table 4.15a. HVLT Form 1.

SIX ALTERNATIVE FORMS FOR THE HVLT

HOPKINS VERBAL LEARNING TEST

Form 1: 4-legged animals, precious stones, human dwellings

Part A: Free Recall

	Trial 1	Trial 2	Trial 3
LION	___	___	___
EMERALD	___	___	___
HORSE	___	___	___
TENT	___	___	___
SAPPHIRE	___	___	___
HOTEL	___	___	___
CAVE	___	___	___
OPAL	___	___	___
TIGER	___	___	___
PEARL	___	___	___
COW	___	___	___
HUT	___	___	___
# Correct	___	___	___

Part B: Recognition

HORSE	ruby*	CAVE	balloon	coffee	LION
house*	OPAL	TIGER	boat	scarf	PEARL
HUT	EMERALD	SAPPHIRE	dog*	apartment*	penny
TENT	mountain	cat*	HOTEL	COW	diamond

True Positives:____/12
#False–Positive Errors, Related: ____/6   Unrelated: ____/6
Discrimination Index: (# True–Pos.) – (# False–Pos.) = _____
*The asterisk above recognition words indicates that this is a categorically related word.

120

Table 4.15b. HVLT Form 2.

Form 2: kitchen utensils, alcoholic beverages, weapons

Part A: Free Recall

	Trial 1	Trial 2	Trial 3
FORK	___	___	___
RUM	___	___	___
PAN	___	___	___
PISTOL	___	___	___
SWORD	___	___	___
SPATULA	___	___	___
BOURBON	___	___	___
VODKA	___	___	___
POT	___	___	___
BOMB	___	___	___
RIFLE	___	___	___
WINE	___	___	___
# Correct	___	___	___

Part B: Recognition

spoon*	PISTOL	doll	whiskey*	FORK	POT
harmonica	can opener*	SWORD	pencil	gun	VODKA
knife*	RUM	trout	BOMB	PAN	gold
WINE	lemon	SPATULA	BOURBON	beer	RIFLE

True Positives:____/12
#False–Positive Errors, Related: ____/6   Unrelated: ____/6
Discrimination Index: (# True–Pos.) – (# False–Pos.) = _____

Table 4.15c. HVLT Form 3.

Form 3: musical instruments, fuels, food flavorings

Part A: Free Recall

	Trial 1	Trial 2	Trial 3
SUGAR	___	___	___
TRUMPET	___	___	___
VIOLIN	___	___	___
COAL	___	___	___
GARLIC	___	___	___
KEROSINE	___	___	___
VANILLA	___	___	___
WOOD	___	___	___
CLARINET	___	___	___
FLUTE	___	___	___
CINNAMON	___	___	___
GASOLINE	___	___	___
# Correct	___	___	___

Part B: Recognition

pepper*	GARLIC	WOOD	drum*	oil*	SUGAR
ball	salt*	priest	chair	COAL	CLARINET
TRUMPET	basement	CINNAMON	FLUTE	electricity*	moon
KEROSINE	VANILLA	GASOLINE	sand	piano*	VIOLIN

True Positives:____/12
#False–Positive Errors, Related: ____/6 Unrelated: ____/6
Discrimination Index: (# True–Pos.) – (# False–Pos.) = _____

Table 4.15d. HVLT Form 4.

Form 4: birds, articles of clothing, carpenter's tools

Part A: Free Recall

	Trial 1	Trial 2	Trial 3
CANARY	____	____	___
SHOES	____	____	___
EAGLE	____	____	___
BLOUSE	____	____	___
NAILS	____	____	___
CROW	____	____	___
BLUEBIRD	____	____	___
SCREWDRIVER	____	____	___
PANTS	____	____	___
CHISEL	____	____	___
SKIRT	____	____	___
WRENCH	____	____	___
# Correct	____	____	___

Part B: Recognition

BLUEBIRD	shirt*	CHISEL	EAGLE	chocolate	robin*
chapel	SCREWDRIVER	CROW	sparrow*	WRENCH	PANTS
NAILS	socks*	child	SHOES	hair	hammer*
CANARY	apple	skirt	saw*	silver	BLOUSE

True Positives:____/12
#False–Positive Errors, Related: ____/6   Unrelated: ____/6
Discrimination Index: (# True–Pos.) – (# False–Pos.) = ____

123

Table 4.15e. HVLT Form 5.

Form 5: occupations/professions, sports, vegetables

Part A: Free Recall

	Trial 1	Trial 2	Trial 3
TEACHER	___	___	___
BASKETBALL	___	___	___
LETTUCE	___	___	___
DENTIST	___	___	___
TENNIS	___	___	___
BEAN	___	___	___
ENGINEER	___	___	___
POTATO	___	___	___
PROFESSOR	___	___	___
GOLF	___	___	___
CORN	___	___	___
SOCCER	___	___	___
# Correct	___	___	___

Part B: Recognition

TENNIS	football*	PROFESSOR	spinach*	lawyer*	submarine
GOLF	DENTIST	LETTUCE	spider	water	BEAN
BASKETBALL	doctor	CORN	baseball*	TEACHER	snake
carrot*	ENGINEER	glove	soccer	POTATO	tulip

True Positives:____/12
#False–Positive Errors, Related: ____/6   Unrelated: ____/6
Discrimination Index: (# True–Pos.) – (# False–Pos.) = _____

124

Table 4.15f. HVLT Form 6.

Form 6: fish, parts of a building, weather phenomena

Part A: Free Recall

	Trial 1	Trial 2	Trial 3
SHARK	_____	_____	_____
WALL	_____	_____	_____
HERRING	_____	_____	_____
RAIN	_____	_____	_____
FLOOR	_____	_____	_____
HAIL	_____	_____	_____
CATFISH	_____	_____	_____
ROOF	_____	_____	_____
SALMON	_____	_____	_____
STORM	_____	_____	_____
CEILING	_____	_____	_____
SNOW	_____	_____	_____
# Correct	_____	_____	_____

Part B: Recognition

HAIL	bass*	SNOW	bank	FLOOR	mustard
window*	CEILING	canyon	RAIN	ladder	STORM
HERRING	SALMON	tornado*	trout*	melon	ROOF
SHARK	hurricane*	elbow	CATFISH	WALL	door*

True Positives:_____/12
#False–Positive Errors, Related: _____/6 Unrelated: _____/6
Discrimination Index: (# True–Pos.) – (# False–Pos.) = _____

125

Table 4.15g. Blank HVLT form.

Form : _____ , _____ , _____ ,

Part A: Free Recall

	Trial 1	Trial 2	Trial 3
	____	____	____
	____	____	____
	____	____	____
	____	____	____
	____	____	____
	____	____	____
	____	____	____
	____	____	____
	____	____	____
	____	____	____
	____	____	____
# Correct	____	____	____

Part B: Recognition

____	____	____	____	____	____
____	____	____	____	____	____
____	____	____	____	____	____
____	____	____	____	____	____

\# True Positives:____/12
#False–Positive Errors, Related: ____/6   Unrelated: ____/6
Discrimination Index: (# True–Pos.) – (# False–Pos.) = ____

REITAN STORY MEMORY HEATON ADAPTATION (RSM)

Heaton, Grant, and Matthews (1991) developed an administration and scoring procedure for a story authored by Ralph Reitan. This adaptation was designed to assess multiple-trial learning and retention. Patients hear and attempt to recall the story until they obtain a score of 15 points on a single trial for a maximum of five trials. Following a 4 hour delay during which other tests are administered, patients are asked again to recall the story. A learning score is computed by dividing the score obtained on the last learning trial by the number of trials administered. A retention or memory score is computed as a percentage loss score comparing the last learning trial with delayed recall. The Heaton et al. adaptation of this test is relatively new. It was normed as part of the development of an extended Halstead-Reitan Battery, and complete information is available in the extended HRB manual.

THE CLINICAL ASSESSMENT OF MEMORY

RIVERMEAD BEHAVIORAL MEMORY TEST (RBMT)

A frequently raised issue in memory assessment is the relationship between laboratory test results and patients' performance of everyday life tasks. Similar issues have been raised about the relationship between neuropsychological test performance in general and predictions of patients' functional capabilities. In response to these concerns, a relatively recent memory battery was developed based on tasks paralleling those encountered in daily living: the Rivermead Behavioral Memory Test (RBMT) (Wilson, Cockburn, Baddeley, & Hiorns, 1989). It was developed to assess everyday memory in a rehabilitation setting and requires no elaborate and expensive equipment. The Rivermead includes the following subtests:

1. *Remembering a Name.* The subject is shown a photograph and told the first and second name of the person depicted. Subjects are told they will be asked to remember the name. Later in the test, the photograph is again shown and the subject is asked to recall the assigned name.

2. *Remembering a Hidden Belonging.* A possession belonging to the individual is borrowed and hidden. The subject is requested to ask the examiner for the object at the end of the session. On completion of the RBMT, the subject is told the test is over. Three parameters of recall are assessed: remembering to request the object, recalling its name, and identifying its location.

3. *Remembering an Assignment.* An alarm is set for 20 minutes. The subject is instructed to ask a particular question about an upcoming matter when the alarm rings.

4. *Picture Recognition.* Line drawings of 10 common objects are shown to the subject, one at a time, for 5 seconds. Later the subject is shown 20 pictures, presented individually, and is asked to identify the original 10.

5. *Prose Recall (Newspaper Article).* The examiner reads a short passage to the subject. The subject is asked to repeat the story and to recall it again later in the test.

6. *Face Recognition.* Pictures of five faces are presented individually to the subject. Each picture is presented for 5 seconds. To facilitate encoding, the subject is asked to say if the

individual pictured is male or female and whether the individual is over or under 40 years of age. Later the subject is shown 10 faces and asked to chose the original 5.

7. *Remembering a Short Route.* The examiner traces a short route within the room. The route is composed of five stops. The subject is told to watch the examiner and do the same thing. The examiner also tells the subject he is going to take an envelope with him. The envelope is marked "MESSAGE" and is shown to the subject. The next to the last stop before returning to the original position is a table. The examiner leaves the envelope on the table when tracing the route. The envelope is then retrieved and placed in front of the subject. The subject is instructed to retrace the route of the examiner. Scores are based on whether subjects can retrace the route immediately and later in the test and on whether they remember to take and deliver the envelope.

8. *Orientation and Date.* As with most assessments of mental status, subjects are asked questions pertaining to general information and orientation to time and place.

The RBMT uses a dual scoring system involving both screening and profile scores. To obtain a screening score, each item is scored pass or fail and assigned a score of 1 or 0. Standard profile scores permit more detailed analysis of patient performance of the individual RBMT subtests. To permit longitudinal testing of patients, four alternative forms are provided.

RELIABILITY AND VALIDITY

Wilson et al. (1989) provided reliability, validity, and normative data for the RBMT. Interrater reliability was assessed by having two raters simultaneously and independently score the performances of 40 subjects. There was 100% agreement between the two raters for both scoring procedures. Alternative-form reliability was established by giving two versions of the test to 118 patients. All of the patients completed Form A; approximately one-third completed each of the three remaining forms. For the Screening Score, correlations between Form A and forms B-D were .86, .80, and .67, respectively. For the standardized Profile Score, correlations were .86, .83, and .88, respectively.

Three methods were used to establish validity. First the performance of brain-damaged individuals was compared to that of

RBMT

controls. Controls performed significantly better on all RBMT measures. Second, RBMT total, screening, and profile scores were correlated with scores from other memory tests. Tests used for comparison included (1) Warrington Recognition Memory Test for words and faces, (2) Digit Span, (3) Corsi Block Span technique, (4) paired-associate learning from the Randt, and (5) the Collins and Quillian sentence verification task. The obtained correlations were uniformly positive, ranging from .24 to .63, exclusive of semantic processing measures. Third, performance on the RBMT was correlated with behavioral ratings of forgetting made over the 2-week period during rehabilitation training. Eighty patients were observed for an average of 35 hours, and memory lapses were recorded. The number of memory lapses correlated .71 with the RBMT Screening Score and .75 with the RBMT standardized Profile Score. In general, RBMT scores correlated more highly with recorded memory lapses and with patient and family ratings of memory difficulty than did the other tests of memory included in the study. However, the word-recognition score from the Warrington Recognition Memory Test yielded similar correlations with both recorded lapses and subjective ratings. The correlation between the Randt paired-associate learning test and subjective ratings of memory impairment was identical to that obtained with the RBMT.

The intent of the RBMT was to provide an ecologically valid assessment of memory. The authors were also concerned with developing a test whose results would have direct applications in rehabilitation. Although the RBMT is based primarily on items mimicking daily activities, additional research is necessary to demonstrate that RBMT scores predict day-to-day performance with greater accuracy than do traditional laboratory measures of memory. Intuitively, tests based on daily living tasks have more face validity and are less intimidating. Nevertheless, the precise advantages of different approaches used to assess memory have yet to be empirically established. In the Wilson et al. (1989) study, the combination of the Warrington Recognition Memory Test for words and the paired-associate learning subtest of the Randt correlated as well with independent memory measures as did the RBMT. Administration time required for both the word-recognition and paired-associates test is considerably less than for the RBMT.

THE PACED AUDITORY SERIAL ADDITION TASK (PASAT)

The Paced Auditory Serial Addition Task (PASAT) is not a formal memory test; however, it is a sensitive measure of information-processing ability. It requires the ability to sustain high levels of concentration and attention as well as the ability to register and rapidly (and mentally) add sequentially presented digits. As a result, it has proved quite useful as a means to factor out attention/concentration deficits from memory deficits when interpreting ambiguous results from more traditional tests (e.g., the WMS-R). The PASAT, developed by Gronwall & Sampson (1974) and validated on head-injured patients using a return-to-work criterion (Gronwall & Wrightson, 1981), can be used clinically to help determine the appropriateness of returning to work after traumatic brain injuries. However, there are significant age effects, with performance deteriorating significantly in elderly subjects as a result of what Wrightson and Gronwall (1981) termed "neuronal fall-out." In addition, performance varies as a function of intellectual ability, and brighter subjects are able to perform the necessary calculations significantly faster. There is an especially strong correlation between PASAT performance and performance on those WAIS subtests that require nonverbal processing speed (Kanter, 1984).

Gronwall and Wrightson (1980) also demonstrated the cumulative effect of repeated traumatic injuries to the brain by showing that PASAT performance was markedly more impaired in patients who had suffered a second brain insult than in matched controls with a history of a single traumatic brain injury.

PASAT stimuli are presented via audiotape and consist of a series of randomized single (1–9) digits. Examinees are asked to add each number presented in the series to the digit that immediately preceded it. For example, if the examiner reads the numbers "2–8–6–1–9," the subject's correct responses, beginning as soon as the examiner says "8," are "10–14–7–10." The digits are presented at four rates of speed, each differing by four tenths of a second, and ranging from one every 1.2 seconds to one every 2.4 seconds. There is a 30-second delay between each of the four trials. The patient's performance can be evaluated in terms of (a) the percentage of correct responses or (b) the mean score.

PASAT

THE CLINICAL ASSESSMENT OF MEMORY

ADMINISTRATION OF THE PASAT

There are several versions of the PASAT available, and this has made it difficult to compare studies that utilize different versions for research. The original version developed by Gronwall and his colleagues involved sequential presentation of the identical sequence of 60 digit pairs, potentially enhancing the PASAT's documented practice effect (Stuss, Stethem, & Poirier, 1987). We recommend the version developed by Levin et al. (1987), which reduced the total number of digit pairs to 49, including four separate sets, and the use of norms collected for this test by Brittain et al. (Brittain, LaMarche, Reeder, Roth, & Boll, 1991). Instructions for Levin's version of the PASAT (Levin et al., 1987) are presented below.

A sheet of paper is presented to the subject with the following numbers printed on it:

$$1 \quad 3 \quad 7 \quad 4 \quad 2 \quad 1 \quad 9$$

These numbers are presented right side up to the subject (upside down to the examiner).

The examiner says: **This is a test of attention. You are going to hear numbers on the tape recorder. The numbers are never going to be less than 1** (Examiner points to number 1 at the beginning of the number series) **and are never going to be more than 9** (Examiner points to the number 9 at the end of the number series). **In other words, they are all single digit numbers.**

You will hear a number (Examiner points to the first number at the beginning of the number series). **Then you will hear another number** (Examiner points to the second number in the number series). **I want you to add them together and give me the total, out loud, so I can hear you. (Examiner writes the number "4" between the 1 and the 3).**

$$1 \quad + \quad 3 \quad 7 \quad 4 \quad 2 \quad 1$$
$$4$$

Then you will hear another number. (Examiner points to the next number in the number series). **I want you to add it to the last number that you heard on the tape recorder.**

The subject will answer either with a 10 (correct answer) or an 11 (incorrect answer). If the subject correctly responds "10," the

132

examiner says **"That's right,"** and enters the 10 between the 3 and the 7.

1	+	3	+	7	4	2	1	9

4   10

Now if the next number you hear is a 4, you would tell me ____ (expecting them to say "11"). If the response is correct, the examiner says **That's right**, and proceeds to finish the example in a similar manner. However, if the subject incorrectly responds "11" to the 3 + 7 presentation, the examiner should point to the 3 and then to the 7, saying: **No, you added to the last total. I want you to remember to add to the last number you heard on the tape recorder.** If the subject is still having problems understanding the instructions, then a new random number series is given.

After the sample is successfully administered, the examiner says: **There are four* trials. In the first one, the numbers come slowly. Each trial gets a little faster. It is important to remember that if you lose your place, and many people do, that you can start over by adding the next two numbers you hear on the tape recorder.**[1]

At the end of trials 1, 2, and 3, there is a 30 second pause. At these points, the examiner says: **That was the end of that trial. The next one is just like that, only a little faster.** Testing is continued until all trials are completed.

Some subjects may add the first and second numbers, giving a correct total, then add the third and fourth number correctly, then add the fifth and sixth numbers correctly, and so on. Numbers are being added as a set rather than as a successive series of numbers. After the third error, the tape is stopped and rewound to the beginning. The examiners reviews the instructions, saying: **What you are doing is correct. However, you are missing adding these numbers** (pointing to the omitted pairing). The testing is restarted and continued to completion, even if the subject continues to respond incorrectly. Corrected responses receive credit.

---

[1]Two, three, or four trials may be given.

133

Some subjects may keep a running total. If this continues to occur after the third error, the tape is stopped and rewound. The examiner reviews the instructions, saying: **Remember to always add the number you hear to the last number you heard on the tape recorder.** The test is restarted and continued to completion, even if the subject continues to respond incorrectly. Corrected responses receive credit.

Other subjects may cease responding, appearing to "give up." The examiner should encourage the subject by saying: **Add the next two numbers you hear**. The tape should continue running, and the use of this encouragement should be done with obvious moderation.

Of course, it is necessary to use a tape recorder and a prerecorded audiotape to present the PASAT stimuli. If the reader has a reasonable sense of rhythm, a timer, and tape recorder, with some practice it is possible to make an adequate tape by reading the digits presented in Table 4.16 at the rate indicated in the series heading.

Scoring of the PASAT

A number of useful summary scores can be calculated from PASAT raw data. These include the percentage and total number correct for each of the four series and the overall total. In addition, the mean seconds per correct response across trials and number of errors for each series should also be calculated.

To complete "seconds per correct response" do the following:

1. Series A: $2.4 \times 49/$ # Correct =
2. Series B: $2.0 \times 49/$ # Correct =
3. Series C: $1.6 \times 49/$ # Correct =
4. Series D: $1.2 \times 49/$ # Correct =

Norms for the PASAT

Several recent studies have been conducted specifically to provide normative data for the Levin (1979) adaptation of the PASAT. Roman et al. (Roman, Eduall, Buchanan, & Patton, 1991) collected norms using a sample of 143 healthy individuals, including 62 persons aged 18 to 27 (58% female), 40 aged 33 to 50 (50% female), and 41 aged 60 to 75 (51% female). Education level for this sample was 12 to 18 years of formal

134

Table 4.16. PASAT stimuli and answers.

Series A (2.4/s)		Series B (2.0/s)		Series C (1.6/s)		Series D (1.2/s)	
9	5 (11)	2	8 (11)	4	4 (9)	3	5 (7)
1 (10)	8 (13)	4 (6)	4 (12)	8 (12)	6(10)	2 (5)	1 (6)
4 (5)	9 (17)	5 (9)	2 (6)	6 (14)	3 (9)	6 (8)	6 (7)
2 (6)	4 (13)	4 (9)	1 (3)	2 (8)	6 (9)	5 (11)	9(15)
8 (10)	3 (7)	3 (7)	9 (10)	2 (4)	3 (9)	4 (9)	4(13)
6 (14)	1 (4)	1 (4)	8 (17)	9 (11)	2 (5)	3 (7)	8(12)
5 (11)	2 (3)	8 (9)	3 (11)	3 (12)	9(11)	1 (4)	5(13)
3 (8)	6 (8)	6(14)	5 (8)	4 (7)	1(10)	6 (7)	9(14)
4 (7)	3 (9)	9(15)	6 (11)	5 (9)	8 (9)	5 (11)	2(11)
9 (13)	4 (7)	2(11)	9 (15)	8 (13)	5(13)	9 (14)	6 (8)
1 (10)	8 (12)	9(11)	8 (17)	1 (9)	4 (9)	8 (17)	1 (7)
3 (4)	9 (17)	8(17)	4 (12)	6 (7)	9(13)	4 (12)	3 (4)
6 (9)	5 (14)	6(14)	3 (7)	3 (9)	6(15)	2 (6)	4 (7)
8 (14)	1 (6)	1 (7)	2 (5)	8 (11)	2 (8)	1 (3)	2 (6)
2 (10)	2 (3)	3 (4)	5 (7)	6 (14)	4 (6)	2 (3)	3 (5)
5 (7)	8 (10)	4 (7)	1 (6)	2 (8)	3 (7)	4 (6)	9(12)
1 (6)	1 (9)	5 (9)	6 (7)	4 (6)	5 (8)	9 (13)	5(14)
8 (9)	2 (3)	2 (7)	1 (7)	1 (5)	8(13)	3 (12)	6(11)
6 (14)	5 (7)	1 (3)	8 (9)	9 (10)	1 (9)	6 (9)	8(14)
9 (15)	3 (8)	9(10)	5 (13)	5 (14)	5 (6)	8 (14)	1 (9)
2 (11)	9 (12)	4(13)	6 (11)	1 (6)	6(11)	5 (13)	6 (7)
4 (6)	6 (15)	5 (9)	3 (9)	9 (10)	9(15)	4 (9)	4(10)
3 (7)	4 (10)	6(11)	2 (5)	8 (17)	8(17)	3 (7)	9(13)
5 (8)	3 (7)	2 (8)	9 (11)	2 (10)	3(11)	8 (11)	2(11)
6 (11)	6 (9)	3 (5)	4 (13)	5 (7)	1 (4)	2 (10)	3 (5)

Source: Levin adaptation (Levin, 1979).

training, and IQ averaged 107 to 110. Norms from this study are presented in Table 4.17.

Additional normative data were collected by Brittain et al. (1991). Subjects in this study consisted of 526 healthy adults, aged 17 to 88 years. Education level ranged from 10 to 16 years, and IQ averaged 101 to 106 in this sample. Normative data consisted of seconds per correct response and errors per trial for age by IQ. These data are presented in Table 4.18.

Interpretation of the **PASAT**

The PASAT is a measure of the rate at which cognitive information is processed. It measures "channel capacity," the amount of information that can be handled at one time. Mental processing of information will be inadequate either if the number of

135

Table 4.17. Norms for the Levin et al. (1979) adaptation of the PASAT.

Presentation Speed	PASAT Series				
	2.4 s	2.0 s	1.6 s	1.2 s	Total
Young Adult (18–27 n = 27)					
Raw score M/SD	45/ 4.5	39/ 7.8	36/ 7.7	28/ 6.7	148/ 23.5
Percent correct M/SD	91.68/ 8.9	79.53/ 16.2	72.79/ 15.9	57.92/ 13.8	75/ 12.0
Middle Aged Adult (33–50 n = 40)					
Raw Score M/SD	44/ 4.9	38/ 7.6	33/ 8.9	28/ 9.3	144/ 27.0
Percent correct M/SD	90.70/ 10.3	77.50/ 15.3	68.22/ 18.2	57.22/ 18.9	73/ 14.0
Older Adult (60–75 n = 41)					
Raw score M/SD	37/ 9.1	31/ 9.2	27/ 8.5	20/ 6.1	115/ 29.9
Percent correct M/SD	75.95/ 18.6	63.04/ 18.9	54.95/ 17.4	41.63/ 12.2	59/ 15.3

Source: Roman et al. (1991).

items demanding simultaneous attention is too great or if the rate of processing is inadequate.

PASAT Profiles for Head-Injury Patients

Postconcussion patients consistently perform well below control group standards when assessed immediately after injury or after return to consciousness. However, in almost all cases of mild head injury, scores return normal within 30–60 days (Lezak, 1983).

PASAT results can be used as an indicator of the efficiency of information processing following concussion. This information can be used to help determine when a patient is able to return to a normal level of social and vocational activity without experi-

Table 4.18a. Norms for PASAT Series A (2.4/s).

Age (Years)		n	<90 Time	Errors (secs)	n	IQ 90–109 Time	Errors (secs)	n	>109 Time	Errors (secs)
< 25	M	7	3.85	15.43	89	3.37	10.79	49	2.90	16.63
	SD		1.50	9.45		1.50	9.13		1.12	7.24
25–39	M	15	5.67	18.80	95	3.19	9.78	54	2.81	6.37
	SD		6.67	11.43		1.19	8.16		0.58	6.08
40–54	M	17	6.37	26.35	47	3.42	10.79	31	2.73	5.65
	SD		3.29	9.89		1.57	9.35		4.53	4.53
> 54	M	18	6.56	28.83	54	4.97	21.78	50	3.80	14.24
	SD		2.65	6.84		2.05	10.45		1.66	10.36

Table 4.18b. Norms for the PASAT Series B (2.0/s).

Age (Years)		n	<90 Time	Errors (secs)	n	IQ 90–109 Time	Errors (secs)	n	>109 Time	Errors (secs)
< 25	M	7	3.52	18.71	89	3.20	14.84	49	2.90	11.06
	SD		1.13	9.16		1.74	8.66		1.75	8.81
25–39	M	15	4.21	20.47	95	3.15	14.98	54	2.65	10.74
	SD		2.88	10.24		1.43	8.28		0.55	6.81
40–54	M	17	5.72	28.06	47	3.14	15.15	31	2.57	9.97
	SD		3.10	8.57		1.12	8.48		0.52	7.18
> 54	M	18	5.28	28.39	54	4.26	23.61	50	3.47	16.54
	SD		1.93	6.70		1.44	7.86		1.94	9.32

Table 4.18c. Norms for the PASAT Series C (1.6/s).

Age (Years)		n	<90 Time	Errors (secs)	n	IQ 90–109 Time	Errors (secs)	n	>109 Time	Errors (secs)
< 25	M	7	3.01	20.71	89	2.88	19.10	49	2.28	12.59
	SD		0.91	8.75		0.98	8.43		0.60	8.28
25–39	M	15	3.85	24.87	95	3.16	19.26	54	2.34	13.31
	SD		2.23	8.23		2.74	8.47		0.74	7.66
40–54	M	17	4.83	29.82	47	3.11	18.36	31	2.40	14.84
	SD		2.55	6.64		2.64	9.21		0.53	7.48
> 54	M	18	4.15	28.50	54	3.49	25.04	50	3.27	20.90
	SD		1.51	4.87		0.97	6.08		1.99	8.50

Source: Brittain et al. (1991).

Table 4.18d. Norms for the PASAT Series D (1.2/s).

Age (Years)		n	<90 Time Errors (secs)		n	IQ 90–109 Time Errors (secs)		n	>109 Time Errors (secs)	
< 25	M	7	3.38	29.00	89	2.67	24.22	49	2.07	18.59
	SD		1.56	7.21		1.03	7.77		0.59	7.52
25–39	M	15	3.07	28.67	95	3.35	25.64	54	2.20	20.61
	SD		0.75	5.47		5.86	7.14		0.56	7.18
40–54	M	17	4.60	32.76	47	2.70	25.34	31	2.28	21.61
	SD		2.71	6.90		0.85	6.68		0.54	7.13
> 54	M	18	3.95	32.44	54	3.39	29.26	50	2.74	25.12
	SD		1.59	4.76		1.30	6.42		1.01	7.22

Source: Brittan et al. (1991).

encing undue stress, or when a modified activity schedule should be adopted.

Crossen and Wiens (1988) have presented PASAT data for head-injured clients (see Table 4.19). These researchers found that the PASAT was significantly more sensitive in assessing the effects of head trauma than the WMS-R Attention /Concentration composite index. The authors concluded from their study that the PASAT was more sensitive than the WMS-R in detecting subtle closed head injury effects because the PASAT has been designed to detect problems in sustained attention and concentration. The test produces an "attention overload" associated with the required rapid and sustained pace of performing men-

Table 4.19. Comparison data for head injured vs. healthy patients.

	PASAT Speed (s)	Error Scores Head Injured (n = 8) M	SD	Healthy Normals (n = 42) M	SD
Trial 1	2.4	18.4	10.2	5.8	4.5
Trial 2	2.0	24.1	7.1	11.2	7.0
Trial 3	1.6	26.0	8.7	13.7	7.2
Trial 4	1.2	32.0	6.3	20.2	8.0

Source: Crossen & Wiens (1988).

tal operations. Mean error scores for 49 possible items on each PASAT trial for the Crossen and Weins (1988) head injury study are presented in Table 4.19.

An alternative administration procedure involves letting the patient complete the test at his or her own rate (i.e., the test is unpaced). Here the examiner records pauses of 5 seconds and longer. The paced delivery format identifies patients whose responses are slowed as well as those who have a tracking disability. The unpaced delivery is more likely to identify those patients whose defective performance is primarily due to a tracking defect (Lezak, 1983).

THE CLINICAL ASSESSMENT OF MEMORY

VISUOSPATIAL MEMORY

Verbal memory and language are important skills and deficiencies in these areas are quickly perceived by both patients and family members. In contrast, spatial deficits and visuospatial memory deficits are most often discovered only when directly evaluated with appropriate tests. For this reason, it is important for assessment batteries to include tests sensitive to various aspects of visuospatial memory such as the Rey-Osterreith Complex Figure Test, Benton Visual Retention Test, and the figural memory portions of the WMS-R and MAS.

Many visual memory tests require patients to draw. This procedure can confound the interpretation of deficient performance, because the patient's failure may relate to spatial defects rather than memory problems. Tasks based on recognition may also be affected by perceptual difficulties and visual inattention. Consequently, clinicians must pay close attention to the quality of nonverbal memory test performance in order to estimate the relative contributions of memory and perceptual deficits. The examination must also include spatial tasks that do not involve memory to aid in the differentiation.

To minimize the possibility of verbal mediation, most visual recall test stimuli consist of abstract designs or nonsense figures. However, even when these figures are quite complex or unfamiliar, they do not fully control for verbal mediation. It is virtually impossible to design nonsense figures that do not elicit verbal associations.

BENTON VISUAL RETENTION TEST (BVRT)

The Benton Visual Retention Test (BVRT) consists of three alternative but equivalent versions that may be administered under different conditions, including simple copying and reproducing from memory after various delay intervals. Norms are available that take into account the subject's WAIS IQ scores. Benton (1962) reported an overall hit rate of about 70% in a study distinguishing brain damaged from control subjects. He also noted that the test was most efficient in identifying right-hemisphere-injured and diffusely injured patients. The BVRT has been found effective in a number of different populations. Using the BVRT, the user can obtain information on both memory and spatial abilities.

There is considerable evidence suggesting that the BVRT is effective in discriminating groups of patients with brain damage from those with psychiatric disorders (Benton, 1974). As with other tests of visual functioning, patients with right-hemisphere lesions tend to perform more poorly than do patients with left-sided brain damage. In addition, patients with posterior damage to the parietal-occipital region do more poorly than those with anterior dysfunction. However, the clinician is warned that the above statements reflect statistical associations and are not hard-and-fast rules (Berg, Franzen, & Wedding, 1987).

The BVRT was first published in 1955 and is still widely used for testing visual retention and brain dysfunction. It was initially designed as a test of impairment of visual memory; however, patients with right-hemisphere damage (especially in the parietal-occipital region) who have consequent problems with perceptual organization and visuospatial processing also do poorly on the BVRT.

Administration Procedure A (the most popular) consists of a 10-second exposure of a card following which the subject must reproduce the drawing from memory. Eight of the designs consist of three separate shapes (triangle, square, circle) in which one of the shapes has been displaced to one side or the other. Patients with *unilateral neglect* routinely fail to draw the outlying design on one side (whether right or left). This type of unilateral spatial neglect frequently occurs in patients who have a lesion in the contralateral cerebral hemisphere.

BVRT

141

THE CLINICAL ASSESSMENT OF MEMORY

Extensive normative data from 600 "normal" subjects from Iowa are available for administration A. Norms are presented in the BVRT manual for ages 8–64. The test's reliability of .95 is extremely high, and it shows good stability over 6 months (.77). The test assesses visuomotor ability, visuospatial perception, visual and verbal conceptualization, immediate memory span, and delayed recall.

The constructional skills required by the BVRT may be more demanding than the memory component measured by this test. Therefore, it should always be used as part of a battery and never as a single screening test. Benton (1974) has made this point, noting that a substantial proportion of patients with demonstrable cerebral disease perform adequately. The exact proportion depends on the characteristics of the sample of patients under study. If the sample consists of patients with "organic brain syndromes" and dementia in a state hospital, one is likely to find defective performance in all of the sample. If the sample is restricted to nonpsychotic patients with adequate premorbid intelligence who are being seen in the neurological department of a general hospital, the proportion showing normal performance will be in the range of 40% to 60%. However, despite the problem of false negatives, the BVRT is an excellent test, more sensitive than either Memory for Designs or the Bender Gestalt.

SCORING AND INTERPRETATION OF THE BVRT

Scoring of the BVRT is relatively straightforward and includes (a) number of correct reproductions (Number Correct score) and (b) errors (omissions, distortions, perseverations, rotations, misplacements, and size errors).

Number of Correct Reproductions

Each design is judged on an *all-or-none* basis and given a score of 1 or 0. Therefore, the range of possible scores for any single form of the test is from 0 to 10.

The principles underlying the scoring of each design together with samples of correct and incorrect reproductions, are presented in detail in the BVRT manual, and these examples should be studied carefully by anyone administering the test. However, as a general rule, *the scoring standards are lenient because the major intent is to measure the subject's capacity to retain a visual impression, not to assess drawing ability.* Thus, the size of the reproduction as a whole, as compared with the original design, is not considered in the scoring. However, within a specific design, the *relative size* of the figures (as compared with each other) is taken into account.

The Error Score

The Error Score system of evaluation classifies errors by type and provides for a total error score. This system, in addition to providing a measure of general efficiency of performance, facilitates analysis of the *qualitative* characteristics of a subject's performance.

The specific types of potential errors have been grouped into six major categories: omissions, distortions, perseverations, rotations, misplacements, and size errors. The complete scoring system is presented in the BVRT manual, which should be used in conjunction with the interpretive comments below.

Rotations

Rotational errors historically have been a favorite "organic sign" for many psychologists. Because rotations appear relatively frequently in the productions of brain-diseased patients, they readily attract the attention of the examiner. However, these errors occur in the productions of many control subjects as well. *Stabilization rotation* (the drawing of an angle so that it rests on a side) occurs more frequently than any other type of rotation and is commonly encountered in both control and brain-diseased subjects.

The ratio between stabilization and other types of rotation may differ substantially between patients and controls. Control subjects make about five times more stabilization errors than other types of rotational errors, whereas brain-impaired subjects make only about twice as many stabilization rotations relative to other types of rotational errors.

Errors of Size

Normal adults demonstrate wide variations in the proportional size of major and peripheral figures, but the peripheral figure is almost always drawn as appreciably smaller than the major figures, with the major figures approximating the size of the model.

Omission of a Peripheral Figure

This error generally has significant implications for diagnosis, particularly if it is *not* accompanied by a verbalization by the patient that the figure has been forgotten, thus implying a lack of awareness that such a figure was included in the exposed design. It would seem that the peripheral figure either was not perceived at all when the complex design was presented or, if it was perceived, the perception was so weak that not even a momentary trace of it persisted.

The failure to reproduce the peripheral figure has been related to a general constriction in the dynamic visual field that is found in many brain-diseased patients, particularly those with parietal-occipital lesions.

Occasionally, deficits of this type are found in pure form; that is, the patient's reproductions of the major figures of all of the designs are correct, but at the same time not a single peripheral figure is drawn. If patients are reminded after the test that most of the designs included a peripheral figure, they will often state that they did not remember seeing the figure. If another form of the test is given to them, usually there will be fewer omissions of the peripheral figure (although such omissions may still occur despite the patient's deliberate attempts to attend to them); but their reproduction of the figure is usually uncertain and often incorrect, either in form or in placement. It is interesting to note that *these patients are usually able to copy the designs quite accurately, the deficit appearing only when they are required to reproduce them from memory.*

SCORING THE RECORD AND USING THE NORMS TABLES

Norms for Administration A are presented below. They are derived from Lezak (1983) and Benton (1974). Benton's original group of subjects consisted of 600 adult Iowans from Des Moines and Iowa City.

Number Correct

Taking into account age and IQ level, the patient's score is compared to the norms listed in the Table 4.20 to decide if the score falls in the impaired range. The table is read as follows: For a 50-year-old subject whose premorbid IQ is estimated as supe-

Table 4.20. Adults Expected Number of Correct Responses Adjusted for Estimated Premorbid IQ & Age.

	Expected no. correct, by age:		
Estimated premorbid IQ	15–44	45–54	55–64
110 and up (superior)	9	8	7
95–109 (average)	8	7	6
80–94 (low avg.)	7	6	5
70–79 (borderline)	6	5	4
60–69 (mild MR)	5	4	3
59 & lower (MR)	4	3	2

rior (i.e., 110 or more) the expected Number Correct Score is 8. The patient's obtained score is compared with this score.

Benton (1974) suggested that a score 2 points below the number of expected correct responses "raises the question of impairment"; scores 4 or more points below the expected score are viewed as a "strong indication" of impairment.

Table 4.21 presents adult norms for the *error* score for Administration A. As with the Number Correct Score, interpretation of a subject's performance is made on the basis of an "expected" score appropriate for his or her age and assumed original or premorbid intellectual endowment. Simplification of designs, including a disregard of size and figure placement, has been associated with a generalized behavioral regression in patients with bilateral or diffuse damage. A patient whose error score exceeds the expected score, based on age and intelligence, by 3 or more points can be suspected of being impaired, and an error score exceeding the expected level by 5 or more points is considered a "strong indication" of brain dysfunction.

A wealth of clinical information is available from careful inspection of BVRT reproductions. For example, impaired immediate-memory or attention disorders are most likely to appear as simplifications, simple substitutions, or omissions of the designs. Normal subjects exhibit these tendencies as well but not to the same degree. Unilateral spatial neglect tends to appear as

145

Table 4.21. Expected error scores on the BVRT.

Estimated Premorbid IQ	Expected number of errors, by age			
	15–39	40–54	55–59	60–64
110 & up (superior)	1	2	3	4
105–109 (high average)	2	3	4	5
95–104 (average)	3	4	5	6
90–94 (low average)	4	5	6	7
80–89 (dull average)	5	6	7	8
70–79 (borderline)	6	7	8	9
60–69 (mild MR)	7	8	9	10
59–below (MR)	8	9	10	11

a consistent omission of the figure on the same side of the design, whereas construction deficits most often manifest as defects in the execution or organization of the drawings. Rotations and consistent design distortions generally indicate a more basic perceptual problem.

Perseverations signal the need to look elsewhere in the patient's testing protocol for other examples of perseveration on different tasks. Widespread perseveration suggests a monitoring or activity-control problem, whereas perseveration limited to performance on the BVRT is usually indicative of a specific visual or immediate memory impairment in a patient who is trying hard to either compensate for or cover up brain dysfunction.

Patients with right-hemisphere damage generally have copying error scores that are worse than those of patients with left-hemisphere lesions. In addition, patients with more posterior damage in the parietal-occipital region do more poorly than do those with more anterior dysfunction.

Simplification of designs, including a disregard of size and figure placement, has been associated with a generalized behavioral regression in patients with bilateral or diffuse damage. Lezak (1983) found that patients with bilateral frontal lobe damage

146

had error scores (4.6) that exceeded both those of patients with right-hemisphere lesions (3.5) and those with left-hemisphere lesions (1.0). The overall error score for the patients with left-sided damage fell within the normal range.

The performance of schizophrenic patients varies markedly on the BVRT. However, one common diagnostic sign is "autistic" performance—that is, reproductions that have no clear relevance to the original design or ones in which the patient draws objects, symbols, or unduly elaborate designs. Such reproductions are generally made only by schizophrenic patients or by confabulating organic patients.

Evaluation of depressed patients is always a clinical dilemma. However, performance on the BVRT tends to be reasonably good if the patients are encouraged and display at least moderate motivation.

Malingering patients make more distortion errors and fewer omission, perseveration, and size errors than do brain-damaged patients. They also tend to produce bizarre features that are rarely seen in the drawings of patients with genuine brain disease.

Age can have a marked effect on BVRT performance. For example, Benton (1974) found that in the age range 65–75, the mean BVRT score was 3 points below the expected score for a comparable group of subjects under the age of 45, whereas the mean error score was 7 points above the expected score for the younger group (Benton, 1974). Benton also found that defective drawing skills and task adjustment (due to education or relevant social experience) can confound results. He also cautions that poor performance on the BVRT may occur in subjects who have experienced cultural deprivation or in subjects from non-Western cultures.

Recently, Youngjohn, Larrabee, and Crook (1993) have published age and education-correction norms for the BVRT Administration A. Their study included 1128 adults with an age range of 17 to 84 (M = 58), and education range of 12 to 25 years (M = 16). Their derived norms are quite close to Benton's original values. In addition, their sample included 53 individuals in the 70+ age range. Norms for this group are shown in Table 4.22

They also presented the regression equations for predicting expected BVRT scores (+/- SE) for both correct and error scores.

Table 4.22. Age and Education-Correction Norms for the BVRT Administration A.

Yrs. of Education	Total Correct Mean & SD		Total Errors Mean & SD	
12–14	5.62	(1.73)	7.28	(3.55)
15–17	6.06	(1.84)	6.74	(4.34)
18+	6.22	(1.57)	6.33	(3.63)

Their formulae for predicting a specific individual's score is as follows:

Predicted BVRT # correct (+/− 1.57) =
7.87 − .045 (age) + .098 (years of education)

Predicted BVRT # errors (+/− 2.88) =
1.73 + .088 (age) + .126 (years of education)

Administering the BVRT (Part A)

The patient is given a fresh sheet of paper, approximately the size of the stimulus card, for each design. The sheet is removed after the patient completes each drawing, and a clean sheet is not given to the patient until it is time to draw the next figure. Patients who have difficulty following instructions should be given the first three designs for practice.

The patient is told that he or she will be shown a card on which there are one or more figures, then is instructed to study the card for 10 seconds and to draw the stimulus items immediately after the card is removed. The design book should be positioned at an angle of about 60 degrees from the surface of the table to permit optimal viewing by the subject. It should not be placed flat on the table. The clinician should number the drawings to indicate orientation of the drawing on the paper.

Occasionally, a subject will start to draw the first design before a full 10 seconds have elapsed. He or she should be stopped at this point and told to study the card for the full time allowed. The examiner may make a comment such as "I know this design is an easy one, but the others are harder, and I want you to get into the habit of looking at the card for the full ten seconds."

Each card is presented without comment, except that before introducing Design III (the first to include two major figures and a peripheral minor figure), the examiner should say, "Do not forget to draw everything you see." If the subject omits the peripheral minor figure in Design III, the examiner should make the same statement before introducing Design IV.

The subject is permitted to make erasures or corrections. No spontaneous praise is offered, but reassurance may be given if the subject asks about the quality of his or her performance. Administration A requires that each design from Form D be exposed for 10 seconds, followed by immediate reproduction from memory by the subject.

DELAYED RECOGNITION

Gary Kay (1989) created a delayed-recognition task by mixing figures from all three forms and presenting them to the patient in a randomized order. The patient is instructed to say "old" if they've seen the design before and "new" if they haven't. In a study with 60 normal, healthy adults, aged 22–75, less than 5% of normals made more than two false-negative responses or four false-positive responses.

The format used for ordering and scoring recognition trials is presented in Table 4.23. Note that Form C stimuli are included as target recognition figures.

It may be helpful to examine a patient's responses by laying them out in a two-by-two table as follows.

Table 4.23. Format for ordering and scoring recognition trials when the BVRT is used to measure delayed recognition.

1.	E8	11.	D4	21.	E5
2.	D3	12.	E4	22.	D2
3.	C8	13.	C3	23.	C4
4.	E3	14.	D5	24.	D7
5.	D9	15.	C9	25.	E1
6.	C1	16.	C2	26.	C7
7.	E7	17.	D10	27.	E6
8.	C5	18.	E10	28.	C6
9.	D8	19.	D6	29.	E9
10.	E2	20.	C10	30.	D1

THE CLINICAL ASSESSMENT OF MEMORY

Table 4.24

	TRUE	FALSE
OLD STIMULI	Hit (a)	Intrusion (c)
NEW STIMULI	Correct Rejection (b)	Miss (d)

Potential responses outlined in Table 4.24 are explained below.

(a) True Old: C figure is presented, and subject correctly says, "old" (Maximum of 10 correct responses).

(b) True New: D or E figure is presented, and subject correctly says, "new" (Maximum of 20 correct responses).

(c) False Old: D or E figure is presented, and subject incorrectly says, "old" (Maximum of 20 errors).

(d) False New: C figure is presented, and subject incorrectly says, "new" (Maximum of 10 errors).

REY-OSTERRIETH AND TAYLOR
COMPLEX FIGURE TEST (CFT)

The Rey-Osterreith "complex figure" test (CFT) was devised by Rey (1941) in an effort to investigate both perceptual organization and visual memory in brain-damaged individuals. Osterrieth (1944) standardized Rey's procedure and obtained normative data from the performance of 230 normal children, with ages ranging from 4 to 15 years, and 60 adults in the 16–60 age range (Lezak, 1983). Osterrieth also gathered data from a small group of adults (43) who had sustained traumatic brain damage.

ADMINISTRATION OF THE REY-OSTERRIETH CFT

Administration of the Rey-Osterrieth test requires Rey's figure (Figure 4.2), three blank sheets of paper, and five or six colored pencils. The patient is first asked to copy the figure, which has been placed so that its length runs along the patient's horizontal plane. The examiner watches the performance closely. Each time a section of the figure is completed, a different-colored pencil is handed to the patient, and the order of colors is recorded. After the patient is satisfied that the copied figure is complete, both the figure and drawing are removed from the patient's field of vision. After 3 minutes, the subject is given a second sheet of paper and is asked to draw the design from memory.

A long-delay recall trial follows 20–60 minutes after the 3 minute short-delay recall trial. Here again, the subject is given a blank sheet of paper and asked to draw the design from memory. It is important to interpose tests that are "nonspatial" during the delays to avoid interference. The authors have found tests such as the Controlled Oral Word Association Test (FAS) to be appropriate for filling the 3-minute delay interval. Tests such as the AVLT and CVLT are appropriate for administration during the 20–60-minute interval.

QUALITATIVE SCORING AND INTERPRETATION

Osterrieth (1944) originally analyzed the drawings in terms of the patient's method of procedure as well as specific copying errors. Seven procedural types were identified.

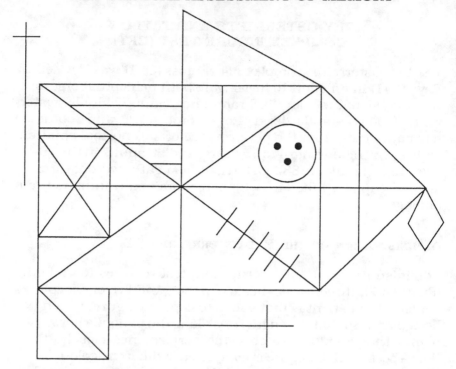

Figure 4.2. Rey-Osterrieth Complex Figure Test. From Osterrieth, P. A. (1944). Le test de copie d'une figure complex. *Archives de Psychologie, 30,* 206–356. Reproduced by permission.

1. Subject begins by drawing the large central rectangle and details are added in relation to it.
2. Subject begins with detail attached to the central rectangle or with a subsection of the rectangle, completes the rectangle and adds remaining details in relation to the rectangle.
3. Subject begins by drawing the overall contour of the figure without explicit differentiation of the central rectangle and then adds internal details.
4. Subject juxtaposes details one by one without an organizing structure.
5. Subject copies discrete parts of the drawing with no semblance of organization.
6. Subject substitutes the drawing of a similar object, such as a boat or a house.
7. Subject produces an unrecognizable drawing.

In Osterrieth's (1944) sample, 83% of the adult control group followed procedure types 1 and 2, 15% used Type 4, and one individual followed Type 3. More than 50% of the children used procedure types 1 and 2. More than 63% of the traumatically brain-injured group also followed type 1 and 2 procedures, although there were a few more type 3 and 4 subjects in this group and one of Type 5.

Three of four aphasic patients and one with senile dementia gave Type 4 performances; one aphasic and one presenile dementia patient followed Type 5 procedure (Berg et al., 1987). The performance of brain-damaged subjects could be distinguished from the performance of normals primarily by the fact that the large rectangle was not recognized or reproduced by the brain-damaged patients. Because the main line clusters were not perceived, parts of the main lines and details were drawn intermingled, working from top to bottom and from left to right.

Visser (1973) observed that stroke patients have a fragmented or piecemeal approach to copying the figure, reflecting their inability to process as much information at one time as do normals. Thus, brain-damaged patients tend to deal with smaller visual units, building the figure by accretion. Many ultimately produce a reasonably accurate reproduction in this manner, although the piecemeal approach increases the likelihood of size and relationship errors.

Messerli, Seron, and Tissot (1979) studied 32 patients whose lesions were entirely localized within the frontal lobes. Seventy-five percent of these patients produced copies of the Rey-Osterrieth Complex Figure that were significantly different from the model. The most frequent error was the repetition of an element that had already been copied, an error resulting when the patient would lose track of what had been drawn because of a disorganized approach. In one-third of the defective copies, a design element was transformed into a familiar representation (e.g.,the circle rendered as a face). Perseveration occurred less often, usually showing up as additional cross-hatches (Scoring Unit 12) or parallel lines (Scoring Unit 8). Omissions were also noted.

Binder (1982) investigated Rey-Osterrieth performance in patients with lateralized lesions. He found that patients with lesions restricted to the left hemisphere tend to break up the design into units that are smaller than normally perceived, whereas right-hemisphere damage makes it more likely that elements will be omitted altogether. However, on recall of the complex figure, patients with left-hemisphere damage who may have copied the figure in a piecemeal manner tend to reproduce the basic rectangular outline and the structural elements as a configural whole, suggesting that their processing of all of these data is slow. Given time, these patients ultimately reconstitute the data as a gestalt. This reconstitution is less likely to occur with right-hemisphere-damaged patients, who, on recall, continue to construct poorly integrated figures.

Patients with right-brain damage tend to produce designs with partial omissions (e.g., fewer dots or lines than called for), whereas left-brain-damaged patients tend to simplify by rounding angles (e.g., giving curved sides to the diamond of the figure), drawing dashes instead of dots (which are more difficult to execute), or leaving the cross of the Rey figure in an incomplete, T-shaped form. Of the 32 simplifications made by patients with left-hemisphere damage, however, only 5 were made with the right hand, and 3 of those errors were made by patients who had residual right-upper-limb weakness. All others were made by the nonpreferred left hand of hemiparetic patients. These data suggest that, for the most part, simplification errors of patients with left hemisphere damage are the product of the left hand's deficient control over fine movements; that is, *simplification in left-sided-lesion patients is a defect of execution, not one of perception or cognition.*

Errors made by patients with frontal lobe lesions reflect disturbances in their ability to program their approach to copying the figure. Patients with parietal-occipital lesions, on the other hand, have difficulty with the spatial organization of the figure. When given a plan to guide their approach to the copy task, the patients with frontal damage improved markedly. The patients with posterior lesions also improved their copies when provided spatial reference points. However, use of spatial reference points did not improve the copies made by the patients with frontal damage, nor did those with parietal-occipital lesions benefit from a program plan.

It is important to note that the above findings and general principles should be considered strictly as qualitative guidelines. This is particularly important in light of the findings of Bennett-Levy (1984), who studied determinants of performance on the Rey-Osterreith CFT with 107 healthy subjects. He found that in a "normal" population, a more or less disorganized piecemeal approach to the copy of the figure was common. Probably the most important effect of the approach to the copy procedure has to do with recall score. A piecemeal approach may result in a high copy score but will generally be related to a poor recall trial.

QUANTITATIVE SCORING OF THE REY-OSTERRIETH CFT

An accuracy score, based on a unit scoring system (see Table 4.25 and Figure 4.3), can be obtained for each test trial. The scoring units refer to specific areas or details of the figures that have been numbered for scoring convenience. Since the reproduction of each unit can earn as many as two points, the highest possible score is 36. After the age of eight, a score of 30 should be earned; the average adult scores for ages 16 to 70 normally range between 32–35 (Spreen & Strauss, 1991).

The memory trial on the Rey Osterrieth is scored in the same manner. A comparison of the scores for each trial will aid in determining the presence of visuographic or visual-memory defects, as well as their relative severity.

The accuracy score provides a good measure of how well the subject reproduces the design, regardless of the approach used. Since the memory trial of the CFT is scored in the same manner, the accuracy score permits a comparison between the different trials of the test. For example, although almost half of the 43 traumatically brain injured adult patients in Osterrieth's sample achieved "copy" scores of 32 or better, one-third of this group scored significantly lower. On the memory trial, fewer that one-third of these subjects were able to achieve the normal group's mean score of 22. In general, there was a wider disparity between the copy and memory scores of the brain injured group than in the normal group of 60 persons aged 16–60.

Some patients will perform relatively better on the memory than the copy task, suggesting delayed perceptual organization or slowed ability to adapt to new tasks. Patients with severe psychiatric disorders may add bizarre embellishments to their drawings, interpret details concretely, or fill in parts of the design with solid color. Behavior of this kind is extremely rare in brain damaged patients.

Table 4.25. Scoring System for the Rey-Osterrieth Complex Figure Test.

Units	Copy	3 Min Delay	20–60 Min Delay
1. Cross upper left corner, outside of rectangle	____	____	____
2. Large rectangle	____	____	____
3. Diagonal cross	____	____	____
4. Horizontal midline of 2	____	____	____
5. Vertical midline	____	____	____
6. Small rectangle within 2, located to the left	____	____	____
7. Small segment above 6	____	____	____
8. Four parallel lines within 2, upper left	____	____	____
9. Triangle above 2, upper right	____	____	____
10. Small vertical line within 2, below 9	____	____	____
11. Circle with 3 dots within 2	____	____	____
12. Five parallel lines with 2 crossing 3, lower right	____	____	____
13. Sides of triangle attached to 2 on right	____	____	____
14. Diamond attached to 13	____	____	____
15. Vertical line within triangle 13 parallel to right vertical of a	____	____	____
16. Horizontal line within 13, continuing 4 to right	____	____	____
17. Cross attached to 5, below 2	____	____	____
18. Square attached to 2, lower left	____	____	____
Total Score	____	____	____

Source: Lezak (1983).

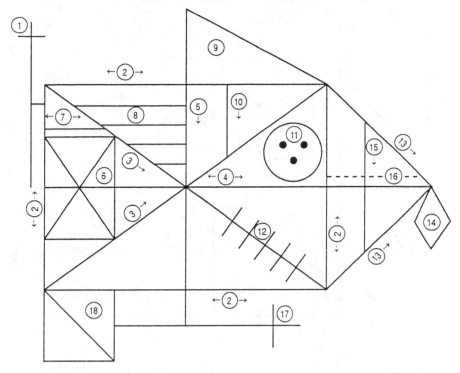

Figure 4.3. Quantitative scoring of the Rey-Osterrieth CFT.

SCORING

Each of the 18 units in Table 4.25 is considered separately. Each unit is scored for accuracy and relative position within the whole of the design. For each unit, count as follows:

Correct or placed properly	2 points
Correct but placed poorly	1 point
Distorted or incomplete, but placed properly	1 point
Recognizable but placed poorly	½ point
Absent or not recognizable	0
Maximum possible score	36 points

It is also possible to calculate a percent recall score that provides an option for removing the effects of level of performance

157

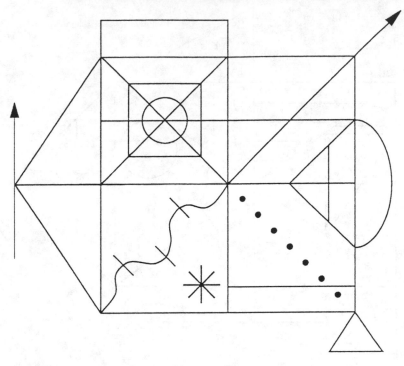

Figure 4.4. The Taylor Complex Figure. (*Source:* Lezak, 1983.)

on the copy trial from the recall trials. Lezak (1983) offered the following formula for this purpose:

$$(CF \text{ recall}/CF \text{ copy}) \times 100$$

An alternative form is available, the Taylor Complex Figure (Figure 4.4). Administration for the Taylor figure is the same as for the Rey-Osterreith CFT. Details on scoring of the Taylor Complex Figure are provided in Table 4.26 and Figure 4.5.

Osterreith's (1944) percentile norms for accuracy scores for adults are provided in Lezak (1983), and are reproduced along with Loring's norms (Loring, Martin, & Kimford, 1990) in Table 4.27.

The delay can be 3–60 minutes for Table 4.27. Within that range, the performance of normal patients was characterized by a difference of about 1–2 points between immediate and delayed

Table 4.26. Scoring system for the Taylor Complex Figure.

	Copy	3 Min Delay	20–60 Min Delay
1. Arrow at left of figure	___	___	___
2. Triangle to left of large square	___	___	___
3. Square, which is the base of figure	___	___	___
4. Horizontal midline of large square, which extends to 1	___	___	___
5. Vertical midline of large square	___	___	___
6. Horizontal line in top half of large square	___	___	___
7. Diagonals in top left quadrant of large square	___	___	___
8. Small square in top left quadrant	___	___	___
9. Circle in top left quadrant	___	___	___
10. Rectangle above top left quadrant	___	___	___
11. Arrow through and extending out of the top right quadrant	___	___	___
12.. Semicircle to right of large square	___	___	___
13. Triangle with enclosed line in right half of large square	___	___	___
14. Row of 7 dots in lower right quadrant	___	___	___
15. Horizontal line between 6th & 7th dots	___	___	___
16. Triangle at bottom right corner of lower right quadrant	___	___	___
17. Curved line with 3 cross-bars in lower left quadrant	___	___	___
18. Star in lower quadrant	___	___	___
Total Score	___	___	___

Source: Lezak (1983).

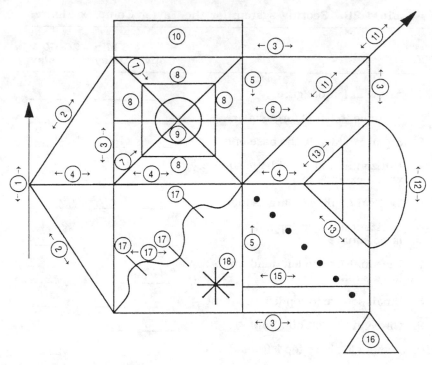

Figure 4.5. Quantitative scoring guide for the Taylor Complex Figure.

recall trials. In contrast, the norms from Loring et al., (1990) reflect the importance of conducting a short-delay recall trial. The authors' interpretation of the above was that immediate recall produces a facilitatory effect on both quantitative and qualitative delayed-recall performance. They warn that using normative information should take into account this important testing procedure difference.

Spreen and Strauss (1991) presented normative data for a 30-minute delayed recall of the Rey-Osterreith Complex Figure. It is interesting to note that the norms presented in Lezak (1983) are comparable to the Spreen and Strauss norms for the 16–30-year-old group. However, it should also be noted that these norms may not be appropriate for individuals outside this age range. For example, several studies have shown that 30-minute recall scores normally decrease on the average by 2–4

Table 4.27. Osterrieth's 1944 percentile norms for adults on the Complex Figure. Memory trial norms are for delays of 3 to 60 minutes. The Loring, 1990, norms include a copy, 30 delayed recall, and a 30-minute recall trial. The (+) indicates a recall trial that followed a 30-second recall procedure; the (–) indicates a recall trial that followed only the copy procedure.

Osterrieth 1944 Norms n = 60										
Percentile	10	20	30	40	50	60	70	80	90	100
Copy trial										
Score	29	30	31	32	32	33	34	34	35	36
Memory trials 3–60 Min										
Score	15	17	19	21	22	24	26	27	28	31
Loring et al. 1990 Norms n = 87										
Copy Trial	34	35	36	36	36	36	36	36	36	36
Memorial Trials										
30-Second	21	24	26	28	29	29.5	30.5	32	33.0	36
30-Minute (+)	22.5	25	28	29	30.5	31	32	33	35.0	36
30-Minute (–)	16	19.5	20	21	23	24.5	26	28	30.5	32

Source: Lezak (1983).

points for each decade beyond the age of 40. This decrease is correlated with normal aging, not neuropathology.

When applying norms for the Rey-Osterreith to scores derived from administration of the Taylor, an adjustment of about 5 points for the recall trial should be made (Spreen & Strauss, 1991). This is because recall on the Rey-Osterreith is somewhat harder, even though copy administrations of the two figures are of equivalent difficulty.

INTERPRETATION OF THE COMPLEX FIGURE TESTS

Patients whose lesions are on the left tend to show preserved recall of the overall structure of the figure with simplification and loss of detail. Patients with right-sided damage tend to lose many of the elements of the design, making increasingly impoverished reproductions of the original figure as they go from the immediate to the delayed-recall trial. Those right-hemisphere-

Table 4.28. Rey Osterrieth Complex Figure Test performance in head injured and normal individuals.

	Head-Injured (n = 10)		Healthy Normals (n = 71)	
	M	**SD**	**M**	**SD**
10' Recall	14.8	8.32	22.9	4.9

damaged patients who have visuospatial problems or who are subject to perceptual fragmentation will also increasingly distort and confuse the configurational elements of the design. Patients with head injuries, especially patients with frontal lobe damage, tend to perseverate, confabulate, personalize, or otherwise distort the design that first appears on the initial copy or the immediate recall trial. The distortions are exaggerated with repeated recall.

Crossen and Wiens (1988) examined Rey-Osterrieth CFT performance in 10 head-injured and 71 normal individuals and obtained the results presented in Table 4.28.

VERBAL FLUENCY

Although not typically thought of as a test of memory, word fluency can be considered a measure of retrieval. Tests of word fluency fall into two general categories: (1) retrieval employing phonemic categories and (2) retrieval employing semantic categories. With phonemic categories, patients are asked to retrieve as many words as they can beginning with a particular letter of the alphabet. With semantic categories, subjects are asked to retrieve as many words as possible that represent a specific logical category, (e.g., articles of clothing). Typically, patients are given 1 minute in which to generate as many words as possible that fit the defined category. Often, responses are recorded in 15-second segments to track the consistency of the individual's word production. Word fluency may be impaired in a variety of neurological conditions not necessarily associated with aphasia. The inability to retrieve words within categories is often an early symptom of Alzheimer's disease (Cummings & Benson, 1983).

The Word Fluency test from the Neurosensory Center Comprehensive Examination for Aphasia (Spreen & Benton, 1977) is frequently employed as a measure of word retrieval. A similar test, the Controlled Oral Word Association Test, is part of the Multilingual Aphasia Examination (Benton & Hamsher, 1983). Scores for both tests are corrected for age and education. Performance is not affected by the subject's sex.

In some studies (e.g., Borowski, Benton, & Spreen 1967), control subjects of low ability were found to perform less well than brighter brain-damaged patients. This highlights the need to account for the patient's premorbid verbal skill when evaluating verbal fluency.

The Animal Naming subtest of the Boston Diagnostic Aphasia Examination (Goodglass & Kaplan, 1983a) allows patients 90 seconds in which to produce the names of animals. However, only the patient's best consecutive 60-second performance is scored. Aphasic patients tend to perform in an uneven fashion. Their ability to produce animal names tapers quickly, despite periodic bursts in which they produce correct responses. Goodglas and Kaplan (1983b) stated that the average adult is able to name approximately 18 animals within their most productive

163

60-second period. However, age- and education-based norms are not provided.

The Controlled Oral Word Association Test and the Set Test are generally considered to be tests for aphasia. However, *verbal fluency difficulty also is often characteristic of patients with memory dysfunction*. For example, in one study patients with Korsakoff's syndrome could produce the names of only 9.1 animals on the Set Test—in contrast to normal controls, who generated an average of 12.5 animal responses. These results stand in marked contrast to the relatively good performance of the Korsakoff's syndrome patients on the WAIS-R vocabulary subtest (average score of 10).

CONTROLLED ORAL WORD ASSOCIATION TEST (FAS)

The Controlled Oral Word Association Test (the "FAS") was published by Benton and Hamsher (1983) and is a measure of verbal fluency. It consists of three word naming trials using the letters *F*, *A*, and *S*, in that order. Patients are asked to respond with as many words as they can think of that begin with the designated letter, omitting proper nouns, numbers, and the same word with different suffix.

SCORING

The total number of all correct words pronounced during the three 1-minute trials is recorded. This sum is adjusted for age, sex, and education (by adding additional points from Table 4.29) and is then converted into percentile scores using Table 4.30.

Table 4.29. Correction values for age and education on the FAS.

Education (Years completed)	AGE					
	50–54		55–59		60–64	
	M	F	M	F	M	F
Less than 9	9	8	11	10	14	12
9–11	6	5	7	7	9	9
12–15	4	3	5	4	7	6
16+	—	—	1	1	3	3

Source: Adapted from Lezak (1983).

Table 4.30. FAS Summary Table.

Percentile Adjusted Scores	Range	Classification
53+	96+	Superior
45–52	77–89	High normal
31–44	25–75	Normal
25–30	11–22	Low normal
23–24	5–8	Borderline
17–22	1–3	Defective
10–16	<1	Severe defect
0–9	<1	Nil-Trace

Source: Adapted from Lezak, 1983.

There is marked variability of performance at the lower education levels, so the performances of persons with less than a high school education must be interpreted with caution. .

The instructions for the Controlled Word Association Test are presented in Table 4.31.

Table 4.31. Instructions for the Controlled Word Association Test.

"I want to see how many words you can say beginning with a certain letter in one minute. Don't say proper nouns or numbers, or the same word with a different ending. The letter is F, Begin!"

If patients have difficulty in understanding the task it can be explained with examples, using a non-designated letter. After the first (F) trial has been completed the A and S trials are administered. The examiner keeps a record of patients' verbal responses by writing them down.

Alternative instructions: **"I will say a letter of the alphabet. Then I want you to give me as many words that begin with that letter as quickly as you can. For instance, if I say "B" you might give me "bad, battle, bed"...I do not want you to use words which are proper names such as "Boston, Bob, or Brylcream." Also, do not use the same word again with a different ending such as "eat and eating." Any questions? (pause) Begin when I say the letter. The first letter is F. Go Ahead."**

Begin timing immediately after saying "go ahead". Allow one minute for each letter. Say "fine" or "good" after each one minute performance. If the patients tend to discontinue before the end of the minute encourage them to try to think of more words. If there is a silence of 15 seconds repeat the basic instructions, and the letter.

FAS

THE CLINICAL ASSESSMENT OF MEMORY

THE SET TEST (SET)

The Set Test was initially described by Isaacs and Kennie (1973). Since that time it has become widely popular because it is straightforward, easily administered, and simple to understand, and it has considerable face validity. The patient is asked to name as many items as possible from four successive categories: colors, animals, fruits, and towns. The patient names items in the first category until 10 item names are given or until no more can be remembered, at which point the next category is announced, and so on.

The instructions are simply to **"Name as many [animals] as you can."** Only 1 minute is allowed per category, so the entire test takes at most 5 minutes with instructions. The maximum correct score is 40 (because no more than 10 items are recorded for each category).

Isaacs and Kennie (1973) studied healthy subjects over the age of 65. These subjects averaged 31.2 items overall, and 95% of the subjects had scores greater than 15. In contrast, demented patients averaged fewer than 26 correct responses. Lower scores were associated with illness and to a lesser extent, low socioeconomic status. However, depressed patients were found to perform in the normal range on this test.

As an alternative approach, the examiner may want to add the animals category to the FAS test and time it as a 60-second trial. Normal adults should be able to name more than 18 animals in 60 seconds. Elderly control and mildly demented patients can typically name more animals than FAS words.

Word fluency, as measured by FAS and the SET tests, has proved to be a sensitive indicator of brain dysfunction. Frontal lesions, regardless of site, tend to depress fluency scores, with left frontal lesions resulting in lower word production than do right frontal lesions. Benton (1968) found that patients with left frontal lesions produce on average almost one-third fewer FAS words than do patients with right frontal lesions; bilateral lesions tended to lower verbal productivity even more. Patients with Alzheimer's disease display reduced capacity to generate words on tests of verbal fluency. In contrast, verbal fluency holds up when symptoms of depression mimic organic deterioration (i.e., in pseudodementia).

VERBAL AND NONVERBAL SELECTIVE REMINDING TASKS

A variation to the list-learning approaches thus far presented is the Selective Reminding Task (SRT) procedure developed by Buschke (1973) and refined by Buschke and Fuld (1974). The primary difference between the SRT and other supraspan learning procedures such as the AVLT and the CVLT is that in the SRT assessment procedure, the patient is read the "to-be-learned" list only once, in the beginning (Ivnik, 1991). On subsequent trials, only those words from the list that were not recalled by the patient during the immediately preceding trial are repeated.

The selective reminding procedure assumes that once a word has been recalled it has been learned. Only unlearned (i.e., unrecalled) words are presented on subsequent trials. After each trial, the examiner repeats all of the words the patient omitted in that trial. The reminding and the recall trials continue until the patient recites the whole list or until 12 trials have been administered.

The selective reminding procedure structures the list-learning task in a manner intended to differentiate word storage (i.e., learning) from word retrieval (i.e., recall). The SRT is designed to provide a variety of estimates of both storage and retrieval. These measures include "long-term storage" (words recalled on each learning trial), "total long-term storage" (the sum of words recalled across all learning trials), "consistent long-term retrieval" (number of words recalled at any specific trial that were recalled on all preceding trials), and "total consistent long-term retrieval" (sum of the "consistent long-term retrieval" scores across trials) (Ivnik, 1991).

VERBAL SELECTIVE REMINDING TEST (VSRT)

The purpose of the Verbal Selective Reminding Test (VSRT) is to measure verbal learning and memory during a multiple-trial list-learning task. Several versions of the test exist, but the one most commonly used was developed by Hannay and Levin (1985). This version consists of four alternative forms. Each form consists of 12 unrelated words. The Form 1 list is the one that has been used the most frequently in screening batteries, and there is a growing number of sources for norms for this list.

SET

VSRT

Table 4.32. SRT Forms 1–4 for Adult Administration.

Form 1	Form 2	Form 3	Form 4
bowl	shine	throw	egg
passion	disagree	lily	runway
dawn	fat	film	fort
judgment	wealthy	discreet	toothache
grant	drunk	loft	drown
bee	pin	beef	baby
plane	grass	street	lava
county	moon	helmet	damp
choice	prepare	snake	pure
seed	prize	dug	vote
wool	duck	pack	strip
meal	leaf	tin	truth

Source: Hannay & Levin (1985).

Table 4.32 provides a listing of Hannay and Levin's (1985) four alternative forms. It should be noted that *Form 1 was found to be approximately 10% more difficult than forms 2, 3, and 4.* One way to address this dilemma when using the alternative forms was suggested by Larrabee, Trahan, Custiss, and Levin (1988), who recommended reducing the raw score performance on forms 2, 3, and 4 by 10%, then calculating percentiles of performance based on the Form 1 norms constructed by Larrabee, Kane, Schuck, and Francis (1985) and presented later in this chapter.

The Buschke (1973) procedure has been extended to include a *cued-recall* trial after the 12th or last selective reminding trial, a *multiple–choice recognition* test that immediately follows the cued-recall trial, and a *30-minute delayed-recall* trial (Hannay & Levin, 1985). Unfortunately, there is no commercial source for these testing materials. However, it is not difficult to develop one's own recording forms for the basic VSRT test.

Administration

The total time for administration of the VSRT is approximately 30 minutes; however, there is no specific time limit for this test. The procedure involves reading a list of 12 words to the patient and then having the patient recall as many of the words as possible. Each subsequent learning trial involves the selective presentation of only those items that were not recalled on the immediately preceding trial. The list of 12 words is read to the patient over 12 selective reminding trials or until the patient is able to recall the entire list on three consecutive trials.

In the extended version of this test (Hannay & Levin, 1985), a cued-recall trial, multiple-choice recognition, and 30-minute delayed recall are included. The following procedure was modeled after the one described by Buschke (1973), and the extended procedure described by Larrabee et al. (1988).

Administration of the SRT begins when the examiner reads the list of 12 words to the patient. Note that *the entire list is read only once*, that is, only on the first trial prior to the recall challenge. Thereafter, on subsequent trials, only the words not recalled by the patient are read. The order of recall is recorded as the patient repeats the words he or she remembers on a given trial. Intrusions (i.e., words not on the list) are also recorded. If the patient on a given trial repeats only the words that were read by the administrator (i.e., the "missed" words), he or she is reminded to recite as much of the entire list as he or she can remember, including the words recalled previously. This usually happens only on Trial 2.

The following instructions should be read to the patient immediately preceding administration of the test.

> **I'm going to read you a list of words. Listen carefully because when I'm finished, I'll expect you to repeat as many of them as you can. After you've told me all the words that you can remember, I'll tell you the words that you missed. Then I'll ask you to again tell me as many of the words as you can remember from the entire list, which include the ones that you told me and the ones that you missed.**

Read the list at a rate of 2 seconds per word; then say, **"Now tell me as many of the words as you can remember."** Record the words recalled by writing the sequence in which they are recalled in the column for that trial; then say, **"These are the words you missed, listen."** Read the words that were missed (i.e., not recalled) from top to bottom of the list, then say, **"Now tell me the complete list again, including the words you said last time."**

Repeat this sequence until the test is complete (i.e., up to 12 trials). If the patient recalls all 12 words correctly on three consecutive trials, discontinue and score the test as though all 12 trials had been administered. Do not tell the patient the number of words in the list or the number of trials. If the patient says a word that is not on the list, just continue without telling him or her that the word is not one of the words on the list.

Prompting

Larrabee et al. (1988) maintains that prompting is appropriate during the SRT and makes the following recommendations.

1. If the patient responds with a particular word on four trials in a row without being reminded, then fails to give the word on the following trial, the administrator is allowed to prompt by saying, **"there is a word you have given me quite a few times, but you have not said it yet."**
2. The administrator is also allowed to ask the patient to **"run through the list out loud"** on each trial to make sure the subject had not left out anything.

Cued Recall

After the regular version is completed, a cued-recall trial may be presented as an additional trial. This procedure is an extension of the original Buschkc (1973) SRT and may be considered a testing option.

The cued recall consists of presenting the first two letters from each of the original words and asking the question **"Which word started with the letters____?"** (e.g., *pa* [for passion]). The administrator literally says the *names* of the letters, not the sound of the two-letter set. However, on Form 1 the word *bee* can be readily identified by the letters *be*, hence, this cue should be omitted from the cued-recall procedure. A listing of cued-recall words is presented in Table 4.33 for the four alternative forms. Each of the letter sets should be printed on 5 × 7 unlined index cards and presented one set at a time. Patients are allowed to return to previous cards if they ask to do so.

Multiple-Choice Procedures

The multiple-choice recognition procedure immediately follows the cued-recall trial. This task requires the patient to discriminate the target word from three foil words (i.e., a phonemic foil, a semantic foil, and an unrelated foil). Sets of four words are

Table 4.33. Cued Recall letters for SRT Forms 1–4.

Form 1	Form 2	Form 3	Form 4
BO	SH	TH	—
PA	DI	LI	RU
DA	FA	FI	FO
JUD	WEA	DI	TO
GR	DR	LO	DR
—	—	BE	BA
PL	GR	ST	LA
COU	MO	HE	DA
CH	PRE	SN	PU
SE	PR	DU	VO
WO	DU	PA	ST
ME	LE	—	TR

Source: Hannay & Levin (1985).

presented on 5 × 7 unlined index cards, and the patient is asked, **"Which of these four words was on the list that you have been learning?"** Patients are allowed to return to previous cards is they ask to do so. Further, cues that fail initially to elicit the target word are routinely presented a second time after each cue has been given the first time. A listing of multiple-choice words originally presented by Hannay (1986) is presented in Table 4.34

Delayed Recall

Following a 30-minute period of visual memory testing (e.g., the Benton Visual Retention Test), a delayed "free" recall trial is administered. Here the patient is asked "Remember the word list that you learned previously? Will you please tell me as many words for that list as you can remember?" This is done without prior cuing or reminding; in addition, it is important that a nonverbal intervening task is selected for the 30-minute delay.

Scoring

Scoring of the VSRT appears to be more formidable than it actually is, and the reader is encouraged to try the following procedures before being intimidated by the scoring form presented in Table 4.35. These instructions are intended to provide a practi-

Table 4.34. Multiple choice items for the Selective Reminding Test.

Example of how items would be displayed on a card:

(1)	bowl	(2)	dish
(3)	bell	(4)	view

Multiple-Choice Items for SRT Forms 1–4

Form 1

a) bowl, dish, bell, view;

b) love, poison, conform, passion;

c) dawn, sunrise, bet, down;

d) pasteboard, verdict, judgment, fudge;

e) grand, grant, give, jazz;

f) see, sting, fold, bee;

g) pain, plane, pulled, jet;

h) county, state, tasted, counter;

i) voice, select, choice, cheese;

j) flower, seed, herd, seek;

k) date, sheep, wool, would;

l) mill, queen, food, meal.

Form 2

a) shine, glow, chime, cast;

b) dispute, disappear, contour, disagree;

c) fat, oil, trail, fit;

d) stopwatch, affluent, wealthy, worthy;

e) trunk, drunk, stoned, blunt;

f) fin, peg, wake, pin;

g) glass, grass, plan, lawn;

h) moon, beam, spark, noon;

i) propose,ready prepare, husband;

j) award, prize pot size;

k) bark, bird, duck, luck;

l) leap, ranch, blade.

Form 3

a) throw, toss, through, plate;

b) flower, lilt, intent, lily;

c) film, movie, slave, kiln;

d) waver, cautious, discreet, distinct;

e) soft, loft, attic, tack;

f) beet, meat, clue, beef;

g) stream, street, speed, road;

h) helmet, armor, bacon, velvet;

i) smoke, serpent, snake, pool;

j) hoed, dug, hay, dog;

k) blank, bundle, pack, puck;

l) ton, shirt, foil, tin.

Form 4

a) egg, shell, beg, source;

b) airline, runner, darling, runway;

c) fort, castle, sink, fork;

d) boldness, dentist, toothache, headache;

e) blown, drown, float, rib,

f) body infant, middle, baby;

g) larva, lava, echo, rock;

h) damp, moist, hook, stamp;

i) purse, clean, pure, bare;

j) ballot, vote, dish, note;

k) chain, peal, strip, slip

l) trust, rise, fact, truth.

Source: Hannay (1986).

Table 4.35. Scoring sheet for the Verbal Selective Reminding Test.

Verbal Selective Reminding Test–Form 1
Name_____ Date_____ Administrator_____

	1	2	3	4	5	6	7	8	9	10	11	12	CR	M.CH	30"	R
1. BOWL																
2. PASSION																
3. DAWN																
4. JUDGEMENT																
5. GRANT																
6. BEE																
7. PLANE																
8. COUNTY																
9. CHOICE																
10. SEED																
11. WOOL																
12. MEAL																

	1	2	3	4	5	6	7	8	9	10	11	12	SUM
TOTAL RECALL													
LTS													
STR													
LTS													
CLTR													
RLTR													
INTRUSIONS													
REMINDERS													

CUED RECALL (TOTAL)_____

MULTIPLE CHOICE (TOTAL)_____

30" RECALL (TOTAL)_____

COMMENTS:

_____

Source: Hannay (1986).

173

cal method for scoring the VSRT. Please note that a red-ink pen is recommended for underscoring and differentiating a variety of scores.

1. Mark all blank spaces on the scoring sheet with a large X.
2. Add the number of words recalled down each column and enter the totals in the row marked Total Recall [TOT RECALL].
3. Examine across each word row (1–12). When two trials are recalled consecutively, underscore in red those trials and all subsequent trials in that row (regardless of whether the word has been consistently recalled or not). This represents the long-term storage score (LTS).
4. Trace each word row backward, (i.e, from right to left), and place an arrow in the numbered square following the last square with an X. There should be *no* arrows in the 12th column. This represents the score for consistent long-term retrieval (CLTR).
5. Moving down each column, count the squares with numbers (recalled words) that are underlined in red and enter the total in the row marked LTR. This is the score that represents long term retrieval.
6. Subtract the LTR row from the TOT RECALL by column, and enter the results in the row marked STR (i.e., short-term retrieval). When the lines marked LTR and STR are added together, they will equal the line marked TOT RECALL.
7. Add down the columns only those numbered blocks having arrows, and enter the totals in the row marked CLTR (i.e., consistent long-term retrieval).
8. Count down each column those squares with an X or a number *underlined in red* and enter the totals in the row marked LTS (i.e., long-term storage).
9. Subtract the row marked CLTR from the LTR row by column and enter the remainder in the row marked RLTR (i.e, random long-term retrieval).
10. Sum across the LTS row and enter the total in the total (i.e., sum) block.
11. Sum across the CLTR row and enter total in the total (i.e., sum) block.

Normative Data

Larrabee et al. (1988) collected normative data on 271 persons between the ages of 18 and 91 for Form 1 of the VSRT (Levin, Benton, & Grossman, 1982) and found that performance was significantly related to age and gender. These authors subsequently generated gender corrections by age- and education-matched pair analyses of the VSRT performance of 80 males and 80 females. Normative findings are grouped by seven age cohorts: 18–29, 30–39, 40–49, 50–59, 60–69, 70–79, and 80–91.

The authors note that the mean values for LTR and STR and for CLTR and RLTR do not sum to the exact mean value for total correct, and small discrepancies exist because different gender corrections were used for the respective scores. A matched-pair regression analysis of the normative data suggests age and gender have significant effects on VSRT performance. Age is the more dramatic of the two variables, especially in the 50 and older age group. Education appears to be relatively unimportant and has no significant effect on VSRT performance. The Larabee et al. (1985) norms are presented in Table 4.36.

Validity Studies of the VSRT

Buschke (1973) developed the selective reminding technique to assess retrieval, registration, and consolidation components of memory. To date, research has not supported the independence of all measures derived from the selective reminding procedure. Studies typically show these scores to be highly correlated and to load on a single verbal memory factor.

The selective reminding procedure has been used by a number of investigators to study memory impairment associated with a variety of neurological disorders and to monitor both the positive and negative effects of drugs. For example, the selective reminding procedure has been used to study memory deficits associated with Huntington's disease, Alzheimer's disease, multiinfarct dementia, head injury, asymptomatic seropositive HIV infection, and schizophrenia (Kane & Kay, 1991). They have demonstrated sensitivity to the effects of left temporal lobe lesions and have been used to assess drug effects for the treatment of patients with attention and memory disorders. These procedures have also been used to screen for drug-related cogni-

Table 4.36. Verbal Selective Reminding Norms.

				Age Groups			
Measures	18–19	30–39	40–49	50–59	60–69	70–79	80–91
Age							
Mean	22.55	34.62	43.71	54.17	66.00	74.49	83.48
SD	(3.30)	(2.69)	(2.91)	(2.74)	(2.47)	(2.97)	(3.10)
Education							
Mean	12.88	14.90	14.71	12.92	13.40	13.46	13.22
SD	(1.73)	(2.47)	(2.72)	(1.98)	(3.57)	(3.78)	(3.76)
N	51	29	31	24	50	59	27
Female/male	23/28	15/14	19/12	22/2	33/17	38/21	23/4
Total							
Mean	128.18	124.59	125.03	121.62	114.82	105.27	97.96
SD	(9.16)	(13.40)	(12.00)	(10.46)	(15.77)	(16.67)	(17.49)
LTR							
Mean	122.16	118.14	118.55	112.71	101.52	89.95	77.22
SD	(13.12)	(20.64)	(17.96)	(16.10)	(24.68)	(29.23)	(26.26)
STR							
Mean	6.14	6.72	6.48	8.96	13.52	17.47	20.74
SD	(4.82)	(7.59)	(6.72)	(6.40)	(9.52)	(10.41)	(9.62)
LTS							
MEAN	124.00	121.62	122.45	116.67	107.00	95.54	87.48
SD	(10.47)	(18.36)	(15.64)	(14.52)	(21.79)	(24.86)	(25.26)
CLTR							
Mean	115.12	107.93	107.10	101.50	88.92	69.68	54.96
SD	(19.67)	(27.62)	(26.62)	(22.39)	(35.85)	(35.96)	(29.04)
RLTR							
Mean	8.12	10.10	11.19	10.79	14.66	20.71	22.19
SD	(9.42)	(9.73)	(11.34)	(9.25)	(11.83)	(14.37)	(10.70)
Reminders by Examiners							
Mean	16.00	18.10	19.03	22.25	28.12	36.95	43.46
SD	(8.42)	(13.12)	(11.26)	(10.06)	(15.16)	(15.17)	(15.77)
Intrusions							
Mean	.84	.97	1.81	1.17	3.90	4.22	3.30
SD	(1.29)	(1.43)	(3.10)	(1.49)	(7.29)	(5.76)	(5.09)
Cued Recall							
Mean	—	—	—	—	9.58[a]	8.95[b]	8.16[c]
SD	—	—	—	—	(1.93)	(2.12)	(2.22)
Multiple Choice							
Mean	12.0	12.0	12.0	12.0	11.96	11.85	11.93
SD	(0.0)	(0.0)	(0.0)	(0.0)	(0.20)	(0.58)	(0.27)
Delayed Recall							
Mean	11.53	10.66	11.03	10.83	9.58	9.05	8.37
SD	(.83)	(1.97)	(1.43)	(1.40)	(2.46)	(2.62)	(2.45)

Correction values for raw scores of males must be calculated as illustrated below before entering normative tables.

Total = +5; LTR = +9; STR = –4; LTS = +7; CLTR = +13; RLTR = –5; Reminders = –5; Intrusions = 0; Cued Recall = 0; Multiple Choice = 0; Delayed Recall = +1. (Caution: *Do not correct LTS or CLTR if raw score is 0.*) [a]n=31; [b]n=38; [c]n=19. *Source:* Larrabee et al. (1985).

tive impairment. In all cases, the selective reminding procedure was sensitive to alterations in memory. The results of these experimental studies correspond to the authors' clinical experience that the selective reminding procedure is sensitive to subtle changes in memory functioning. As with a majority of neuropsychological measures, an individual's premorbid intellectual level must be factored into interpreting performance on selective reminding procedures. Bishop, Dickson, & Allen (1990) demonstrated moderate correlations between selective reminding performance and psychometric intelligence in a group of 60 college students. Individuals of low-average intelligence tended to score one standard deviation below the mean, using the norms compiled by Larrabee et al. (1985, 1988).

The VSRT has proved useful in the assessment of head injury. Not surprisingly, VSRT performance is significantly impaired following severe closed head injury (Levin, Grossman, Rose, & Teasdale, 1979), and the degree of long-term memory impairment 1 year after severe head injury was shown to be significantly correlated to the overall level of disability. Furthermore, patients who were able to resume normal work and social functioning performed within the normal range on the VSRT. Performance on consistent recall was severely impaired in patients who were judged to be moderately to severely disabled at the time of the study.

Using the VSRT technique, Levin and colleagues (1979) were able to differentiate the efficiency with which patients who had sustained head trauma of varying degrees of severity learned a list of 12 high-frequency words. They used four measures: *long-term storage* (the number of words recalled in each of 12 trials); *total long-term storage* (the sum of words in storage across trials); *consistent long-term retrieval* (from storage, the number of words recalled in any given trial that were recalled on all subsequent trials without reminding); and *total consistent long-term retrieval* (the sum of the latter scores). It is interesting to note that on long-term storage, only the seriously damaged group did not continue to show improvement across all 12 trials but leveled off (with an average recall of approximately six words) by the sixth trial. The mildly impaired group achieved an almost perfect one-word-per-trial lag throughout. However, the moderately impaired group showed a much less consistent retrieval pattern than that of the mildly impaired group (Lezak, 1983).

In addition to the above application, the VSRT measure of LTR and CLTR have proved useful in distinguishing mild dementia from normal aging (Spreen & Strauss, 1991).

COMPUTERIZED VERSIONS OF THE VERBAL AND NONVERBAL SELECTIVE REMINDING TASKS (NSRT)

Following the model of the VSRT presented by Buschke (1973), Kane and Perrine (1988) developed a computer program that presented designs on a computer video screen and made subsequent presentation contingent upon the subject's previous performance. In essence, this is a Buschke selective reminding paradigm using nonverbal stimuli for the primary "to-be-learned list." During the development of this variation of the SRT procedure, Kane and Perrine tested a series of designs for difficulty of verbal encoding by asking normal subjects to describe a series of abstract designs. Reaction times were recorded along with the nature of the subjects' responses. Designs that were difficult for the subjects to describe were chosen for the nonverbal analog to the traditional VSRT. To avoid confounding memory with visual construction deficits, a recognition paradigm was implemented.

In the present version of this test, Kane and Kay (1992) developed three independent forms to be used along with automated data output. In addition, they also created an automated version of the VSRT with the same "look and feel" as its nonverbal counterpart employing the recognition memory paradigm.

The Nonverbal Selective Reminding Test (NSRT) (Kane & Kay, 1992) is based on three sets of 21 abstract designs. For each form of the test, 7 designs are designated as targets and 14 as distractors. During the learning phase, the computer presents the designs, one at a time, for 2.5 seconds. The computer then presents a 21-design array that includes the seven targets. The subject's task is to identify the seven target designs. Positions of the figures in the 21-design array change for each recall trial. During the learning phase of the test, the subjects have 3 minutes per trial to complete their selections. When a design is selected, the box outlining the design turns red. Subjects are permitted to change their response during a trial and "unselect" a choice. In this case, the box surrounding the design returns to its normal color. Both initial learning and delayed recognition tasks are included.

NSRT

THE CLINICAL ASSESSMENT OF MEMORY

AUTOMATED VERBAL SELECTIVE REMINDING TEST

The automated VSRT runs in a parallel fashion to the NSRT except that the three sets of 21 designs are replaced by three sets of 42 words. All 126 words are concrete nouns with a Thorndike and Lorge (1944) rating of AA or AAA. The subject's task is to learn a 14-word list presented in the selective reminding format. Each target word in the list is paired with two distractors beginning with the same letter, having the same number of letters, and having an identical Thorndike-Lorge rating. Test directions are presented on an instruction screen. The administrator stays with the subject during the test and provides prompts during the instruction phase as needed. Practice trials precede testing administration to assist the subject in comprehending the selective reminding format.

Norms for the automated VSRT and NSRT are not available at present; however, formal normative studies are being conducted.

We believe that measures of this type are creative approaches to the measurement of memory impairment and may tap dimensions of memory not assessed with more traditional measures. In fact, factor-analytic studies (Kane & Perrine, 1988) have suggested that a unique nonverbal factor is being measured by the NSRT. Other studies (e.g., Kane & Kay, 1992) suggest that the NSRT is a promising measure of nonverbal recognition memory and potentially useful for detecting lateralized memory impairment. The factor analytic data demonstrating independence of the NSRT scores from a more general spatial memory factor are especially provocative.

AN ABBREVIATED VERSION OF THE SRT: THE MIAMI SELECTIVE LEARNING TEST (MSLT)

Russell has recently constructed an abbreviated version of the VSRT. This test is called the Miami Selective Learning Test (MSLT) and is modeled on the Buschke and Fuld (1974) selective reminding procedure. Russell created the MSLT because he believed tests such as the CVLT are too long and tedious, and there appears to be contamination of the half-hour memory by the interpolated memory test (Russell, personal communication, 1992). He also felt that the Buschke method had the advantage of measuring storage rather than just retention. The MSLT consists of a primary list of 12 unrelated words and a recognition list of 36 words. The administration includes six selective reminding trials, a half-hour free-recall trial, and a recognition trial. Norms and computer scoring for the MSLT are available and may be purchased from Western Psychological Services (WPS).

MSLT

THE CLINICAL ASSESSMENT OF MEMORY

SELF-REPORT QUESTIONNAIRES

SUPPLEMENTING THE STANDARDIZED ASSESSMENT METRICS

This section contains a summary and selected "structured" subjective-report scales. These measures were designed to supplement formal memory assessments. This section also includes a listing of some general assessment considerations.

SELF-REPORT

Many "standardized" tests fail to predict everyday memory and cognitive functioning in the "real world," and they are not ecologically valid. However, this limitation does not necessarily mean we should not use them. As Gregory (1987) stated, "It is far better to use an imperfect measure, mindful of its limitations, than no measure at all." He further suggests that "examiners should not rely exclusively upon formal tests but should supplement such measures with self-report questionnaires."

Kapur and Pearson (1983) conducted an interesting study demonstrating commonalities between the memory complaints of brain-damaged and normal subjects. The results of this study are presented in Table 4.37.

Other relevant information that will help in the assessment will be found in answers to the following.

1. Does the patient have a memory problem?
2. How severe is the impairment?
3. Is the impairment more than we should expect with normal aging?

Table 4.37. The most common memory complaints from patients (listed in order of frequency).

Brain-Damaged	Normal Controls
1. Forgetting people's names	1. Forgetting to do something
2. Forgetting recent events	2. Forgetting people's names
3. Forgetting a spoken message	3. Forgetting a spoken message
4. Forgetting to do something	

Source: Adapted from Kapur and Pearson (1983).

4. How can the information help structure rehabilitation and management programs?
5. Is the residual memory deficit going to affect job performance or help address legal issues such as compensation for head injury?
6. Is the patient's report of memory difficulties reliable?

It is important that the clinician always assess the patient's reports of memory failure in context. For example, depressed patients often complain about loss of memory; however, their complaints are often unfounded. Depression and memory complaints are correlated, but actual memory ability is not severely impaired in depressed patients. It will be helpful to use encouragement to elicit better performance from these patients. In addition, the following tests are those least affected by depression: digit span, repeating a paragraph, and paired associate learning.

Older subjects are often more upset about their memory failures, and may perceive what is "normal forgetfulness" (e.g., misplacing one's keys or eyeglasses) as a sign of an early stage of senility or other pathology.

THE COGNITIVE DIFFICULTIES SCALE (CDS)

The Cognitive Difficulties Scale (CDS) is a straightforward and helpful tool to assess memory difficulties (McNair & Kahn, 1983). It is presented in Table 4.38. The CDS is an adjunct to the initial interview rather than a formal psychometric instrument from which a score is derived and analyzed. It was designed to assess the effects of tricyclic antidepressants that often affect memory, especially in elderly patients. It can be used to help screen for difficulties in attention, concentration, psychomotor coordination, orientation, recent memory, and long-term memory.

The CDS is a qualitative tool, and the clinician should use common sense and clinical judgment to further evaluate any response checked 2, 3, or 4. If there is not time for a formal evaluation using the CDS, a brief questionnaire will often suffice. An example of this approach to assessing memory problems is presented in Table 4.39.

Table 4.38. The Cognitive Difficulties Scale

Below are statements describing everyday inefficiencies, lapses of attention or memory, and related functions that people often notice about themselves. Please rate the degree to which each statement describes your typical or usual behavior during the past (days, weeks, etc.). Use the following scale and record your answers in the blanks provided.

4 = Very often   1 = Rarely
3 = Often   0 = Not at all
2 = Sometimes

___ 1. I have trouble recalling frequently used phone numbers.
___ 2. I put down things (glasses, keys, wallet, purse, papers) and have trouble finding them.
___ 3. When interrupted while reading, I have trouble finding my place again.
___ 4. I need a written list when I do errands to avoid forgetting things.
___ 5. I forget appointments, dates, or classes.
___ 6. I forget to return phone calls.
___ 7. I have trouble getting my keys into a lock.
___ 8. I forget errands I planned to do on my way home.
___ 9. I have trouble recalling names of people I know.
___ 10. I find it hard to keep my mind on a task or job.
___ 11. I have trouble describing a program I just watched on television.
___ 12. I don't say quite what I mean to say.
___ 13. I fail to recognize people I know.
___ 14. I have trouble getting out information that's at the tip of my tongue.
___ 15. I have trouble thinking of the names of objects.
___ 16. I find it hard to understand what I read.
___ 17. I miss the point of what other people are saying.
___ 18. I forget names of people soon after being introduced.
___ 19. I lose my train of thought as I listen to somebody else.
___ 20. I forget steps in recipes I know well and have to look them up.
___ 21. I forget what day of the week it is.
___ 22. I forget to button or zip my clothing.
___ 23. I need to check or double-check whether I locked the door, turned off the stove, etc.
___ 25. I cannot keep my mind on one thing.
___ 26. I need to have instructions repeated several times.
___ 27. I leave out ingredients when I cook.
___ 28. I have trouble manipulating buttons, fasteners, scissors or bottle caps.
___ 29. I misplace my clothing.
___ 30. I have trouble sewing or mending.
___ 31. I find it hard to keep my mind on what I'm reading.
___ 32. I forget right away what people say to me.
___ 33. When walking or riding, I forget how I've gotten from one point to another.
___ 34. I have trouble deciding if I've received the correct change.
___ 35. I forget to pay bills, record checks, or mail letters.
___ 36. I have to do things very slowly to be sure I'm doing them right.
___ 37. My mind just goes blank at times.
___ 38. I forget the date of the month.
___ 39. I have trouble using tools (hammer, pliers) for minor household repairs.

Source: Adapted from McNair and Kahn (1983).

Table 4.39. A Structured Questionnaire for Examining Memory Difficulties.

STRUCTURED QUESTIONNAIRE FOR EXAMINING MEMORY DIFFICULTIES

How is your memory for the following things?

Is it **better**, the **same**, or **worse** than it was before your current problems?

1. Knowing the time of day, the day of the week, month of the year.
2. Knowing where you are when you travel around town.
3. Remembering appointments, meetings, or engagements.
4. Remembering that you have already met someone when you are introduced to them again
5. Remembering something that a friend or spouse has told you.
6. Remembering where you have put things.
7. Remembering the names of people you have known and interacted with for some time.
8. Remembering recent events you have heard on the news.
9. Remembering to do something that you had intended to do.
10. Remembering the names of famous people whose pictures you have seen many times.

Source: Adapted from Gregory (1987).

CHAPTER FIVE

Summary: Practical Guidelines for Memory Assessment

Robert Kane, Dennis Reeves, and Danny Wedding

GENERAL CONCEPTS IN MEMORY ASSESSMENT

Thus far in this text we have presented an overview of general theoretical models, terminology, and neuroanatomy related to memory processes. In this final chapter we introduce guidelines for a practical approach to clinical memory assessment. We begin with a discussion of types and levels of assessment and a review of the mental status examination as it applies to the evaluation of memory. We then present a model for the evaluation process. In the last portion of the chapter, we present a brief overview of selected tests. Our intent here is to provide convenient guidelines for test selection and a quick overview of memory tests and their essential characteristics.

When planning the assessment, it should be kept in mind that memory is not a unitary construct and that memory loss is almost never complete. For example, some patients have a retrograde amnesia (a loss of memory for remote events) as well as an anterograde amnesia (deficit for learning new material). Others have primarily an anterograde component. Some patients have a specific deficit confined to the learning of verbal or nonverbal material. In addition, memory problems may occur at different stages of learning such as registration, storage, or retrieval. Finally, loss of mental efficiency accompaning the aging process can magnify the ordinary disparities in performance levels between these various functions (Weintraub & Mesulam, 1985).

With these principles in mind, an assessment of memory should cover, at minimum, immediate memory span, learning capacity, and retention for recently learned information and recall of long-stored information. The examination of memory must be sufficiently broad to detect different deficit patterns without being overwhelmingly lengthy.

The guidelines introduced in this chapter were derived from everyday practice as experienced by the authors and are based on the premise that the assessment instruments presently available allow one to assess the following:

1. Learning (encoding and storage of material)
2. Recall versus recognition of memory items.
3. Material-specific memory (i.e., differentiating learning and recall of verbal and nonverbal material).
4. A "primary" memory problem versus a memory problem attributable to deficits in attention, organization, malingering, or emotional or psychiatric disturbances.

By "primary memory problem" we mean difficulty in encoding, storing, or retrieving information resulting from damage to specific temporal or other memory structures and not attributable to deficits in attention or organization.

In reviewing specific assessment procedures, we intentionally do not cover techniques commonly used in experimental laboratories to study differences in implicit and explicit memory or procedural learning. As valuable as these techniques may be, they have only recently become available as normed procedures (e.g., The Colorado Neuropsychology Tests) that can be implemented as part of a clinical assessment (Davis, Bajszor, & Squire, 1992). Consequently, additional experience and data are needed to

187

evaluate the utility of these procedures for standard clinical practice.

We also refrained from detailing specific tests of remote memory. Earlier we noted that different patterns of remote memory disturbance have been associated with some neurological diseases. However, the assessment of remote memory has been problematic. It is difficult to know at what point an individual acquired a particular bit of information. Remote memory tests based on items such as old TV programs (Lezak, 1983) rely on similarity in personal habits between patients and control subjects. All such tests require constant updating and are expensive in both money and time to maintain. As important as remote memory may be, its standardized measurement remains a challenge.

In most cases, remote memory can be sufficiently assessed through the clinical interview. Patients can be questioned about past events of presumed personal significance. Obtaining validation of the patient's answers from an independent source is usually required. Nevertheless, data obtained using this method has to be viewed with caution. What was important to the patient may not have been important to the individual verifying the patient's answers. In addition, different interpretations of past events are common in the non-brain-impaired population. For the purposes of this book, we have limited ourselves to a discussion of procedures used to assess the ability to learn and retain new information. Clinically, most patients lose the ability to acquire new information before they experience problems accessing previously learned material.

GENERAL CONSIDERATIONS

PATIENT HISTORY AND CHARACTERISTICS

Knowledge of the patient's medical history and demographic information is not a requirement unique to neuropsychological assessment. Nevertheless, this information is essential for interpretation of test results. Standardized tests rely on a comparison of the patient's scores to normative data based on relevant characteristics such as age and education. Relating test findings to the patient's history aids in understanding their significance for diagnosis, prognosis, and intervention. Knowing the patient's background and medical condition can be important for test selection. Therefore, a brief discussion of the background information useful for the assessment of memory follows.

As stated above, the patient's medical and social history can provide important data relevant to both the selection and interpretation of memory tests. Critical variables include age, education level, intellectual level, and cultural background. In addition, it is important to have an accurate history of significant illnesses, injuries, or surgeries and knowledge of the patient's psychiatric status. The latter is particularly important because mood disorders such as depression are generally associated with memory impairment and can be mistaken for dementia. If it is known from prior history that the patient has had recurrent episodes of depression, such information can help guide construction of a battery designed for differential diagnosis and help the clinician avert a serious misdiagnosis.

It is also helpful to know whether there is potential monetary or other secondary gain associated with confirmation of a deficit. A severe and unexpected memory deficit associated with a mild closed head injury may be better understood if the clinician has knowledge of the patient's potential gain if the neuropsychological findings suggest brain damage.

In addition, it is important to know the names and dosages of any medications a patient may be taking. Further, it is important to ascertain if the patient is well rested and how susceptible to fatigue effects he or she may be. Many medications, general fatigue or sleep deprivation, and severe stress can adversely affect results in the absence of organic impairment.

Finally, it is important to consider the patient's general health and potential physical limitations. One must be careful to note any sensory or motor impairment that would prohibit administration of written or auditory tests. The examining clinician must also ascertain if English is the patient's first language. Inadequate language competence can adversely affect test results independent of organic or functional impairment.

In summary, the behavioral effects of brain damage vary with lesion characteristics, patient background, and individual differences in brain anatomy and physiology. Consequently, the importance of obtaining a thorough history to aid in the examination process and interpretation of results cannot be overstated.

THE CLINICAL ASSESSMENT OF MEMORY

LEVELS OF NEUROPSYCHOLOGICAL ASSESSMENT

Data gained from the history and during the interview can be effectively used to help determine the appropriate level of memory examination for a given patient. According to Kay and Horst (1988), there are at least three levels of assessment with respect to neuropsychological functioning and the assessment of memory. These include the comprehensive neuropsychological evaluation, neuropsychological screening, and the mental status examination.

The *comprehensive neuropsychological evaluation* (CNE) refers to an in-depth, objective assessment of a wide range of cognitive, perceptual, motor, and emotional behaviors that reflect the integrity of cortical functioning. The CNE often includes the use of standardized batteries such as the Halstead-Reitan or Luria Nebraska neuropsychological assessment batteries. These batteries are usually augmented by the administration of other instruments, with the complete evaluation taking from 4 to 7 hours. The purpose of the CNE is to provide information regarding the presence and extent of brain impairment, patterns of cognitive strengths and weaknesses, lesion chronicity, localization and possible etiologies. It also provides useful data for rehabilitation planning.

In contrast, *neuropsychological screening* is aimed at detecting the presence of organically based impaired functioning. This procedure involves the administration of a circumscribed group of tests and typically takes approximately 45–90 minutes to complete. The purpose of a screening battery is to provide "cost effective" formal data that will assist in deciding whether to recommend more comprehensive diagnostic procedures. It should be noted that abbreviated screening batteries may fail to detect mild, subtle, or nonspecific deficits.

Compared to neuropsychological screening, the *mental status examination* (MSE) is a briefer, qualitative, impressionistic assessment procedure that supplements the neurological examination or psychiatric interview. In this capacity, the MSE serves as a qualitative screening procedure that can alert clinicians to the presence and/or level of neurocognitive impairment and the need for more formal neuropsychological assessment. The MSE is frequently used in the acute-care inpatient hospital setting to monitor rapid and short-term changes in the patient's condition during routine and daily rounds. Examples of patients needing this type of evaluation include those with known brain lesions; patients with a history of recent onset seizures, behavior change, and/or head trauma; patients with an equivocal diagnosis of neurological disease; and psychiatric inpatients (especially those with a recent onset of psychiatric disturbance).

Another rationale for administering the MSE is to help rule out possible confounding factors, such as level of alertness or agnosia (i.e., the inability to identify an object as opposed to the ability to "remember" its name), that can influence memory test performance. For example, patients with difficulty maintaining alertness will invariably have difficulty with any cognitive task presented to them. With respect to memory tests, they won't be able to store information because of their attention deficit. Patients with visual object agnosia will have difficulty recognizing objects. Consequently, they will have difficulty naming and will appear unable to recall the object when asked. In these cases, it is a fundamental basic skills deficit (e.g., attention and object recognition) that results in the patient's poor memory test performance.

Once confounding factors have been ruled out, the use of the MSE for memory assessment is based on the premise that patients who consistently fail MSE memory items typically have some form of memory impairment. However, more definitive statements regarding the adequacy of an individual's memory or the nature of the impairment can be made only by following the MSE with a standardized assessment instrument or integrating formal instruments in the MSE/interview procedure (Berg et al., 1987; Lezak, 1983).

INTEGRATING THE MENTAL STATUS EXAMINATION WITH TESTS OF MEMORY

It is now known that many of the cherished, time-honored MSE items have limited sensitivity to cognitive and memory impairment (Kay & Horst, 1988). In the paragraphs that follow, we present items that can be incorporated into the memory portion of the MSE and that have empirically established sensitivity with respect to memory problems. In addition, we provide guidelines on how to combine formal testing with the clinical interview and MSE during neuropsychological screening.

THE CLINICAL ASSESSMENT OF MEMORY

In most MSEs, the evaluation of memory includes items that are classified according to temporal dimensions (i.e., immediate, delayed, and remote), stimulus modality, and involvement of new learning. The most common MSE memory item has the patient repeat a list of three or four unrelated words. The patient is told to remember the words because they will have to be repeated at a later time. The initial repetition of the word list provides a measure of registration or immediate recall. The task demand of this aspect of the exam is related to encoding but provides no information regarding storage or retrieval processes. As a result, repetition of a brief word list is relatively insensitive to neurocognitive insult and does not differentiate between normals and patients with mild to moderate dementia.

In contrast, delayed recall of a word list or sentence is highly dependent upon storage and retrieval. Following an interval (usually filled with other activities), the patient is asked to repeat the list. The intervals used in these tests typically range from 5 to 30 minutes. Normal subjects are generally able to recall four out of four words at 10 minutes and three out of four words at 30 minutes. In contrast, demented patients will not be able to recall more than two items. Delayed recall of less than three out of four items is generally considered abnormal (Kay & Horst, 1988).

Alternatively, a sentence-recall procedure may be used instead of a list of words. The results with sentences are comparable to those obtained with the word lists: Immediate recall is not discriminative, whereas delayed recall is one of the most sensitive measures.

Immediate and delayed recall of a paragraph-length story is uncommon in mental status testing. However, it is a standard neuropsychological procedure that is easily integrated into a more extended MSE/screening evaluation. The most frequently administered stories are the Logical Memory items from the Wechsler Memory Scale (WMS), the Babcock Stories, and the Cowboy Story (Lezak, 1983). Examiners should avoid using stories from memory batteries such as the WMS-R or Memory Assessment scales if there is a possibility that they may later wish to administer the entire battery to the patient. Use of stories out of the context of their standard administration as part of a battery may invalidate the use of normative data tables that accompany these batteries.

Generally, intact subjects are able to recall only a third of the content immediately after listening to a story and immediate recall of the stories is not a good screen for organic dysfunction. Immediate story recall often fails to discriminate patients with brain damage from those with affective disorders. In contrast, delayed story recall appears to be a useful procedure that is differentially sensitive to brain dysfunction. For example, on the WMS, depressives average 1 point less on delayed recall, whereas patients with neurological disorders average 5 points less on delayed recall, compared to their immediate recall scores. The critical variable is not the total material recalled after 30 minutes but the percentage of information retained. Normal subjects generally recall two-thirds or more of the material on delay compared to their initial recall (Kay & Horst, 1988). Further, delayed recall is one of the testing methods least affected by age and intelligence, and it is one of the best measures for predicting the presence of cerebral pathology.

Immediate recall of nonverbal material is rarely tested in the MSE. However, use of items from the Benton Visual Retention Test (BVRT) make such an addition a practical and valuable adjunct for rapid memory screening. Typically, the patient is shown a geometric design for a brief period (i.e., 10 seconds) and then is instructed to draw the design from memory. Performance on this test is significantly affected by normal aging. Although norms are not available for abbreviated versions of the BVRT, the complete test is well recognized as a sensitive measure of brain dysfunction. In addition, the designs can potentially be used to assess delayed recall or recognition. The BVRT is a stand-alone test. Its administration as part of the MSE does not affect later test selection.

Another approach to assessing immediate nonverbal memory is the delayed recall of objects hidden in the examiner's office. Following a 10-minute delay a patient can be expected to locate at least three to five objects. Patients with memory disorders frequently complain that they misplace things and this mental status procedure has face validity for many patients. The issue of face validity or relevance is especially important in the assessment of the elderly.

Recall of personal information is generally used in the MSE to assess remote memory. Although adding to the thoroughness of the examination, these items are notoriously insensitive to neurocognitive dysfunction. Tests of historic events, current events, and religious or cultural information are also occasionally used to assess recent and remote memory. Tests developed in the United States generally ask the patient to name the current and past president. However, studies cited by Kay and Horst (1988) demonstrate that recall of the current president's name was relatively difficult for hospital control patients and is not a sensitive test for brain dysfunction. In contrast, the patient's ability to name the previous president along with one's own date of birth was a relatively sensitive item set for the MSE level of assessment. This brief test-item set appears to be reasonably good for discriminating between memory-impaired and normal subjects. In addition, Kay and Horst (1988) noted that performance on these items do not appear highly correlated with IQ.

Tests of learning are rarely used in the MSE. However, these measures are sensitive and functionally relevant and can be integrated into the MSE with little additional effort. One method for assessing verbal learning is the use of paired associates. This procedure involves presentation of a list of paired words (i.e., *rope* and *potato*). After a brief delay the patient is asked to say the word that was paired with the first word. This list of paired words can be repeated until the patient learns the word pairs, and the patient's progress across trials can be recorded.

Another popular method in neuropsychology for assessing verbal memory involves learning a word list to criterion. After a set interval, the patient is tested for recall and recognition of the material. This approach provides the examiner with information regarding the patient's capacity to learn with repetition and also yields information regarding the stability of the patient's recall. Testing the subject's recognition of the word list is very useful in differentiating between normal aging and pathological memory dysfunction. Normal subjects generally perform well on recognition testing. In contrast, patients with Alzheimer's dementia perform poorly on recognition tests and tend to make intrusion (non-list word) errors in their recall.

The examiner may choose to integrate formal tests of memory into the interview and MSE. This procedure creates a testing format that avoids stressing memory-impaired patients who may be concerned about their deficits. Nonmemory aspects of the evaluation can be accomplished in time periods separating initial from delayed recall. Thus, considerable mental status information can be obtained quite naturally during the initial interview and history. For example, rather than simply noting the patient's report of his or her years of schooling, the examiner can ask for dates of school attendance, information about academic success, need for special help or special classes, and other relevant information. The examiner can also inquire about dates and types of employment, special training, entry into service, and how long after finishing school these events took place. Information also can be obtained about the patient's living situation and support network. As mentioned earlier, it is often the case that the examiner will be unable to verify biographical and historical information. However, internal inconsistencies or vagueness can indicate problems with remote memory. When the patient's memory test performance is consistent with the estimated premorbid level and present general level of functioning, the examiner can assume learning and memory are basically intact. Conversely, deficits on the general review of memory call for detailed investigation, involving systematic comparisons between functions, modalities, and the length, type, and complexity of the material.

With the large number of tests available, having a procedural model for memory assessment is useful for guiding selection of tests and MSE items. It also serves to facilitate the interpretation of results. Such a model should account for verbal learning and memory functioning and must account for basic memory processes of encoding, storage or consolidation, and retrieval. It must also account for more general cognitive skills subserving learning and retrieval (e.g., attention and language).

A model for the integrated MSE/test-based screening of memory functions is presented in Table 5.1. It is adapted from Kay and Horst (1988) and includes a list of functions pertinent to the assessment of memory along with MSE and screening items of demonstrated sensitivity.

The testing procedures outlined above constitute a neuropsychological screening-level assessment of both attention and memory. This combined MSE/test-based procedure can be completed at bedside if necessary, provides answers to many neurodiagnostic questions, and will help identify those patients who require more thorough neuropsychological evaluation. It can be used with a wide variety of patients with various neurological conditions, and routine use will permit the clinician to become comfortable with expected levels of performance.

Table 5.1 A model for memory assessment.

ATTENTION/IMMEDIATE MEMORY

Verbal
Digit Span
Repeat a list of words
Repeat a sentence
Follow multiple step instruction (also a measure of verbal comprehension)
Repeat a paragraph-length story

Non-Verbal
Visual memory span
Draw geometric designs immediately following exposure
Immediate recall for location of 2 or 3 objects and their location hidden in the examiner's office.

RECENT MEMORY

Personal Information and Current Events
Last meal eaten
Last movie or television show seen
Current events in the news

Learning
Paired associates, word list, or sentence presented on multiple trials until learned to criterion

Delayed Recall Procedures (20 to 60 minutes)
Recall of paragraph length story, word-lists, or parired associates
Recall of objects or their location hidden in the examiner's office
Recall and/or recognition of geometric designs

REMOTE MEMORY

Personal Information and Past Events
School attended
Religious/Cultural/Historical Events
Presidents

TEST SELECTION FOR MEMORY SCREENING

As is the case with many neuropsychological procedures, memory test selection is frequently a matter of the examiner's personal preference because there is little empirical data comparing testing procedures (Kane, 1991). Since the classic studies of Milner and Scoville (Milner, 1970; Scoville & Milner, 1957), neuropsychologists have included measures of both verbal and nonverbal memory as part of a flexible assessment battery. Milner and Scoville demonstrated that verbal and nonverbal memory are differentially affected by lesions on different sides of the brain. There are a large number of techniques that can be used to screen for verbal memory and learning problems. The almost unlimited possibilities for combining different kinds of verbal stimuli with input and output modalities and presentation formats have resulted in an explosion of verbal memory tests. Many of them were developed in response to specific clinical problems or research questions. Only a few have received enough use or sufficiently careful standardization to have reliable norms. Moreover, because of the lack of systematic comparisons between different verbal memory tests, their relative utility and potential interchangeability are unknown. For this reason, our discussion of specific assessment tools will be limited to those few tests that have been reasonably well normed and that have been demonstrated clinically useful.

In the sections that follow, we present a brief overview of available memory tests and batteries in an effort to provide the reader with a quick reference for making decisions regarding which tests or test batteries to use in a given assessment.

THE WECHSLER MEMORY SCALE AND THE WMS-R

The Wechsler Memory Scale and now the Wechsler Memory Scale-Revised are the most frequently used batteries in the assessment of memory. The WMS and WMS-R are composed of subtests designed for assessing both verbal and nonverbal memory. The major advantages of using the WMS-R are that it was standardized with age-based norms, the nonverbal subset includes nonconstructional items, summary scores include measures of immediate and delayed recall of verbal and nonverbal memory, and it provides an assessment of attention/concentration independent of memory.

THE CLINICAL ASSESSMENT OF MEMORY

Recent studies that have focused on issues of validity and diagnostic potential of the WMS-R have shown the battery to be useful in the assessment of a variety of patient subgroups. These include patients with amnesic disorders, Alzheimer's disease, and Huntington's disease.

The WMS-R contains improvements over the original scale. However, recognition and remote memory are not assessed, and the measurement of nonverbal memory is deficient. Further, the WMS-R has not been found very useful in differentiating patients with left and right temporal lobe lesions.

THE MEMORY ASSESSMENT SCALES

The Memory Assessment Scales (MAS; Williams, 1991) is the most recent general memory battery to become available. The MAS was constructed to assess aspects of memory considered useful in clinical practice. The MAS includes measures of (1) visual and verbal attention span (short-term memory), (2) verbal and nonverbal learning and immediate memory, and (3) delayed memory for verbal and nonverbal material. The MAS also includes measures of recognition memory, provides for analyses of intrusions during learning, and assesses the subject's use of categorical grouping during retrieval. The present authors have found the MAS to be especially useful when testing older patients because several of the subtests have good face validity and are more readily accepted by this group. In addition, the MAS provides a useful computer scoring option.

Because the MAS is a relatively new memory battery, it has not yet been employed in very many independent investigations with different neurological patient groups. Nevertheless, the MAS appears to be a promising general memory assessment battery. As Larrabee (1991) noted in his review of the MAS, the battery's normative sample is more than twice the size of that used in developing the WMS-R. Unlike the WMS-R, the MAS manual provides age- and education-based normative tables. In addition, measures of verbal memory have been introduced to help bridge the gap between clinical assessment and theoretical conceptualizations of memory disorders.

SELECTIVE REMINDING TESTS

Buschke (1973) developed the selective reminding technique to assess the retrieval, registration, and consolidation components of memory. To date, research has not fully supported the independence of all measures derived from the selective reminding procedure. Studies typically show scores to be highly correlated and to load on a single verbal memory factor.

The selective reminding procedure has been used by a number of investigators to study memory impairment associated with a variety of neurological disorders and to monitor both the positive and negative effects of drugs. For example, the selective reminding procedure has been used to study memory deficits associated with Huntington's disease, Alzheimer's disease, multiinfarct dementia, head injury, asymptomatic seropositive HIV infection, and schizophrenia (Kane, 1991).

REY AUDITORY VERBAL LEARNING TEST

The Rey Auditory Verbal Learning Test (AVLT) is a measure of learning and retention and can be used to assess recall and recognition aspects of memory. The AVLT consists of 15 unrelated words administered over five trials. Following the fifth trial, a 15-item interference list is presented and recall for those items is assessed. The subject is then asked to recall the original list. The structure of the AVLT permits an analysis of learning and retention. The use of a list-learning technique yields a learning curve. Recording order of recall allows for assessing both primacy and recency effects. Use of the interference list permits assessment of both proactive and retroactive interference. Recognition memory can be assessed in addition to retrieval by using the above-mentioned techniques. A delayed-recall administration may also be added to the AVLT.

The AVLT has been found useful in the assessment of patterns of memory impairment associated with a variety of clinical populations. These include Huntington's disorder, Korsakoff's syndrome, and head trauma patients; individuals with attention deficit disorder; schizophrenics; and nonpsychotic psychiatric patients.

199

THE CLINICAL ASSESSMENT OF MEMORY

CALIFORNIA VERBAL LEARNING TEST

The California Verbal Learning Test (CVLT; Delis et al., 1987) is another test of verbal learning and memory designed to incorporate findings from memory research into clinical assessment. The CVLT is administered by asking the subject to learn a list of 16 words over five trials. The words are presented as a shopping list to more closely mirror everyday life demands. Free-recall procedures are followed by cued recall in which the subject is supplied with the category names from which the words were selected. Longer-term recall is also assessed with the CVLT. Following a delay of 20 minutes, the subject is asked to recall items from the original list; first without cues and then with cues. Finally, recognition memory is measured.

One reason for using neuropsychological measures based on theories of brain functioning is to provide a more refined assessment of deficits associated with different neurological conditions. Conversely, the ability of a test to demonstrate distinct deficit patterns in different patients documents the construct validity of a test. The CVLT has proved useful in the study of memory impairment associated with a variety of neurobehavioral conditions, includinng Alzheimer's disease (AD) and Parkinson's disease (Kramer, Blusewicz, Brandt, & Delis, 1985; Kramer et al., 1986). A consistent difference in the two disorders was noted in that AD patients made a greater number of intrusion errors. Impaired recognition memory was noted in both dementia subtypes. Other studies have shown the CVLT to be useful in characterizing memory impairment associated with head injury (Crossen, Novack, Trenerry, & Craig, 1988) and with elderly patients with suspected dementia who may benefit from treatment of depression (Morris, Stoudemire, Kaplan, & Cohen-Cole, 1986).

Despite the recent development of the CVLT, research has clarified its factor structure and demonstrated patterns of performance associated with different neurological conditions.

HOPKINS VERBAL LEARNING TEST

The Hopkins Verbal Learning Test (HVLT) was created by Brandt (1991). It too was modeled after the AVLT; however, it is shorter (e.g., a 12-item list), takes about 10 minutes, and has six alternative forms. It was designed for patient groups that cannot sustain the level of effort required by the longer list-learning tests.

CONTROLLED ORAL FLUENCY TESTS

Although not typically considered a formal memory test, Word Fluency can be considered a measure of retrieval. Typically, patients are given 1 minute in which to furnish as many words as they can that fit the defined category. Word Fluency may be impaired in a variety of neurological conditions not necessarily associated with aphasia. The inability to retrieve words within categories is often an early symptom of Alzheimer's disease (Cummings & Benson, 1983).

The Word Fluency Test from the Neurosensory Center Comprehensive Examination for Aphasia (Spreen & Benton, 1977) is frequently employed as a measure of word retrieval. A similar test, the Controlled Oral Word Association (also referred to as the "FAS"), is part of the Multilingual Aphasia Examination (Benton & Hamsher, 1983).

Berg, Franzen, and Wedding (1987) warn that in some studies (e.g., Borowski, Benton, & Spreen, 1967), control subjects of low ability were found to perform less well than brighter brain-damaged patients. This result highlights the need to account for the patient's premorbid verbal skill when evaluating verbal fluency.

The Animal Naming subtest of the Boston Diagnostic Aphasia Examination (Goodglass & Kaplan, 1983a) allows patients 90 seconds in which to produce the names of animals. However, only the patient's best consecutive 60-second performance is scored. Aphasic patients tend to perform in an uneven fashion. Their ability to produce animal names quickly tapers, despite periodic bursts in which they produce correct responses (Goodglass & Kaplan, 1983b). Goodglass & Kaplan (1983b) stated that the average adult is able to name approximately 18 animals within their most productive 60-second period. However, age- and education-based norms are not provided.

THE RIVERMEAD

A frequently raised issue in memory assessment is the relationship between laboratory test results and patients' performance of everyday life tasks. Similar issues have been raised about the relationship between neuropsychological test performance in general and predictions of patients' functional capabilities. In response to these concerns, a relatively recent memory battery was developed based on tasks paralleling those encountered in daily living. This is the Rivermead Behavioral Memory Test (RBMT; Wilson, Cockburn, Baddeley, & Hiorns, 1989). It was developed to assess everyday memory in a rehabilitation setting. It approaches this task without dependence on elaborate and expensive equipment. It requires patients to remember a name, remember a hidden belonging, remember an assignment, recognize a picture, remember a newspaper article, recognize a face, remember a short route, and be oriented.

The intent of the Rivermead was to provide ecologically valid assessment of memory. The authors were also concerned with developing a test whose results would have direct application in rehabilitation. Although the RBMT is based primarily on items mimicking daily activities, additional research is necessary to demonstrate that these items predict day-to-day performance with greater accuracy than do traditional laboratory measures of memory. Intuitively, tests based on daily living tasks have face validity for patients and may be less intimidating. Nevertheless, the precise advantages of different approaches used to assess memory have yet to be empirically established.

HEATON ADAPTATION OF THE STORY AND FIGURE MEMORY TESTS

The Heaton et al. (Heaton, Grant, & Matthews, 1991) adaptation of the Reitan story and the Wechsler Memory Scale Form-I drawings permits the assessment of verbal and figural learning and retrieval. An advantage of the Heaton et al. procedure is that these are parallel techniques for administering and scoring both the verbal and figural memory tests, and the authors provide age-, education-, and sex-based norms. The disadvantage is that norms for delayed retention are based on a 4-hour interval between initial learning and later recall. Consequently, these procedures are more easily employed as part of a comprehensive neuropsychological evaluation. Examiners also must be careful about test selection during the 4-hour delay to avoid unwanted interference effects.

BENTON VISUAL RETENTION TEST

The Benton Visual Retention Test (BVRT) consists of three alternate but equivalent versions that may be administered under different conditions, including simple copying and reproducing from memory after various delay intervals (Lezak, 1983). Norms are available that take into account the subject's WAIS IQ scores. The BVRT appears most effective in identifying right-hemisphere injury and diffusely injured patients. In addition, patients with posterior damage to the parietal-occipital region do more poorly than those with anterior dysfunction. There is considerable evidence suggesting that the BVRT is effective in discriminating groups of patients with brain damage from those with psychiatric disorders (Benton, 1974). However, the clinician is warned that the above statements reflect statistical associations and are not hard-and-fast rules (Berg et al., 1987).

THE REY-OSTERREITH COMPLEX FIGURE TEST

The "complex figure" devised by Rey (1941) and standardized by Osterreith (1944) was designed to investigate both perceptual organization and visual memory in brain-damaged individuals. The test consists of copying the figure and then redrawing it from memory at 3- and 30-minute delay intervals. Often colored pencils are used during the construction of the task to aide in defining the subject's strategy and approach to constructing the figure. Age-corrected norms are available for copying and for 30-second, 3-minute, and 30-minute recall trials. This test has proved useful for general screening of spatial construction skills and visual memory.

A CLOSING STATEMENT

This book was written to provide a theoretical understanding of memory and practical knowledge to facilitate its assessment. To this end, we provided the reader with information about various aspects of memory, including its anatomical underpinnings and component processes. We have tried to familiarize the reader with the vocabulary of memory to facilitate a basic understanding of fundamental concepts, and we have discussed those factors that influence a patient's performance on tests of memory. We also tried to provide guidlines for different levels of memory assessment and for selecting tests appropirate to different patients and referral questions.

The examination of memory can vary from a basic mental status examination to a comprehensive evaluation. Each has its place. However, to evaluate memory successfully, one must understand both its various components and the techniques available for its assessment. We hope this book has made understanding the complex domain of memory easier and has provided practical and empirically based guidelines to facilitate clinical evaluation.

References

Aggleton, J. P. (1991). Anatomy of memory. In T. Yanagihara & R. C. Pertersen (Eds.). *Memory disorders: Research and clinical practice.* New York, Marcel Dekker, Inc.

Albert, M. S., & Lafleche, G. (1991). Neuropsychological testing of memory disorders. In T. Yanagihara & R. C. Pertersen (Eds.). *Memory disorders: Research and clinical practice.* New York, Marcel Dekker, Inc.

Anastasia, A. (1988). *Psychological testing* (6th ed.). New York: Macmillan.

Battig, W. F., & Montague, W.E. (1969). Category norms for verbal items in 56 categories: A replication and extension of the Connecticut category norms. *Journal of Experimental Psychology, Monograph, 80,* 1–46.

Bennett-Levy, J. (1984). Determinants of performance on the Rey-Osterreith Complex Figure Test: An analysis, and a new technique for single-case assessment. *British Journal of Clinical Psychology, 23,* 109–119.

Benton, A. L. (1973). The visual retention test as a constitutional praxis task. *Confederation of Neurology, 22,* 141–155.

Benton, A. L. (1968). Differential behavioral effects in frontal lobe disease. *Neuropsychologia, 6,* 53–60.

Benton, A. L. (1973). The measurement of aphasic disorders. In A.C. Velasquez (Ed.) *Aspectos patologicos del lengage* (pp. 141–192). Lima: Centro Neuropsicologico.

Benton, A. L. (1974). *Revised Visual Retention Test: Clinical and Experimental Applications* (4th Ed.). New York: Psychological Corporation.

Benton, A. L. (1979). Behavioral consequences of closed head injury. In G. L. Odom (Ed.), *Central nervous system trauma re-*

search status report (pp. 230–231). Bethesda, MD: NINCDS, National Institutes of Health.

Benton, A. L. , & Hamsher, K. (1983). *Multiligual Aphasia Examination*, Iowa City: AJA Associates.

Berg, R., Franzen, M., & Wedding, D. (1987). *Screening for brain impairment: A manual for mental health practice*. New York: Springer Publishing Co.

Binder, L. M. (1982). Constructional strategies on complex figure drawings after unilateral brain damage. *Journal of Clinical Neuropsychology, 4*, 51–58.

Bishop, E. G., Dickson, A. L., & Allen, M. T. (1990). Psychometric intelligence and performance on selected reminding. *Clinical Neuropsychologist, 4*, 141–150.

Blessed, G., Tomlinson, B. E., & Roth, M. (1968). The association between quantitative measures of dementia and senile change in the cerebral gray matter of elderly subjects. *British Journal of Psychiatry, 114*, 797–811.

Bolla-Wilson, K., & Bleecker, M. L. (1986). Influence of verbal intelligence, sex, age, and education on the Rey Auditory Verbal Learning Test. *Developmental Neuropsychology, 2*, 203–211.

Borowski, J. G., Benton, A. L., & Spreen, O. (1967). Word fluency and brain damage. *Neuropsychologia, 5*, 135–140.

Brandt, J. (1991). The Hopkins Verbal Learning Test: Development of a new memory test with six equivalent forms. *The Clinical Neuropsychologist, 5*, 125–142.

Brittain, J. L. , LaMarche, J. A., Reeder, K. P., Roth, D. L., & Boll, T. J. (1991). The effects of age and IQ on the Paced Serial Addition Task (PASAT). *Clinical Neuropsychologist, 5*, 163–175.

Brown, G. G., Kieran, S., & Patel, S. (1989). Memory functioning following a left medial thalamic hematoma. *Journal of Clinical and Experimental Neuropsychology, 11*, 206–218.

Brown, G. G., Sawyer, J. D., Nathan, A., & Shatz, M. W. (1987). Effects of lateralized cerebral dysfunction on the Continuous Paired-Associates Test. *Journal of Clinical and Experimental Neuro-psychology, 9*, 680–698.

Buschke, H. (1973). Selective reminding for analysis of memory and learning. *Journal of Verbal Learning and Verbal Behavior, 12*, 543–550.

Buschke, H., & Fuld, P. A. (1974). Evaluating storage, retention, and retrieval in disordered memory and learning. *Neurology*, 24, 1019–1025.

Butters, N., Salmon, D.P., Cullum, C.M., Cairns, P. Troster, A.I., Jacobs, D., Moss, M., & Cermack, L. S. (1988). Differentiation of amnestic and demented patients with the WMS-R. *The Clinical Neuropsychologist*, 2, 121–132.

Butters, N., Wolfe, J., Granholm, E., & Martone, M. (1986). An assessment of verbal recall recognition and fluency abilities in patients with Huntington's disease. *Cortex*, 22, 11–32.

Casson, I. R., Siegel, O., Sham, R., Campbell, E. A., Tarlau, M., & DiDomenico, A. (1984). Brain damage in modern boxers. *The Journal of the American Medical Association*, 251, 2663–2667.

Corkin, S., Growdon, J., Sullivan, E., Nissen, M., & Huff, F. (1986). Assessing treatment effects: A neuropsychological battery. In Poon, L. W. (Ed.). *Handbook for clinical memory assessment of older adults*. Washington DC: American Psychological Association.

Corwin, J. (1993). On measuring discrimination and response bias: Unequal number of targets and distractors and two classes of distractors. *Neuropsychology*.

Crook, T., Ferris, S. H., Crook, T., & McCarthy, M. (1979). The misplaced-object task: A brief test for memory dysfunction in the aged. *Journal of the American Geriatrics Society*, 27, 284–287.

Crook, T., Ferris, S. H., McCarthy, M., & Rae, D. (1980). The utility of digit recall tasks for assessing memory in the aged. *Journal of Consulting and Clinical Psychology*, 48, 228–233.

Crossen B., Novack T. A., Trenerry, M. R., & Craig, P. L. (1988). California Verbal Learning Test (CVLT) performance in severely head-injured and neurologically normal adult males. *Journal of Clinical and Experimental Neuropsychology*, 10, 754–768.

Crossen J. R., & Wiens A. N. (1988). Residual neuropsychological deficits following head-injury on the Wechsler Memory Scale—Revised. *The Clinical Neuropsychologist*, 2, 303–399.

Cullum, C. M., Butters, N., Troster, A. I., & Salmon, D. P. (1990). Normal aging and forgetting rates on the Wechsler Memory Scale-Revised. *Archives of Clinical Neuropsychology*, 5, 23–30.

Cummings, J. L. (1985). *Clinical neuropsychiatry*. New York: Grune & Stratton.

Cummings, J. L., & Benson, D. F. (1983). *Dementia: A clinical approach.* Boston: Butterworths.

Darley, F. L. (1964). *Diagnosis and appraisal of communication disorders.* Englewood Cliffs, NJ: Prentice-Hall.

Davis, H., Bajszor, G., & Squire, L. R. (1992). *Manual for the Colorado neuropsychology tests.* Colorado Springs: H. P. Davis.

deLeon, M., Ferris, S., George, A. E., Reisberg, B., Kricheff, I. I., & Gershon, S. (1980). Computed tomography evaluations of brain-behavior relationships in senile dementia of the Alzheimer's type. *Neurobiology of Aging, 1,* 69–79.

Delis, D. C., Kramer, J. H., Kaplan, E., & Ober, B. A. (1987). *CVLT Adult Version 1 Manual.* San Antonio: The Psychological Corporation.

deRosiers, G. (1992). Primary or depressive dementia: Psychometric assessment. *Clinical Psychology Review, 12,* 307–343.

Eisdorfer, C. (1986) Conceptual approaches to the clinical testing of memory in the aged: An introduction to the issues. In L. W. Poon (Ed.). *Handbook for clinical memory assessment of older adults* (pp. 23–26). Washington DC: American Psychological Association.

Elwood, R. W. (1991). The Wechsler Memory Scale—Revised: Psychometric characteristics and clinical application. *Neuropsychology Review, 2,* 179–201.

Ferris, S. H., Crook, T., Clark, E., McCarthy, M., & Rae, D. (1980). Facial recognition memory deficits. *Journal of Gerontology, 35,* 707–714.

Ferris, S. H., Crook, T., Flicker, C., Reisberg, B., & Bartus, & R. T. (1986). Assessing cognitive impairment and evaluating treatment effects: psychometric performance tests. In L. W. Poon (Ed.), *Handbook for clinical memory assessment of older adults.* Washington DC: American Psychological Association.

Fischer, J. S. (1988). Using the Wechsler Memory Scale-Revised to detect and characterize deficits in multiple sclerosis. *The Clinical Neuropsychologist, 2,* 149–172.

Folstein, M. F., Folstein, S. E., & McHugh, P. R. (1975). Mini-Mental State: A practical method for grading the cognitive state of patients for the clinician. *Journal of Psychiatric Research, 12,* 189–198.

Gaffan, D. (1974). Recognition impaired and association intact in the memory of monkeys after transection of the fornix. *Journal of Comparative Physiological Psychology, 86,* 1100–1109.

Geffen, G., Hoar, K. J., O'Hanlon, A. P., Clark, C. R., & Geffen, L. B. (1990). Performance measures of 16- to 86-year-old males and females on the Auditory Verbal Learning Test. *Clinical Neuropsychologist, 4,* 45–63.

Gregory, R. J. (1987). *Adult intellectual assessment.* Boston: Allyn and Bacon.

Goodglass, H., & Kaplan, E. (1983a). *Boston Diagnostic Aphasia Examination.* Philadelphia: Lea & Febiger.

Goodglass, H., & Kaplan, E. (1983b). *The assessment of aphasia and related disorders.* Philadelphia: Lea & Febiger.

Gronwall, D. M. (1977). Paced Auditory Serial-Addition Task: A measure of recovery from concussion. *Perceptual and Motor Skills, 44,* 367–373.

Gronwall, D. M., & Sampson, H. (1974). *The psychological effects of concussion.* Auckland: Oxford University Press.

Gronwall, D. M., & Wrightson, P. (1980). Duration of post-traumatic amnesia after mild head injury. *Journal of Clinical Neuropsychology, 2,* 51–60.

Gronwall, D. M., & Wrightson, P. (1981). Memory and information processing after closed head injury. *Journal of Neurology, Neurosurgery, and Psychiatry, 44,* 889–895.

Hannay, J. H., (1986). *Experimental techniques in human neuropsychology.* New York: Oxford University Press.

Hannay, J. H., & Levin, H. S. (1985). Selective Reminding Test: An examination of the equivalence of four forms. *Journal of Clinical and Experimental Neuropsychology, 7,* 251–263.

Heaton, R. K., Grant, I., & Matthews C. G. (1991). *Comprehensive norms for an expanded Halsted—Reitan Battery: Demographic corrections, research findings, and clinical applications.* Odessa, FL: Psychological Assessment Resources.

Huppert, F. A., & Kopelman, M. D. (1989). Rates of forgetting in normal ageing: A comparison with dementia. *Neuropsychology, 27* (6), 849–860.

Issacs, B., & Kennie, A. T. (1973). The Set Test as an aid to the detection of dementia in old people. *British Journal of Psychiatry, 123,* 467–470.

Iverson, S. D. (1976). Do hippocampal lesions produce amnesia in animals? *International Review of Neurobiology, 19,* 1–49.

Ivnik, R. J. (1991). Memory testing. In T. Yanagihara & R. C. Petersen (Eds.), *Memory disorders.* New York: Marcel Dekker, Inc.

Kandel, E. R. (1976). *Cellular basis of behavior.* San Francisco: Freeman.

Kane, R., & Kay, G. G. (1992). Computerized assessment in neuropsychology: A review of tests and test batteries. *Neuropsychology Review, 3*(1), 1–118.

Kane, R. L., & Perrine, K. (1988). Construct validity of a nonverbal analogue to the Selective Reminding Verbal Learning Test. *Journal of Clinical and Experimental Neuropsychology, 10,* 85.

Kanter, G. (1984) PASAT performance and intelligence: A relationship? *International Journal of Clinical Neuropsychology, 6,* 84.

Kapur, N., & Pearson, D. (1983). Memory symptoms and memory performance of neurological patients. *British Journal of Psychology, 74,* 409–415.

Kay, G. G. (1989). A procedure for testing delayed recognition memory for the Benton Visual Retention Test. *Unpublished Manuscript.*

Kay, G. G., & Horst, R. (1988). Evaluating cognitive function: A review of mental status tests, neuropsychological procedures, and performance-based approaches. *Technical Report of the Federal Aviation Administration.* Contract DT FA-02-87-C-87069; Faa/95-51-730-01/730-35a-g.

Kessler, H. R., Lauer, K., & Kausch, D. F. (1985). The performance of multiple sclerosis patients on the California Verbal Learning test. *Paper presented at the International Neuropsychological Society Meeting,* San Diego.

Kolb B., & Wishaw, I. Q. (1990). *Fundamentals of human neuropsychology* (3rd Edition). New York: W. H. Freeman.

Kramer, J. H., Blusewicz, M. B., Brandt, J., & Delis, D. C. (1985). The assessment of multiple memory processes in Alzheimer's disease. *Paper presented at the International Neuropsychological Society Meeting.* San Diego.

Kramer, J. H., Delis, D. C., Blusewicz, M. J., Brandt, J., Ober, B. A., & Strauss, M. (1986). Verbal memory errors in Alzheimer's and Huntington's dementias. *Unpublished manuscript.*

REFERENCES

Larrabee, G. J. (1991). Review of the Memory Assessment Scales. *Bulletin of the National Academy of Neuropsychology, 8*, 12–15.

Larrabee, G. J., Kane, R. L., Schuck, J. R., & Francis, D. J. (1985). Construct validity of various memory testing procedures. *Journal of Clinical and Experimental Neuropsychology, 7*, 239–250.

Larrabee, G. J., Trahan, D. E., Custiss, G., & Levin, H. S. (1988). Normative data for the verbal selective reminding test. *Neuropsychology, 2*, 173–182.

Levin, H. S., Benton, A., & Grossman, R. G. (1982). *Neurobehavioral consequences of closed head injury.* New York: Oxford University Press.

Levin, H. S., Grossman, R. G., Rose, J. E., & Teasdale, G. (1979). Long-term neuropsychological outcome of closed head injury. *Journal of Neurosurgery, 50*, 412–422.

Levin, H. S., Mattis, S., Ruff, R. M., Eisenberg, H. M., Marshall, L. F., Tabaddor, K., High, W. M., & Frankowski, R. F. (1987). Neurobehavioral outcome following minor head injury: A three-center study. *Journal of Neurosurgery, 66*, 234–243.

Lezak, M. (1983). *Neuropsychological assessment* (2nd ed.). New York: Oxford University Press.

Lishman, W. A. (1978). *Organic psychiatry: The psychological consequences of cerebral disorder.* Oxford, England: Blackwell.

Loring, D. W., Lee, G. P., Martin, R. C., & Meador, K. J. (1989). Verbal and visual memory index discrepancies from the Wechsler Memory Scale-Revised: Cautions in Interpretation. *Psychological Assessment, 1*, 198–203.

Loring, D. W., Martin, R. C., & Kimford, J. M. (1990). Psychometric construction of the Rey-Osterrieth Complex Figure: Methodological considerations and interrater reliability. *Archives of Clinical Neuropsychology, 5*, 1–14.

Loring, D. W., & Papanicolaou, A. (1987). Memory assessment in neuropsychology: Theoretical considerations and practical utility. *Journal of Clinical and Experimental Neuropsychology, 9*, 340–358.

Luria, A. R. (1981). *Higher cortical functions in man* (2nd Ed). New York: Basic Books.

Martinez, J. L., & Kesner, R. P. (1986). *Learning and memory: A biological view.* Orlando: Academic Press.

McNair, D., & Kahn, R. (1983). Self-assessment of cognitive defi-

211

cits. In T. Crook, S. Ferris, & R. Bartus (Eds.), *Assessment in geriatric psychopharmacology* (pp. 137–143). New Canaan, CN: Mark Powley & Assoc.

Messerli, P., Seron, X., & Tissot, R. (1979). Quelques aspects des troubles de la programmaton dans le syndrome frontal. *Archives Suisse de Neurologie, Neurochirurgie et de Psychiatrie, 125,* 23–35.

Milberg, W. P., Hebben, N., & Kaplan, E. (1986). The Boston process approach to neuropsychological assessment. In I. Grant & K. M. Adams (Eds.), *Neuropsychological assessment of neuropsychiatric disorders* (pp. 65–86). New York: Oxford University Press.

Mishkin, M. (1978). Memory in monkeys severely impaired by combined but not by separate removal of amygdala and hippocampus. *Nature, 273,* 297–298.

Mishkin, M. (1982). A memory system in the monkey. *Philosophical Translations of the Royal Society of London,* Series B, *298,* 85–95.

Mishkin M., & Appenzeller, T. (1987). The anatomy of memory. *Scientific American, 256,* 80–91.

Morris, R., Stoudemire, A., Kaplan, W., & Cohen-Cole, S. (1986). Validation of the CVLT in a dementia/depressed elderly population. *Paper presented at the meeting of the American Psychological Association,* Washington, DC.

Mungus, D. (1983). Differential clinical sensitivity of specific parameters of the Rey-Auditory-Verbal Learning Test. *Journal of Consulting and Clinical Psychology, 51,* 848–855.

Murray, E. A., & Mishkin, M. Amygdalectomy impairs cross modal association in monkeys. *Science, 228,* 604–606.

Osterrieth, P. A. (1944). La test de copie d'une figure complexe. *Archives de Psychologie, 30,* 206–356.

Petersen, R. C., & Weingartner, H. (1991). Memory nomenclature. In T. Yanagihara & R. C. Petersen, (Eds.) *Memory disorders: Research and clinical practice.* New York: Marcel Dekker.

Poon, L. W. (1985). Differences in human memory with aging: Nature, causes and clinical implications. In J. E. Birren & K. W. Schaie (Eds.), *Handbook of the psychology of aging* (pp. 427–462). New York: Van Nostrand Reinhold.

Poon, L. W. (Ed.) (1986). *Handbook for clinical memory assessment of older adults.* Washington DC: American Psychological Association.

Query, W. T., & Megran, J. (1983). Age-related norms for AVLT in a male patient population. *Journal of Clinical Psychology, 39,* 136–137.

Raskin, A. (1986). Partialing out the effects of depression and age on cognitive functions: Experimental data and methodologic issues. In L. W. Poon, (Ed.) *Handbook for clinical memory assessment of older adults.* Washington DC: American Psychological Association,

Rey, A. (1941). L'examen psychologique dans les cas d'encephalopathie traumatique. *Archives de Psychologie, 28,* 286–340.

Ribot, T. (1882). *Diseases of memory.* New York: Appleton.

Roman, D. D., Eduall, G. E., Buchanan, R. J., & Patton, J. H. (1991). Extended norms for the Paced Auditory Serial Addition Task. *Clinical Neuropsychologist, 5,* 33–40.

Rosenhan, D. L., & Seligman, M. E. P., (1989). *Abnormal psychology.* New York: W. W. Norton.

Ruff, R. M., Quayhagen, M., & Light, R. H. (1988). Selective reminding tests: A normative study of verbal learning in adults. *Journal of Clinical and Experimental Neuropsychology, 11,* 539–650.

Russel, E. W. (1975). A multiple scoring method for the assessment of complex memory functions. *Journal of Consulting and Clinical Psychology, 43,* 800–809.

Russell, E. W. (1988). Renorming Russel's version of the Wechsler Memory Scale. *Journal of Clinical and Experimental Neuropsychology, 10,* 235–249.

Russell, E. (1992). The Miami Selective Learning Test. Personal communication.

Ryan, C., & Butters, N. (1986). The neuropsychology of alcoholism. In D. Wedding, A. M. Horton, Jr., & J. Webster (Eds.), *The neuropsychology handbook: Behavioral and clinical perspectives.* New York: Springer Publishing Company.

Ryan, J. J., Geisser, M. D., Randall, D. M., & Georgemiller, R. J. (1986). Alternate form reliability and equivalence of the Rey Auditory Verbal Learning Test. *Journal of Clinical and Experimental Neuropsychology, 8,* 611–616.

Ryan, J. J., & Lewis, C. V. (1988). Comparison of normal controls

213

and recently detoxified alcoholics on the Wechsler Memory Scale-Revised. *Clinical Neuropsychologist, 2*, 173–180.

Ryan, J. J., Rosenbert, S. J., & Mittenberg, W. (1984). Factor analysis of the Rey Auditory Verbal Learning Test. *Journal of Clinical & Experimental Neuropsychology, 8*, 611–616.

Schacter, D. L., Kaszniak, A. W., & Kihlstrom J. F. (1991). Models of memory and the understanding of memory disorders. In T. Yanagihara & R. C. Petersen, (Eds.) *Memory disorders: Research and clinical practice*. New York: Marcel Dekker.

Scoville W. B., & Milner, B. (1957). Loss of recent memory after bilateral hippocampal lesions. *Journal of Neurology, Neurosurgery, and Psychiatry, 20* , 11–21.

Shapiro, D. M., & Harrison, D. W. (1990). Alternate forms of the AVLT: A procecure and test of form equivalency. *Archives of Clinical Neuropsychology, 5*, 405–410

Shimamura, A. P., & Squire, L. R. (1987). A neuropsychological study of fact learning and source amnesia. *Journal of Experimental Psychology: Learning, Memory and Cognition, 12*, 295–306.

Spreen, O., & Benton, A. L. (1977). Neurosensory Center Comprehensive Examination for Aphasia (revised ed.). Victoria B. C.: University of Victoria.

Spreen, O., & Strauss, E. (1991). *A compendium of neuropsychological tests*. New York: Oxford University Press.

Squire, L. R. (1987). *Memory and brain*. New York: Oxford University Press.

Squire, L. R., & Cohen, N. J. (1984). Human memory and amnesia. In G. Lynch, J. L. McGaugh, & N. M. Weinberger (Eds.), *Neurobiology of learning and memory*. New York: Guilford.

Squire, L. R., & Zola-Morgan, S. (1991). The medial temporal lobe memory system. *Science, 253*, 1380–1386.

Strub, R. L., & Black, F. W. (1988). *Neurobehavioral disorders: A clinical approach*. Philadelphia: F. A. Davis.

Stuss, D. T., & Benson, D. F. (1983). Frontal lobe lesions and behavior. In A. Kertesz (Ed.), *Localization in neuropsychology*. New York: Academic Press.

Stuss, D. T., Stethem, L. L., & Poirier, C. A. (1987). Comparison of three tests of attention and rapid information processing across six age groups. *Clinical neuropsychologist, 1*, 139–152.

REFERENCES

Thompson, R. F. (1987). The cerebellum and memory storage. *Science, 238*, 1729–1730.

Thorndike, E., & Lorge, L. (1944). *The teachers workbook of 30,000 words*. New York: Teacher's College, Columbia University.

Tulving, E. (1983). *Elements of episodic memory*. Oxford: The Claendon Press.

Victor, M., Adams, R. D., & Collins, G. H. (1971). *The Wernicke–Korsakoff syndrome*. Philadelphia: F. A. Davis.

Visser, R. S. H. (1973). *Manual of the Complex Figure Test*. Amsterdam: Swets & Zeitlinger.

Warrington, E. K., & Weiskrantz, L. (1974). The effect of prior learning on subsequent retention in amnesic patients. *Neuropsychologia, 12*, 419–428.

Watson, W. C., (1981). *Physiological psychology: An introduction*. Boston: Houghton Mifflin.

Wechsler, D. A. (1945). A standardized memory scale for clinical use. *Journal of Psychology, 19*, 87–95.

Wechsler, D. (1987). *Wechsler Memory Scale—Revised Manual*. San Antonio: The Psychological Corporation.

Weingardner, H. (1986). Automatic and effort-demanding cognitive processes in depression. In L. W. Poon, (Ed.) *Handbook for clinical memory assessment of older adults*. Washington DC: American Psychological Association.

Weins, A. N., McMinn, M. R., & Crossen, J. R. (1988). Rey Auditory—Verbal Learning Test: Development of norms for healthy young adults. *The Clinical Neuropsychologist, 2*, 67–87.

Weintraub, S., & Mesulam, M. (1985). Mental state assessment of young and elderly adults in behavioral neurology. In M. Mesulam (Ed.) *Principles of behavioral neurology*. Philadelphia: F. A. Davis.

Williams, J. M. (1990). *The Memory Assessment Scale (MAS)*. Odessa, FL: Psychological Assessment Resources.

Wilson, B., Cockburn, J., Baddeley, A., & Hiorns, R. (1989). The development and validation of a test battery for detecting and monitoring everyday memory. *Journal of Clinical and Experimental Neuropsychology, 11*, 855–870.

Youngjohn, J., Larrabee, G., & Crook III, T. (1993). New adult age- and education-correction norms for The Benton Visual Retention Test. *The Clinical Neuropsychologist, 2*, 155–160.

THE CLINICAL ASSESSMENT OF MEMORY

Zola-Morgan, S., Squire, S. L., & Mishkin, M. (1982). The neuro-anatomy of amnesia: Amygdala-hippocampus versus temporal stem. *Science, 218,* 1337–1339.

Index

INDEX